THE
ARENA
OF
MASCULINITY

THE

ARENA

OF

MASCULINITY

Sports,
Homosexuality,
and the
Meaning of
Sex

Brian Pronger

University of Toronto Press

Published in hardcover in Canada by Summerhill Press Ltd. 1990
First published in paperback in Canada by University of Toronto Press 1992
Canadian Cataloguing-in-Publication Data
Pronger, Brian.
    The Arena of Masculinity: Sports, Homosexuality, and the Meaning of Sex
Includes bibliographical references.
ISBN 0-8020-7705-6
1. Sports. 2. Athletics. 3. Homosexuality, Male.
I. Title
GV706.8.P76 1990   796'.80'6642   C90-094690-3
        7667ユ

BASKETBALL PLAYERS (Fig. 8) and WRESTLERS (Fig. 9), World Art copyright © 1989 Douglas Blair Turnbaugh, photographs world copyright © 1989 Douglas Blair Trunbaugh, are in the collection of Douglas Blair Turnbaugh and are reproduced with his permission from his book PRIVATE; *The Erotic Art of Duncan Grant* (Lyle Stuart, 1987).

BATHING 1911 (Fig. 7), The Tate Gallery, London, is reproduced from DUNCAN GRANT AND THE BLOOMSBURY GROUP (Lyle Stuart, 1987) By Douglas Blair Turnbaugh.

The presence of the image of name of any person in this book does not necessarily imply that they are homosexual.

For Jim Bartley

CONTENTS

PREFACE

"To unify in the pursuit of truth is a natural instinct, but dangerous to truth."

—Iris Murdoch

My goal in this book is to offer *an interpretation* of gay and athletic experience. This will be an exploration of the unique perspectives of homosexual men: I want to show how it is that in school, in the locker room, on the baseball diamond, in the weight room . . . the experience of gay men is unique. Although some aspects of this study deal with amateur high-performance and professional sports, the main focus is the common experience of men and boys who swim on local teams, run with the high-school track club, or avoid gym classes. I have paid little attention to famous athletes because this study is directed at the day-to-day experience of ordinary people rather than the rarified lives of sports stars. Athletics is a world that touches almost everyone in our society; the way it affects homosexual men is the focus of this book.

Although this book concentrates on the homosexual experience of sport, its project is perhaps more ambitious. Sport here is a vehicle for exploring the meaning of homosexuality, or indeed, more broadly, of sex and gender in our culture generally. The implications of this study are not limited to homosexuality and sport, although my references will be primarily athletic. For example, my discussion of the gay liberation movement (Chapter Seven) is focused on the experience of gay athletic culture; the fact that I spend very little time on other aspects of gay liberation is not meant to suggest that they are unimportant. Gay sport is just one way of exploring the experience of gay liberation. And the experience of gay liberation is itself an exploration of the meaning of sex and gender in our culture as a whole.

This is a qualitative study. To that end, I conducted interviews with thirty-four men. These were open interviews: the point was not to get specific answers to specific questions, but to encourage these men to talk about their experience as much as possible on their own terms. Because I was interested in looking broadly at the experience that gay men have with athletics, I interviewed men from a variety of athletic backgrounds. All except two coaches identified themselves as gay. The athletic range included international-level high-performance athletes, men who are currently involved in recreational athletics, men who were once recreationally athletic but are no longer, and men who have never enjoyed athletics. I have made no attempt to develop a "statistically valid sample." The definition of *who* is homosexual is intrinsically so ambiguous that a statistical approach to the subject is impossible. I will argue that homosexuality is a way of knowing, a special interpretation of the fundamental myths of our culture. One's sexual and athletic experience emerge through one's fluid, dynamic interpretations of oneself in sexual and athletic culture over time. In the hope of shedding light on the experience of homosexual men and boys in athletics, I have developed a theory for the interpretation of that experience. The interviews have both informed this theory and become its subject.

Many of the men I interviewed were happy to have their names included in the text of this book. Because this study is more cultural than biographical, my decision when to use and when not to use interviewees' names has been primarily a stylistic concern. The tapes of the interviews, as well as their transcripts, have been deposited in the Canadian Gay Archives. A few of the men I interviewed did not want their names used in this book; material from those interviews appears anonymously. Two men asked that the tapes and transcripts be destroyed when I finished with them. Quotations from the interviews have been minimally edited—any editing was for the sake of clarity, grammatical coherence, or brevity.

Lesbians were not included in this study. The experience of women in our culture is fundamentally different from that of men. This is a fact that the literature on homosexuality all too frequently does not consider. The anthropologist Evelyn Blackwood said: "Past research on homosexuality reflects the implicit assumption that lesbian behavior is the mirror-image of male homosexuality. Yet the act of having sex with a member of one's own sex may be culturally defined in rather divergent ways for men and women."[1] The experience of gay men and lesbians in sport is quite different: women athletes are often expected to be lesbians; men athletes are seldom expected to be gay. The coach of a university women's basketball team, at the first practice, announced that no team members "could be lesbian during the season." I can't imagine a *men's* basketball coach saying that at the first practice of his team.

It may be that some of the things I'll say, especially in the section on sexual theory, relate to lesbianism as well as to male homosexuality. When I say things like "homoeroticism is an erotic attraction to men," I'm trying to keep it simple and on topic; I'm not suggesting that male homoeroticism is the only homoeroticism. Not wanting to extrapolate from men's experience to women's, I have remained silent on women's experience, leaving that to those who are more qualified. But I must say that over the last number of years I have spoken to many lesbians in the sports world, and it has become very clear to me that sport is a comfortable place for many women who love women. At a sociology of sports conference I recently attended, I asked a colleague why she had chosen the professional field of sociology of sport and physical education. She said that she had always been involved in sports and was afraid that if she left sports she'd "never see another lesbian again." Unfortunately, there has been a concerted effort in the world of women's sport to keep its extensive lesbian content a secret. I sincerely hope that a woman will soon take issue with that cover-up and write a book about the lesbian experience of sport.

It should be noted that the phenomenon I will describe is culturally specific, referring to a particular time and place in history—namely, contemporary North American middle-class culture. I am going to describe elements of that culture, a culture that I think most everyone would agree is immensely sexist and patriarchal. Some of the things I'm going to describe, especially about women, will sound offensive, but that's because the way the gender order treats women in our culture *is* offensive. Please don't misconstrue this report on patriarchy and misogyny as an endorsement of these.

Many people were of great help in my research. I would like to thank all the men who consented to be interviewed, including: John Argue, Owen Atkinson, Jean-Paul Bernier, Normand Boucher, Claude Cormier, Peter Day, Ross Doswell, Bill Eadie, Bernie Finnigan, David Fitzgerald, Eilert Frerichs, John Goodwin, John Grube, Jamie Hamilton, Dan Healey, Andy Higgins, David Lasker, Gerry Oxford, Randall Pearce, Myles Pearson, Jim Pullen, Rupert Schieder, Thom Sevalrud, George Smith, Patrick Spearing, Thomas Suddon, and Lloyd Sykes.

I sincerely appreciate the critical readings that were given the manuscript by: Jim Bartley, Rick Bebout, Margot Blight, Douglas Chambers, Michael Denneny, Eilert Frerichs, Bob Gallagher, Claude Gratton, Craig Patterson, and especially Muriel Shepherd, who was also of invaluable help in typing the transcripts of the interviews. Of course, any work owes a debt to a multitude of influences, but I must especially thank *The Body Politic* and the lesbians and gay men who made it. That paper and those people, perhaps more than any other influence, helped me to feel the joy of being a gay person and think seriously about the meaning of sex. Without the early encouragement and advice of Bruce Kidd, this book would not have been written. I also appreciate the advice and archival aid of Max Allen. The Canadian Gay Archives was very helpful in my research. I am grateful to have received financial support from the Ontario Arts Council. And the School of Physical and Health Education at the University of Toronto was immensely supportive in appointing me a research fellow in order to facilitate the research.

I

Introduction

"The essence of truth is freedom . . .
Freedom . . . lets beings be the beings they are."
—Martin Heidegger

Incongruous and seductive, the combination of homosexuality and sport makes one wonder about the meaning of sex. This book, while exploring the special athletic experience of homosexual men, also speaks of much more. The gay experience of athletics is a lived metaphor for the more general experience of being gay in a straight world, the experience of being an outsider on the inside, of being a stranger in one's own home. By proposing an understanding of our culture's sexuality, a sexuality based on a grossly unjust order of gender, this book offers a substantial criticism of the way in which we all, heterosexually and homosexually, go about our erotic lives. This is not so much a criticism of people as it is a criticism of the culture that has created an ugly gender order, which, through its myths of power, conceals the truth of our humanity by making us see each other always through the filter of gender.

I believe in the power of human beings to take control of their destiny, to say no to an inauthentic myth that has oppressed them, to make themselves free. To find that freedom we must first understand how it is that these myths control us. This book is an attempt at such an understanding.

*   *   *

At least in one's youth, if not throughout life, having homosexual desire goes hand in hand with hiding it. What is it that's apparently so awful about homosexuality that boys with a personal knowledge of it, be it the product of unrequited desire or ambitions fulfilled, feel they should conceal it? Why, when it is revealed, is it often met with stinging silence or vicious attack? Is it just a shallow ignorance of another way of life, or is it a deep sense of the significance of homosexuality that makes people afraid? Why don't we encourage homosexuality in our culture?

If homosexuality were simply a variation of a common sexual urge, merely a matter of preference, of personal taste, as is often maintained, it is unlikely that our culture would make such a big deal out of it. Homosexuality undermines, in a positive way, the most important myth of our culture. This is a myth upon which all human relations are based. In many respects, this myth determines the way one lives, by giving power and prestige to half the members of our society and denying the same to the other half. This myth permeates not only the most important institutions of our society, such as religion, medicine, law, history, the arts, and athletics, but it is also deeply imprinted on the psyche of every human being in our culture. This myth has been responsible for many centuries of appalling subjugation, oppression, and exploitation. It is, of course, the myth of gender, a sociocultural form that divides power between men and women. The gender myth endows the relatively minor biological differences between males and females with major social significance. Homosexuality, although it by no means relinquishes this myth, subverts it. In our culture, male homosexuality is a violation of masculinity, a denigration of the mythic power of men, an ironic subversion that significant numbers of men pursue with great enthusiasm. Because it gnaws at masculinity, it weakens the gender order. But because masculinity is the heart of homoerotic desire, homosexuality is essentially a paradox in the myth of gender.

In many important respects, the difference between an athlete who is homosexual and one who is heterosexual is nonexistent. Sexuality has no bearing on the hitting of tennis balls, speed of skating, height of jumping, precision on gymnastic apparatus, or any other strictly athletic phenomenon. But in our culture athletics has more than purely athletic significance. And sexuality is

2

not just a matter of the pleasure of flesh meeting flesh. Both sexuality and athletics draw meaning from our culture's myths of sexuality and gender. Because homosexuality and athletics express contradictory attitudes to masculinity, violation and compliance respectively, their coexistence in one person is a paradox, the stuff of irony.

Athletics is traditionally understood as a masculine pursuit. (The evidence for this is overwhelming. For example: women were not permitted in the Olympic Games until 1928 and sixty years later at Seoul they represented only about one quarter of the athletes. There are still many sports in which women are not allowed to participate. Women who do become athletes are often considered unfeminine.) That a man can prove his masculinity in the boxing ring or weight room, on the football field, hockey rink, track, or basketball court, is a well-known dimension of the myth of gender.

As a young gay man, homosexuality and sports seemed like opposites to me. And so for many years I eschewed athletics. My sense of being a gay man had more to do with witty conversations at elegant dinner parties than it did with grunting and sweating in a gym. I had avoided athletics because I didn't want to be part of that straight, masculine world that seemed to me both threatening and inappropriate. Over the years, as I came to accept my homosexuality, to see the many implications of that different sexual worldview, I felt less threatened by straight masculinity and more willing to use traditional masculine forms like athletics in my own untraditional ways.

And so I started running, swimming, and lifting weights. This was a wonderful rediscovery of the joys of movement and physical exertion. I joined a swim team, started going to meets, and immersed myself in athletic culture. Now convinced that a physically active life was worth pursuing, I returned to university to study physical education. During that time, I developed an ever-greater appreciation for a paradox at work not only in my own life, but also more generally, for the ironic significance of homosexuality in our culture.

The athletic world of power, speed, and pain is an expression of the masculine ideals of our culture. My interest in athletics, although focused on the healthy pleasures of physical exertion,

3

also involved an ironic relationship with masculinity: I had no interest in pretending to be straight or masculine, yet there I was in a world rich in traditionally masculine significance, a significance that because of its erotic desirability, I didn't totally reject. Although I took great pleasure in these experiences, their masculine significance for me personally remained dubious. When I meet my gay friends in the weight room, lifting weights, grunting and groaning like everyone else, there is usually a sense of humor about how "butch" we seem. We may look as masculine as the other men in the room and may even be taken for straight, but we are aware of a deep paradox in our sense of masculinity and of the irony inherent in the appearance and reality of our lives.

Not all homosexual men and boys avoid athletics because of its masculine significance. Some, because they have outstanding athletic talent or because they enjoy using their bodies athletically, pursue athletics in spite of its masculine implications. Immersed in that straight world, their experience is one of estrangement: they feel they are alone in an overwhelmingly heterosexual milieu. And the irony of being both athletic and homosexual hangs over them, an incomprehensible cloud.

There are also those who pursue sports *because* it is a traditionally masculine pursuit. For some homosexual men and boys, athletics is a hiding place; as a proving-ground of masculinity, success in athletics is an excellent cover-up. Some will use their athletic ability to convince *themselves* that they are as masculine as their heterosexual peers. And some, intuitively aware of their paradoxical relationship with masculine gender and the disapproval that our culture has of that violation of masculinity, will become athletes to deflect the hatred and criticism that *others* may level if their secret is revealed. As we will see in the next chapter, because athletics is one of the major venues for apprenticeship in the orthodox expression of masculinity, it can be intensely estranging for those who understand the gender myth paradoxically.

My suggestion that homosexuality is fundamentally an issue of gender is at odds with conventional wisdom about it. In 1948, the sexologist Alfred Kinsey and his coworkers published their mammoth statistical study of male sexuality. One of their conclusions was that the stereotype of the homosexual man as effeminate is not born out empirically: many homosexual men behave as "normally masculine" as their heterosexual counterparts. The emerging modern gay rights movement took up that line and argued that homosexuality should be considered acceptable because it is not so unlike heterosexuality; the majority of homosexual men are just as masculine as heterosexual men. When the professional football player David Kopay came out of the closet in 1975, he seemed to be living proof that gay men can be masculine, that homosexuality is not an issue of gender.

And so there has been a recent tendency to accept homosexuality because it is perceived as not being *that* different from heterosexuality: gay people are just like anyone else; they just prefer sexual relations with members of the same sex. That view is seriously misguided. Although the sexual acts may in some ways seem the same as heterosexual ones—kissing, oral/genital sex, and so on—the meanings of these acts are profoundly different. And although homosexual men may seem to behave in as masculine a way as "normal" heterosexual men by playing sports, developing muscles, and so on, the interpretation they give that behavior may be quite distinct.

As I will show in Chapter Three (Sexual Mythology), homosexual desire emanates from a reading of the myths of gender and sexuality that is fundamentally unlike that of heterosexual desire; whereas heterosexuality is an expression of an orthodox relationship with gender myth, homosexuality expresses a paradoxical relationship. I will argue that heterosexual practice is an erotic and social confirmation of the division of power in our culture through the myth of gender. It is, therefore, a poor standard for the determination of the ethical acceptability of other sexual practices. The legitimacy of homosexuality lies not in its similarity to heterosexuality and orthodox masculinity but in its difference. Because the homosexual interpretation of masculinity in general is paradoxical, the masculine implications of sport may also have a special significance to homosexual men.

The notion that the homosexual experience of gender and eros is largely similar to the heterosexual experience represents a decisively wrong turn in thinking about sexuality, one that dwells on the superficial, observable appearance of homosexuality, while ignoring the deep psychic and mythic significance of it.[1] Pride of place has been given to the objective observation of homosexuality rather than to subjective experience. The Kinsey researchers studied *objective* sexuality, that is, they focused on sexual acts, not on the meaning that people find in those acts. A deep understanding of sexual experience, however, will not emerge from statistics that record the objective facts about sexual practice. It is, rather, in the subjective experience of people, in the interpretations that they give their experiences, that a better understanding of sexuality will be revealed.

The emphasis in this book on subjective experience rather than on objective behavior is important. Viewed objectively, any sexual act involving persons of the same physical sex can be considered a homosexual act. But the simple physical fact of a man's penis being in another man's hand, mouth, or anus is, in itself, insignificant. In our culture, there is great import attached to our saying that someone has been involved in homosexuality. What's important is the meaning of homosexuality. What the homosexual act might mean to those involved, to someone who has caught them in the act, or to someone who suspects another of being homosexual can be highly significant.

To many high-school coaches, the surprise discovery of two male athletes in flagrante delicto would have almost earth-shattering significance. To some, it would mean that the team has two faggots, pansies, boys who are less than real men. Having engaged in homosexual activity, the two young athletes have betrayed the pure aspirations of athletics: *mens sana in corpore sano,* a sound mind in a sound body. These boys have the potential to destroy the moral fabric of the team and perhaps the entire school. Even more importantly, their characteristically unmasculine behavior could undermine the macho competitive edge that many coaches work so hard to develop among their athletes.

For the boys involved, on the other hand, this sexual foray may have none of the significance that might overwhelm a coach's vision. There is every possibility that the two lads were simply randy and were caught taking advantage of a warm and friendly hand in the showers, a welcome but not necessarily significant physical release of sexual energy. It is also possible, however, that

6

to one or maybe both of the boys, this sexual meeting had enormous personal significance, that it was the young expression of a profound and largely unexplored world of meaning.

Boys and men can engage in homosexual behavior with each other, but the *content* of that behavior depends on the subjective interpretation of those involved. It is actually the subjective meaning of the behavior and not the behavior itself that, from an orthodox view, is considered troublesome in our culture. The source of that irritation should become apparent in the next chapter.*

This book differs from many of its recent predecessors in sexual theory, which have focused on the historical and social structures that organize, shape, or make possible people's sexual experience. They have looked from the top down, that is, from the society to the individual. I am looking from the bottom up. This book is, if you will, a user's view of the social construction of the myths of gender, sexuality, and athletics as they appear in contemporary North American and Northern European middle-class culture. My concern is with the interpretation that contemporary people give these myths rather than the "objective" social, historical conditions that brought them about.

Essential to this view is the role of the subconscious mind in its intuitive awareness of the workings of our culture. The subconscious consists of thoughts, emotions, and ways of understanding that, for the most part, remain unconsidered. The content of the subconscious is the product of a human being's interaction

---

*A few words about words are in order at this point. Having made a distinction between objective and subjective homosexuality, for the sake of stylistic ease, I will now use just the world "homosexual(ity)" when referring to the subjective world of homosexuality. This is in contrast to the words "objective homosexuality." The word "homosexual" is the creation of nineteenth-century science and, for many, carries with it a host of intellectual assumptions from that period. (I will discuss this in more detail in Chapter Four.) For many years, homosexuality was treated as a clinical phenomenon, a pathology. Gay liberation, trying to wrest homosexuality and therefore the lives of homosexual men from the notion of sickness and the control of medicine, preferred the word "gay" because it did not have clinical associations. The word "gay" signifies more than the homosexual knowledge I have been describing; it refers to a positive attitude to that knowledge within the context of the philosophy and politics of liberation. This, I believe, is an important distinction and so I will use "homosexual" except where I mean to imply the philosophy and politics of gay liberation, in which case, I will use the word "gay."

with culture from infancy. The subconscious develops as each human being struggles with the consonances and dissonances between himself and the culture in which he finds himself. That developmental process constitutes the personality.

As the subconscious develops, so too does a deep appreciation for the significance of the cultural myths that are appropriated by the human being. The myths of gender, sexuality, and athletics operate in the subconscious mind in a prereflective way, their significance is intuitively understood. Most live with these myths, in fact use them daily to understand themselves and their relations to others, without much conscious consideration.

In this book, I will reflect on what is taken for granted. Only upon reflection does meaning become apparent. This is a process of recovering a meaning that has been present but hidden; it is a disclosure, a matter of making explicit that which was implicit.

One of the most important shifts in this book involves a change of paradigms. This is the change from the concept of identity to sensibility. It requires that we see sexuality from a new point of view. Rather than defining a person, "homosexuality" and "heterosexuality" describe modes of being in the world, fluid ways of perceiving or interpreting oneself and others in gendered culture. For the last hundred years or so, homosexuality has been understood as an essence; more recently, under the influence of popular social science, it has been conceived as an identity. As I will suggest in Gay Sensibility (Chapter Four), people do not experience homosexuality as an essence. It's not an identity; it is, rather, a way of being and understanding. Sexuality is not so much a drive as it is an ability to know. To be a homosexual man is to have a special intuitive interpretation of the myths of our culture. That "homosexual knowledge" is fluid; it affects the lives of some people differently at various points. Just as there are different levels and forms of knowledge in any sphere, so too there are levels and forms of sexual knowledge. Some people will pay close attention to their intuitions, following through on their implications, and others will not. And so, the significance of homosexuality varies considerably among those who have these intuitions, shaping their experience of sex and sport.

Having paradoxical intuitions about the myth of gender while being in the midst of an overwhelmingly orthodox world, one can

8

respond to those intuitions by viewing the world in three ways. In Chapter Four, I will describe these views as the triad of gay sensibility; they consist of 1) *de-emphasizing* the impact of the intuitions on one's life and living within the orthodox sphere as much as possible; 2) grasping the *irony* of the paradox; or 3) seeing the world in the context of *changing* the authority of the myths that are the origin of the paradox. Depending on a multitude of influences in their lives, homosexual men will employ these sensibilities exclusively and in various combinations.

The body contact of football, hockey, boxing, and water polo, the practice of gymnastic routines, springboard diving, and figure skating, the attention coaches may lavish on their athletes, the exposure of naked sportsmen in locker rooms and showers, all proceed under the assumption that no one involved is aware of the erotic potential of these phenomena, that everyone is heterosexual. But *only* those involved know what erotic inspiration lurks for *them* behind the ostensible heterosexuality of these situations—and as we shall see in Gay Sensibility (Chapter Four) and Sex and Sport (Chapter Six), sometimes even they don't know.

Sport, as a masculine genre, presents some men with an archetypal mythic form for homoerotic desire: the sexy, muscular, *masculine* athlete. That desire is paradoxical, being at once a reverence for and violation of masculinity. The significance of that paradoxical desire will be explored in Chapter Five (Jocks and Paradox).

Athletic homoeroticism, as I show in Chapter Six, is not confined to the world of fantasy. Homosexual desire on the playing fields or wrestling mats, in the swimming pools or showers of professional, university, or community athletic facilities, is an "unthinkable" secret thought by many. Sustaining that secret is the assumption that everyone is heterosexual. Homosexual men and boys, therefore, usually move about these settings undetected, seeming to be what they are not. Many are not unaware of the irony of being able to move about among muscled naked men in locker rooms and showers incognito. This experience, known as "passing," makes an important contribution to the ironic awareness common to many gay men.

What is it about the homoerotic potential of the athletic world that is so fearful that it must be disguised by the assumption of heterosexuality? It can't be a fear of physical pleasure, since that is one of the principal calls of athletic activity. Nor is it a fear of the experience of masculinity, since it is the attainment of masculinity through sports that is often the inspiration behind outstanding performances and the mythic reward of success. This fear is based on the sacred role of eros (Chapter Three, Sexual Mythology, and Chapter Five, Jocks and Paradox) and the significance that the paradoxical erotic attraction to men has in our culture. Because sport is an apprenticeship in orthodox masculinity, it is ironic to some and fearful to others that that world is also an arena for the paradox of homoerotic experience (Chapter Six, Sex and Sport).

The perception that the world of sports is an exclusively heterosexual one is reinforced by the fact that there are virtually no men in the sports world who are openly homosexual. At the high-performance level, only David Kopay and, more recently, the professional body builder Bob Paris have made a point of making known their homosexuality, intentionally contradicting the assumption that all professional athletes are heterosexual. That few professional athletes followed Kopay's lead of more than a decade ago is telling. Professional sports clubs don't want homosexual athletes compromising their masculine image; homosexual athletes know that and keep their sexuality secret.

To call into question the masculine mythos of athletics by asserting one's homosexuality is to upset the most fundamental beliefs and deep motivations of many coaches, athletes, sports administrators, writers, and fans; it is a break with the established order in sports. The spirit of sport is one of playing by the rules. This often results in a slave-master relationship between athletes and the status quo. Questioning the rules is not part of the game—which means that athletes are frequently reluctant to challenge the unwritten rules, such as compulsory heterosexuality. To see things from another perspective is a kind of failure, a failure to play within the rules. Many coaches seem like gods to their athletes, almost arbitrarily presiding over their athletic futures. What the coach says goes, even if it has little do with the athletic enterprise. And so those athletes with homosexual desire

10

keep that knowledge to themselves and usually go about their business appearing to be heterosexual.

The experience of the paradox has given rise to gay culture (Chapter Seven, Fraternities: Gay Culture, Athletic Culture), one facet of which is gay community sports, an athletic milieu in which gay men can find a resolution to the estrangement that so often characterizes their experience in mainstream athletics. With the confidence of gay liberation, some gay men are able to participate in mainstream athletics openly as gay men.

Over the last decade, a gay fascination with the homoerotic appeal of masculine muscular bodies has mushroomed. Gay men are going to gyms in droves. Gay folk wisdom has it that mature gay men are by and large more muscular and more physically fit than their heterosexual male counterparts. Within homosexual and gay culture, muscles have become the erotic embodiment of the gay ironic sensibility. In the conclusion of this book, we shall see how gay muscles represent the irony and the ecstasy of paradoxical gender power. As symbols of the erotic subversion of masculine power, gay muscles illuminate the fundamental nature of gender power in both homosexual and heterosexual relations.

II

Rookies and Debutantes: Estranged Athletes

*"Football is all very well as a game for rough girls,
but it is hardly suitable for delicate boys."*

—Oscar Wilde

In our society, virtually all men and boys have at least a passing acquaintance with sport. For some it's an important part of their lives. I heard the nine-year-old boy who lives next door to me say to his young friend, "I don't know what I'd do without sports; I was *born* for sports." Others hate sports and get excused from compulsory athletic programs at the first opportunity. One fellow told me, "I remember refusing to go to summer camp just because I knew they'd make me play baseball, which I thought was a fate worse than death." The attitudes people have toward sports involve more than reactions to the purely athletic experiences of hitting a ball, running around a track, or trying to negotiate a piece of gymnastic equipment. Although, certainly, success in these activities may influence one's future disposition toward them, one's attitude toward sports also involves the masculine significance of sport in our culture.

Homosexual men grow up and often continue to live in orthodox, or mainstream, culture. Being gay is not like being from another planet. Homosexual men are immersed in the heterosexual world: their parents are, at least ostensibly, heterosexual; the assumption is that their peers, teachers, and sports heros are heterosexual; most grow up expecting to be heterosexual themselves. For boys in sports, heterosexuality and orthodox masculinity are not only assumed, they are also expected. Usually over time, those with homosexual intuitions come to realize that they don't quite fit in the orthodox world in which they find themselves. This is the dawn of the sense of being different, the birth of estrangement.

Before going on, it's crucial to point out that masculinity is not the only realm of experience men have of sports. There are many powerful and beautiful athletic experiences that have nothing to do with masculinity. Personally, I think there are few experiences more exciting, excruciating, and yet sublime than swimming a 400 individual medley, which is 100m butterfly followed by 100m backstroke, 100m breast stroke, and 100m freestyle, or running hard a long distance in the country—the joy is in the physical activity itself. Many men, however, find it difficult, if not impossible, to see beyond the masculine significance of athletic activity. Gary Shaw, a former University of Texas football player, wrote a revealing book on the psychic and physical horrors of football. It is a perceptive explication of those masculine machinations of sport that can obliterate the fulfillment one might find in it. A few years after quitting football and having put aside the aggressive masculine influence it had on his own athletic enjoyment, he describes the pure genderless, perhaps aesthetic, pleasure of being in an empty stadium, throwing a football to some friends.

> With a sudden calmness, I could see the whole field and the three small figures elegantly brushing its top. As I watched their grace, I could feel the empty stands and their suspension of a lost past. This changeless spell brought an acute sense of temporalness and the feeling of fading with the dusk. Yet just as acute was the sense that this present intimately belonged to both past and future. This time and our movements were one. As I released the ball, with the giving length and completeness of my arm, I could see the beginning of its easy soft arc. And it somehow seemed perfectly

coordinated with the stadium, the ground, early evening and the four of us.[1]

Athletics is a traditional theater for the acting out of myths. The ancient Olympic Games were religious celebrations in which the central myths of Hellenic culture were dramatized. Class and patriarchy, as well as the religious belief that fame (which can be achieved by winning at the Olympics) bestows immortality, were the cultural focus of the ancient games. The similarity between the ancient Olympics and modern-day athletics is limited to the more abstract fact that both are dramatizations of myth. Notions that we take for granted, such as fair play, the virtue of participation in sport for its own sake, and the importance of personal bests, were unknown to the ancients. The ancient games could be quite violent, sometimes being fought to the death, and winning was the only thing that mattered. In fact, if an athlete could intimidate his opponents to the point of their withdrawing from the competition, he was considered successful without even participating in the event.

Sport in contemporary Western culture also dramatizes myths; preeminent among them is the myth of masculinity. One of the men I interviewed said:

Our culture has definitely rewarded those who are very masculine and perform well, and men over women. Male tennis players, male golf players make more money than female golfers do. So there is a reward for masculinity and a punishment, in some way, for femininity. . . . I think also there's an intimidating factor to athletics and the way the program's run: gym teachers calling kids sissies if they can't run laps.

Another, who likes lifting weights and wrestling, said,

The way it's currently constituted in terms of the commercial basis that most sport depends on, and certainly the way it was taught to me in school, sport as it exists now parallels closely the individual, aggressive qualities that are seen as masculine by most people today, so I think that the connec-

15

tion is quite clear. And in team sports, it's not a feminist quilting-bee type group, but rather a bunch of behemoths who, instead of not being aggressive and choosing to be cooperative, are in fact simply pooling their collective aggressiveness and channeling it in one way. So I think there's quite a clear connection between sports and masculinity.

The connection between sports and masculinity has grown out of specific historical circumstances. Contemporary conceptions of manliness and sportsmanship emerged out of the larger economic and social picture of late-nineteenth-century Europe and Great Britain. Pierre de Coubertin, who was the founder of the modern Olympics, the athletic movement that epitomizes the present-day attitude toward sports and much of athletics, appropriated the symbols of the ancient games and recast them in a modern mold that reflected the qualities he admired in English rugby and cricket—qualities that characterized productive citizenship in a burgeoning imperial and industrial society.

These sports had their origins in the rural folk games of the late middle ages. In the mid-to-late nineteenth century, they were fashioned into the first modern sports—characterized by standard rules, a bureaucratic structure, the overemphasis on setting records, and the concept of fair play—by middle- and upper-class males in the increasingly bourgeois institutions of the public school, the university, and the private club. Innovators, organizers, and creative publicists like Coubertin consciously regarded sports as educational, preparing boys for careers in business, government, colonial administration, and the military by instilling physical and mental toughness, obedience to authority, and loyalty to the "team." . . . Education or socialization through sport was consciously understood to be "masculinizing." . . . The most popular nineteenth-century games and contests—football, hockey, lacrosse, track and field, and boxing—were termed "the manly sports."[2]

In the nineteenth century in the United States and Canada, men were concerned that boys were becoming "feminized."

16

North American society was changing from country to city, from farming to industry. Whereas previously most fathers were in fairly close contact with their sons by virtue of being on farms where family and working life were intertwined, in the late nineteenth century fathers were away from home and their sons for long hours while they were at work.[3] The lack of masculine influence at home was exacerbated by the fact that schools were dominated by female teaching staffs. To counteract this feminine influence, in an attempt to preserve a polarized gender order by emphasizing the difference between girls and boys, in the hope that boys would learn more "manly" values, sports were introduced to public-school boys and the adolescent members of organizations like the YMCA.[4]

The legacy of sports as an apprenticeship in masculinity has carried on to the present. In our contemporary setting the masculine myth of sports is made evident in a number of ways. The traditional practice of excluding women indicates that sport is considered a masculine preserve.[5] Women have only recently begun to participate in sports in significant numbers—and at the Olympics, their participation is still less than half that of men. There are many events and some sports in which women are not allowed to participate; women are not allowed to box, even with each other. This discrimination against women is completely unjustified. For instance, women are by far the most successful marathon swimmers; yet the longest distance they are allowed to race in the pool is 800 meters, whereas men swim 1500 meters as their long-distance event. In truth, women are capable of participating in any sport or event that men do. Kenneth Dyer conducted an illuminating social biological study of the athletic performances of men and women in which he has shown not only that women can compete in the same sports as men but also that they are becoming capable of competing *against* men. The reason that women have historically registered athletic performances that are beneath those of men is not because their biological destiny has made them inferior to men but because they have been discriminated against physically, athletically, and psychically. Dyer has shown that in those sports where women have been training with the same intensity as men, they are rapidly coming to parallel men's performances.[6]

There is no sound scientific, physiological evidence that proves that men are inherently physically superior to women. That is, there has been no research that has been able to show that independent of social and cultural influences women are physically disadvantaged. Many studies have tried to do so but, inevitably, they have failed because it is impossible to control for social influences. All the subjects of exercise physiology experiments have been raised and continue to live in social settings where there is an assumed difference between men and women, social settings in which women and men are expected to be different. There has been no biological research conducted on humans independent of culture. It cannot, therefore, be argued that there is any strictly biological difference between the capabilities of men and women.

Usually, it's suggested that women shouldn't compete with men because it wouldn't be fair; men tend to be larger and stronger than women. The fact is that there is a continuum in which there is considerable overlap in the size and strength of men and women. So competition could be made fair by the institution of height, weight, or age requirements, depending on the sport. This is already a common practice in several sports, for example, wrestling and rowing. The segregation of men and women in sport is a technique for maintaining a socially constructed difference between men and women, symbolically preserving through sport the power of men over women.

The segregation of boys and girls, men and women, in sports expresses an important meaning that men and boys find in sports. Bruce Kidd, a gold medalist at the 1962 Commonwealth Games and a former Olympian, recalled the meaning that sport had for him in his youth.

I played sports endlessly as a child. I gobbled up the rules, skills, strategies, and lore, none of which seemed to interest my mother, her friends, or the girls my own age on the street. Certainly we rarely included them. I also learned to accept (rather than question) physical pain, to deny anxiety and anger, and to be aggressive in ways that were clearly valued as "manly." I realize now that I gained an enormous sense of my own power when I could respond to challenges in this way, for it meant I was not "like a girl." In fact, sometimes I teased my mother and sister to tears to confirm that I had succeeded in being different from them. Yet it shows how shaky such personal identity can be, because when I put myself into the emotional state I remember from that period, I realize that I would have been devastated if a girl had played on any of the teams I was so proud to belong to. It would have proclaimed to the world that I was inadequate.[7]

For boys, sport is an initiation into manhood, a forum in which they can realize their place in the orthodoxy of gender culture. Sport gives them a feel for masculinity, a sense of how they are different from girls. For those who wish to emphasize their masculine sense of place, the masculinity of sport is a happy discovery, a way of expressing and exploring an important sense of themselves. But not all boys are comfortable with this rookie masculinity. For some, becoming adult men is more a matter of learning how they are estranged from masculine culture than it is one of becoming snug in its orthodoxy. For these boys, the sporting rights of masculine passage make them poignantly aware of their unease. Sport is a masculine obligation that they may fulfill, sometimes at great psychic and physical cost. And there are some boys who just see sports as a hostile world that is to be avoided. One of my interviewees said:

> My experience was that there was no place for me in the conventional sports structure, either ones that my peers had devised for playing ball hockey in the streets, or in the standard high-school or junior-high school structure.

Athletics, as an expression of orthodox masculinity, can be typified in three categories: violence, struggle, and aesthetics. The most masculine sports are the violent ones—boxing, football and hockey. Less masculine are those in which struggle is a dominant characteristic: one struggles with one's opponents and with oneself without perpetrating violence. Baseball, wrestling, tennis, swimming, and track are sports in which nonviolent struggle with one's opponent(s) is integral to the sport. Typical sports where the struggle is primarily with oneself are field events, golf, archery, and weight lifting. The least masculine sports are those where success is determined by the marriage of skill and aesthetic expression. Such sports are figure skating, diving, gymnastics, and body building. These aesthetic sports are the least masculine because they involve the lowest degree of aggression.

The connection between masculinity, aggression, and violence is well established in our culture. In his book, *Violence and Sport*, Michael Smith says:

> Although there is evidence that female violence is on the rise, violence is essentially a male phenomenon. This is true historically and cross-culturally. Males commit most of the violent crimes [90 percent in North America] and most of the violent delinquency. Males predominate in the occupations requiring violence—soldier, policeman, prison guard, football player. Boys and men push, punch, scuffle, and fight more than girls and women. It is mainly boys and men who play rough, violent games and sports.[8]

Because we live in a "civilized" society,[9] masculine violence is curtailed. Although traditionally, "in the interest of family discipline," men are expected to express themselves violently in the privacy of the home by beating their wives and children, this practice is falling into disrepute, as is evidenced by its frequent exposure in the press and the development of new laws to curtail violence in the home. "Acceptable" violence is now confined to war, movies and television, the boxing ring, playing field, and hockey arena. The violence of sports is often considered a metaphor for the violence of war. In 1972, Richard Nixon called for a new bombing assault on North Vietnam, naming it "Operation Linebacker." In his famous poem "Vitaï Lampada," two verses of which follow, Henry Newbolt draws the metaphor of the playing and battle fields.

> *There's a breathless hush in the Close to-night—*
> *Ten to make and the match to win—*
> *A bumping pitch and a blinding light,*

An hour to play and the last man in.
And it's not for the sake of a ribboned coat,
Or the selfish hope of a season's fame,
But his Captain's hand on his shoulder smote
"Play up! Play up! and play the game!"

The sand in the desert is sodden red,—
Red with the wreck of a square that broke;—
The Gatling's jammed and the Colonel dead,
And the regiment blind with the dust and smoke.
The river of death has brimmed his banks,
And England's far, and Honour a name,
But the voice of a schoolboy rallies the ranks:
"Play up! Play up! and play the game!"[10]

Nothing is more manly than making war, than killing one's opponents. Violent combative team sports are the next best thing. Not only are they a metaphor for war-making, but also they offer the opportunity to hurt, maim, or at least "take another man out [of the game]." The former National Football League linebacker Mike Curtis, known for his aggressive style of play, explains why he finds football rewarding. "I play football because it is the only place where you can hit people and get away with it."[11] Violence is cultivated by the coaches. The University of South Carolina lineman Tommy Chaikin described his line coach, Jim Washburn: "Washburn was hung up on being macho, and he'd say bizarre things to us about manhood and being tough and big and mean. 'Ever think about just ripping someone's head off?' he'd ask us. And, I swear, he was serious."[12]

Described by a gay phys ed student as "butchball," football is a brutal sport. More than three hundred thousand football-related injuries are treated in hospital emergency rooms in the United States annually. In the National Football League, an average of one thousand–six hundred players are forced to miss at least two games each year because of serious injuries.[13] If one goes on to play football through college, the risk of sustaining serious injury is 95 percent. One study of American football has found that each year an average of thirty-two college and high-school football players become paraplegics as a result of the sport.[14] This violence, that is, the desire to hurt and the willingness to be hurt, is fundamental to playing football.

Hockey, as Gordie Howe said, is "a man's game." Violence and fighting constitute major attractions to the game, for it is in violence that masculinity shines. "In a game in which every man's mettle is constantly being probed, the ability to fight is as basic as the ability to skate. That's why so many hockey players train with punching bags."[15] But violence is not a necessary part of the sport as it is in football, where equipment like helmets are effectively used as weapons and each play consists of battle-field formations. Wayne Gretzky has proved that fighting need not characterize excellent hockey playing; when there is a fight he skates away. But athletic competence is actually a secondary feature of hockey, especially in the NHL—the real appeal lies in its significance as a "man's game." The masculine aesthetic of hockey becomes almost sacramental through its violence and bloodshed. "The cold adds a subtle coloration to the violence that is one of the sport's special treats. There is an undeniable *frisson* to the sight of blood on ice—the spilling of the very warm onto the very cold, perhaps—that not even football can match."[16]

Contrary to the popular opinion that aggressive combative sports like football and hockey are an outlet for the diffusion of natural aggressive energies, it has been found that these sports actually contribute to the development of aggressive behavior. "Research with high-school and college athletes finds they are more quick to anger than nonathletes and that those who participate in combative sports, such as hockey and football, respond to frustration with a greater degree of aggression when compared to athletes in noncontact sports and nonathletes."[17] Combative sports are really a training ground for aggressive violent masculinity.

The physical and psychic pain that is at the heart of this kind of masculinity is an imposition. According to Gary Shaw, Dave Meggyesy, and other commentators on football, vulnerable young men are pushed to the limits of physical and psychic abuse by coaches and athletic bureaucracies whose only interest is in winning, regardless of the long- and short-term damage it may cause the athletes.[18] Shaw points out that Darrell Royal, the famous head coach of the University of Texas Longhorns, was successful because of his ability to manipulate "the fears of boys in their late adolescence. Their fears of masculinity, their fears of acceptance, their fears of not being good enough—in short, their need to feel like acceptable men."[19] I interviewed a national track coach (who is heterosexual) who said:

> I played football and hockey because it was masculine. My fear that I would be discovered being afraid was greater than my fear of being hurt, and I was getting hurt all the time because I was much smaller than most everyone else. It hurt a lot to hit and get hit. But I was aggressive. It was part of being male and defining your masculinity and toughness. It's a dehumanizing process.

He also described the perverse attitude that one learns to take to injury and pain, not only that that one experiences oneself, but also among one's teammates.

> When I was coaching high-school football one of the kids broke his leg; he was screaming in pain; his femur was sticking out through his pant leg. We carried him off in a stretcher and went on with the game. It was terrible; a human tragedy had happened there and no one let on that anything bad had happened. They just pushed down their emotions and went on with the game.

Boys and men who are willing to put themselves through such violence do so out of an attachment to the meaning of orthodox masculinity. The pain is worth it because masculinity is worth it. Stressing the importance of masculinity, Vince Lombardi said, "when a football player loses his supreme confidence in his super-masculinity, he is in deep trouble."[20] Homosexual boys can be quite apprehensive about the status of their masculinity. Some may go through the horrors of football in an attempt to conteract suspicions of their extremely vulnerable masculinity. The former American pro football player David Kopay said: "[Football] also provided a convenient way for me—and who can say how many of my teammates?—to camouflage my true sexual feelings for men."[21] Others, and I think the majority, avoid violent sports because they feel no need to pursue an inappropriate world of masculinity.

Homosexual men and boys often feel estranged from sport because of its masculinity. Said one man:

> I didn't have a great predilection for sports. I didn't like competition. I really felt uncomfortable with my male peers. Even before I knew I was homosexual, I knew that I had sexual feelings for men. I was also aware that people were categorizing me as nelly or sissy. And I knew that I just wouldn't enjoy going out and playing football in that kind of atmosphere. I was more comfortable reading.
>
> I very often saw myself as less masculine than the boys who were doing [sports]. I suffered a lot because of that; I really think I undervalued myself because of that and never really felt comfortable being a gentle person, which I feel is the best way to categorize the way I was then.
>
> I was very intimidated by sports then; I felt it was very ungentle. I'm not so intimidated anymore. The moment I was able to drop athletics as a subject, I did, and I didn't go near a gym again until university.

The estrangement that many homosexual boys and men feel can be very intense in team sports, especially those characterized by violence and aggression. Of the thirty-two gay men I interviewed, two had played some football in high school and three had played hockey as children—none had continued playing hockey after puberty. That they did not play hockey after puberty is significant, for it is at puberty that hockey playing becomes truly violent[22] and a serious manifestation of masculinity. Although there is evidence that some particularly ambitious parents encourage their prepubescent boys to play a rough game of hockey, it is at puberty and the onset of adolescence that some boys play rough on their own initiative and take it as an expression of their masculinity. (I personally remember well the difference between older adolescent boys and myself—they would hit and roughhouse in earnest; you could tell that it meant something

24

important to them. Whereas it struck me as an unpleasant and alien kind of behavior.) Only one of the men I interviewed found these sports satisfying. He lived on an air force base where everyone played hockey and his father was the coach. His sisters and even his mother played hockey. When his father was transferred to another base, where hockey was not the major social institution, he stopped playing. Another, who became a competitive swimmer, came from a hockey-playing family—his uncle was in the NHL. He said, "My father's idea of sports is very traditional—camaraderie between the men, the physical contact . . . I gave up hockey; I did it for a few years. I pretended I was going to block people. I went through the motions but didn't believe in what I was doing, so I walked away from it. I got involved in swimming and really enjoyed it." One man who played football quit because "they always want you to play when you're injured and tough it out. 'It doesn't hurt *that* much.' After sophomore year, when I broke my foot playing football, I lost my trust in playing football anymore after that. It wasn't worth it. My big event was track, and the broken foot put my track career back, so I said, 'It's not worthwhile for me in the long run.' "

Not one of the men I spoke to had laudatory things to say about football. Regarding football and hockey, one said,

I would say that there's something masculine about certain sports. Football and hockey. I think these sports are much more red-necked because they are violent. I don't like them as sports, they are noisy, boisterous, based on the desire to see people hit, be hit, and if that's masculine, I don't want any part of it.

A competitive swimmer said,

Homosexuality and football just do not mix—I don't know why. Maybe it's the homophobic tendency of men that they are not comfortable with the idea of doing anything else but massacring one another on the football field.

Many of the men I interviewed said they were uncomfortable with team sports. As a member of a team it's important that one identify with the team, that one see one's goals as being in common with the team. Now, if team goals were simply athletic, then homosexual men and boys would probably have no problem identifying with them. But athleticism is often not the only theme in team sports; orthodox masculinity is usually an important subtext if not *the* leitmotif. Coaches demand that their athletes play like men, even if they are just boys; it's boys' concern about masculinity that is played upon to motivate more aggressive performances. Team dynamics depend on a common commitment to orthodox masculinity. With that commitment go assumptions, not the least of which is the heterosexuality of team members. In such a setting where heterosexuality is assumed, homosexuality is more of an insult than a sexual disposition—football coaches are well known for berating their players with insults: "ladies," "faggots," "pansies." Such childish pejoratives are effective because there is a tacit understanding on the team that no one is homosexual or would want to be known as such. Needless to say, gay men or boys who do not share this contempt for homosexuality will feel uncomfortable with its use as a "motivating" insult. More importantly, because they may not share the same view of orthodox masculinity as others on the team, they will feel estranged from its role in sport and find it difficult to join in the chorus of its masculine leitmotif. Consequently, gay men often avoid team sports. Comments from gay men such as, "I had to play baseball and soccer in school and I didn't like team sports," are not uncommon.

Adding to their estrangement in athletics is the not exceptional experience of gay men being the last picked for teams. One man recalled field day at his public school. "They divided each class into teams and there were six kids on each team. We all stood there and the team leaders decided who they wanted. Finally, I was the last one standing and I had to join a team. When the teacher asked the team leaders how many they had, my leader said, 'Five and a half, 'cause we have Palmer.'" Rather than an intrinsic lack of physical ability, this athletic ineptitude is probably a reflection of the indifference some homosexual boys feel toward sports because of its orthodox masculine leitmotif.

There's the whole nightmare about baseball—trying to be as far out in left field as you could possibly get and then every now and then a ball coming your way and having to pick it up, throw it, run after it, pick it up again, throw it until it finally got back to the starting post, or whatever it is in baseball.

A man who is now quite muscular and a good swimmer said:

I was a real klutz. I was always the last one picked to be in anything. You didn't throw the ball right, you couldn't skate properly, and you were afraid of playing hockey. You didn't want to play hockey. I would say that a lot of gays would be in that category. Mostly, I hated going to [gym classes in high school]. I couldn't stand it. Volleyball, basketball—I didn't understand the rules and [had] no desire to do any of that either.

Even gay men who were in fact fine athletes in individual sports would sometimes be the last picked for teams. Myles Pearson, who swam as an international competitor, recalls how he felt in gym class. "I was a little sissy kid, so in gym classes you'd be the last one chosen on the team to play soccer or dodge ball, or whatever, and the same in high school. I went to a private boy's high school where the ultimate insult was 'you faggot.' And I didn't fit in well there. I don't remember high school warmly. It was the worst time."

Most athletic activities, with the exception of those that are by nature violent, have little or no *intrinsic* connection with orthodox masculinity. But orthodox masculinity often becomes associated with athletics nonetheless. Gay men and boys who are involved in athletics are often aware of the orthodox masculine leitmotif that can make them feel that they are outsiders in sports. Myles, the swimmer, said he felt like an outsider "in the locker room, but not in the pool. In the pool everyone was friends, and swim meets were fine. In the locker room, I think maybe I pulled away rather than was pushed away. Just because locker rooms are a boisterous kind of place; they were telling dirty jokes and talking about the girls in the locker room next to them, and I wasn't interested in participating. I would just be on the sidelines." His experience emphasizes the fact that from a purely athletic point of view, the experience of homosexual men and boys in sports cannot always be distinguished from their heterosexual counterparts. But when the orthodox masculine, and therefore heterosexual, leitmotif comes into play in the athletic environment, a sense of not being part of the action, of being outside, of estrangement, is amplified for homosexual men and boys.

While uncomfortable in team sports, many gay men and boys find individual athletic activity more satisfying.

Being from the north, certain kinds of physical activity were very central and very enjoyable to me—canoeing, rowing, hiking, backpacking, snowshoeing, skiing, these were all part of the regular activity. And I think I've always enjoyed individual performance. I've always got a great deal of enjoyment of this kind out of paddling, being able to do so many miles a day, and doing a real long portage, and the great physical satisfaction of the whole thing, and the sense of well-being. But it's always been individual sports, or sports of that kind, that I shared with two or three other people, I never enjoyed team sports, very much. I never enjoyed hockey, I liked skating. I never enjoyed baseball. I liked hitting the ball. The game at which I was best was tennis. I liked fencing too. These were things that I did by myself as opposed to being a member of a team.

This man found the physical activities themselves, for example, skating and hitting the ball, enjoyable, but it was the team dynamics he found distasteful.

A university-level competitive swimmer said that, unlike his friends, he didn't play team sports much.

I never did play hockey or baseball, which is what all my friends were doing. I swam; started when I was eight. In

28

school, I was very into sports—track—I excelled in sports. Volleyball, badminton, gymnastics. I wasn't seriously into basketball, even though I'm tall. The only team sports were volleyball and curling.

Eilert Frerichs, who grew up on a farm and enjoyed the hard physical labor of farming, hated team sports.

[Team sports] scared me. It may have had to do with comparison with other children, and then in organized sports, in athletics at school, marks were assigned, which is gross. I probably could work in the fields longer than most boys who weren't from the farm, but no marks are assigned to that kind of activity.

And Myles Pearson:

I can remember when we played team sports in elementary school and maybe high school. If you did something wrong the whole team would turn on you, sometimes it was your fault, sometimes it wasn't. That really pissed me off. But I found with track (which I did for one year too), and with swimming, it's a lot more individual. I was a lot more proud of individual medals than I was of relay medals. That's part of why I didn't like team things when I was younger. But later on, I was never really interested in team sports because the boys grew up and were tougher and it was this macho thing that I didn't fit in with and that didn't feel a part of me.

One of the reasons Myles didn't like team sports was that he was aware of the orthodox masculine or "macho" leitmotif that at adolescence becomes the métier for boys in sports. Sensing this leitmotif in team sports, some gay men, even though they are participating on a team, prefer to think of the sport as individual. John Goodwin, once an internationally competitive oarsman, said he thought of rowing as an individual sport even if he was rowing in sixes or eights. "It's a team sport only because you are together in the boat, but you have to go beyond that."

Commenting on the seeming predilection that gay men have for individual sports over team sports, former runner Jim Pullen said:

> I think there are more gay people who are swimmers, runners, and skaters than there are football players and baseball players, partly because it's something you can do on your own. I think if you are uncomfortable being part of the mainstream heterosexual thing, if you are a little different, if you are a little effete, shall we say, and you're interested in sports or you're led to sports, then it's easier to do something on your own, where you don't have eighty people in the locker room together, which is intimidating anyway, I would think. When I talk to my gay friends now, for them, gym class was always a dreaded thing. They would always find some illness or something, anything to avoid going to gym and going through this team thing and playing ball and playing football. So if you were athletically talented you probably got into figure skating or swimming. I think that there are probably more natural things than football where you have to learn to knock people over. You can just go out for a run or a swim. If you are insecure, even the slightest bit, about being involved in any big group thing, especially with a bunch of heterosexual men thumping each other, then, at the very first practice when you've got eighty of them all doing it [trying to make the team] you'd probably avoid it. You'd have to really want to do it in order to suffer through that.

A former varsity swimmer, John Argue, said, "The difference between running, skiing, and swimming and team sports is that you are dealing with your own body in order to get it into as good shape as possible in order to excel, so that it is between you and nature, so to speak. It's an expression of pleasure and well-being. Whereas in team sports, the point is domination over others. . . . In team sports it is quite frightening; one wins by fighting, beating, and pummeling—I don't like that." A university phys ed instructor said, "The gay men I know around here are swimmers, divers, gymnasts. I don't know any gay football players."

*   *   *

The orthodox masculine leitmotif can also be heard in sports that fall into the "struggle" category. The volume at which the leitmotif is played depends not so much on the nature of the sport as it does on the attitude of the athletes and coaches. Some gay men think of swimming and similar sports as very masculine. A varsity level swimmer told me,

> I think swimming is a very masculine sport. I think people who swim are some of the hardest-trained athletes, just because of the element of water. I think your body goes through more. You have to be tough mentally.... Swimmers aren't bulky so some people may tend to think they aren't as masculine, but I'm biased. I guess the most masculine to me are the sports like running . . . anything by itself . . . biking, track.

Another man, a volleyball player, agreed.

> I think, probably, athletes in individual sports like skiing would be more masculine, only because the challenge is so much greater and nobody relies on other people, you're doing it all yourself.

These men consider the attributes of strength, mental toughness, and independence, which are required in the individual sports, to be masculine and, therefore, see these sports as more masculine than violent team sports. But this equation of toughness and masculinity is unsatisfactory because it ignores the importance of violent aggression as the quintessential expression of masculine power. The desire to cast less violent sports as equally masculine as more violent ones reflects a wish to maintain a sort of masculine credibility, a credibility that, ultimately, is dubious.

A swimmer, Gerry Oxford, said he sees nothing particularly masculine about his sport.

> Swimming isn't up there with football; it isn't associated in most people's minds with a traditional masculine kind of

image. Being a good swimmer just earns you scorn in the weight room of Hart House [a university athletic facility]. You are probably a faggot if you are a good swimmer. They'd have trouble saying about a football team, 'You don't play with that *fag* football team, do ya?' Swimming is not a butch enough sport to discredit accusations that you're queer. Athletes, however, wouldn't have this attitude about swimming because they know how hard it is to swim. People have more trouble with a football player being queer; there's something gentle about swimmers—they don't go around beating each other up.

The swimming world was horrified when at the Commonwealth Games, in the presence of the Queen, the world record holder in breast stroke, Victor Davis, kicked over a chair because he was upset that his relay team had been disqualified from a race. Such masculine expression of anger pales next to football players breaking each other's legs or hockey players smashing each other into the boards, knocking themselves unconscious.

Another competitive swimmer said he thought orthodox masculinity was expressed in sports not so much through the sport itself but through a more peripheral machismo. "The camaraderie that borderlines on macho, the bum patting sort of locker-room stuff, is macho. There's a lot of contrived machismo as the trappings of the sport—the image goes with the sport but it's not in the sport. . . . There's nothing particularly macho about swimming; both men and women do it and they do it the same way." He thinks the level of orthodox masculinity depends on the coach and other athletes. "The coach didn't try to motivate the team by references to fags. . . . My coach was a professor of child psychology—so that he was concerned about the development of his athletes as people, not just as swimmers. There were a couple of assholes [on the team] but I think that everyone thought they were ridiculous brutes. . . ."

Being in the midst of the machismo of sports can be estranging. One man said, "Doing basic jock stuff with the guys in the swim club, the 'all-for-one-and-one-for-all' sort of thing, I felt that I was a hypocrite, that I was playing along, doing the team, macho thing, talking about women, and you know it's not your natural thing, and you really are different, and you think absolutely nobody understands me."

The social side of athletics, especially for teenagers and college athletes, is overwhelmingly heterosexual. For most boys, their relationship with girls is a preoccupation of their adolescence. One's teammates form a boys-wanting-girls club. Weekend nights, the club goes out together in Dad's car. With the radio blaring, they cruise the town's main drag, looking for girls. There is a lot of hooting, and many rude comments are hurled at the female passersby. Boys "hanging moons" is de rigueur on such occasions. To most of the boys in the car, this playful baring of posteriors is both funny and "kinda gross." Who, after all, would want to look at a guy's ass? For the homosexually inclined, this teenage experience may be read in several ways. Out with their friends, they *are* members of the boys-wanting-girls club. But secretly, often unconsciously, they are more interested in the *boys* than the girls. And when one of the guys "hangs a moon," the homosexually inclined teenager's laughter is probably a response to more than one interpretation of the significance of a boy's bared bum. But he knows that he must not let on that he is aware of any other significance. And so he hides behind the facade of being a member of the club. The other boys in the club, unaware of the homosexually inclined boy's inclinations, assume that everyone is a member in good standing. That experience of seeming to belong when one senses that one really does not, the experience of keeping one's life a secret, amplifies the feeling of estrangement.

The athletic world is organized under the ironic assumption that everyone is heterosexual. It's a setup that few in that world question. Males and females, for example, are always given separate change and shower facilities; the assumption being, if they were to change and shower together, their heterosexual desires would overwhelm their sense of propriety. Women's teams that have male coaches do not allow them in the showers or changing rooms with the athletes. A male coach of a men's or boys' team, on the other hand, is automatically accorded the privilege of seeing his athletes naked in the locker room and showers.

Frequently, boys on the team will go out together on dates with girls. While the other boys have their arms around the girls, feel-

33

ing this to be advantageous to the fulfillment of their sexual destiny, the homosexual boy is aware that the situation has somewhat less potential. John Goodwin told me that he remembered such dates:

> And girls, although I liked them, weren't doing the same to me that boys were doing. So there'd be a gang that was going out on dates and I'd be with my girlfriend and this boy who I had a crush on and his girlfriend, and what I really wanted was to be with him, not the girl. It got to be awkward at that point.

In situations such as this, a young homosexual man knows that as far as everyone else is concerned he is like them. It makes him poignantly aware, however, that he is not.

The irony of being with girls when one is interested in boys can be intense. Novelist John Fox writes of a young swimmer who, while dancing with a girl at a high-school dance, finds himself fantasizing about having sex with a man in a movie he had seen.

> I liked this brother of Paul Newman in this sort of western movie I saw that took place in the present. There I was dancing this slow dance with Sue, thinking about this guy in the movie and my head was on her neck and I could smell perfume but in my mind this guy is on a rumpled bed in his underwear in the ranch house that's in the movie and it's late in the morning. I, also in my underwear, sit on the bed and reach out, put my hand on his crotch and his cock jumps into my hand and he smiles out one side of his mouth and I have a hard-on and I tried to grind up against Sue but there was nothing *down* there to grind up *against* and her tits were all mushed up against my chest. I lifted my head, looked up at the band playing on the stage and kind of choked, "I'm thirsty."[23]

Having had girlfriends all through high school, wanting to be a member in good standing of the boys-wanting-girls club, when I went to university I thought it was appropriate to continue doing so. Several months into a relationship with a woman, whom I was

34

seeing almost daily, we still hadn't had sex; we hadn't even kissed each other. She was getting frustrated. One night when we were out drinking with the gang, she decided to show her dissatisfaction with my seemingly inactive libido: she put her arms around one of the other fellows at the table and he responded gratefully to her advances. It hit me like a ton of bricks. I was jealous. But it was *my girlfriend* I was jealous of. For weeks, I had had a crush on the guy she was coming on to, although until that moment I hadn't realized it. I remember I couldn't take my eyes off his strong, hairy forearms. My girlfriend was watching me. When she realized what was going on, she started to laugh. Still watching me, she ran her fingers up and down his arms, playing with those brown hairs. Then, with an incredibly devious look in her eyes, she turned her attention from me, said something to him I couldn't hear, and deep-kissed him. I was devastated. My girlfriend was getting the man I wanted. I looked around our table; everyone was drunk. It was boy/girl all the way around and they were all over each other. I couldn't stand it; I grabbed my coat and ran out of the bar.

As time passes, membership in the boys-wanting-girls club becomes more of a strain; it becomes more difficult to reconcile with one's homosexual desires. Eventually some men with homosexual desires, but by no means all of them, relinquish their membership. While they are in the club, they find themselves in a heterosexual world, a world in which they don't belong. Some homosexual boys make a point of avoiding the club, one manifestation of which is the social world of athletics. Others live with the duality of being outsiders on the inside.

The experience of being a "sissy," or at least being known as one, is not uncommon for gay boys and men. A sissy is a man or boy who does not subscribe to the orthodox myth of masculinity; he doesn't think like a "real man." Sissiness isn't necessarily the description of behavior; it's a personal disposition. The word "sissy" is derived from "sister" *(Concise Oxford Dictionary),* hence the "girlish" connotation. "Sissy" is usually considered a pejorative expression, especially when it is hurled as an accusation. But when employed by gay men as self-description, its pejorative sense is undermined. Gay men who have eschewed orthodox masculinity have no problem considering themselves as sissies—they do not, after all, subscribe to orthodoxy in gender and don't, therefore, feel compelled to establish a nonsissy status for themselves. One exercise club very popular with gay men in Toronto was well known as "Sissy Fitness." Certainly, not all gay men welcome the application of sissiness to themselves—some are uncomfortable with their estranged place in gender culture; they prefer to think of themselves as just as masculine as their heterosexual counterparts. Like David Kopay, they may go out of their way to "prove" their orthodox masculinity.

Whereas one might behave in a certain way because one is a sissy, one is not confined to that behavior; a sissy may behave effeminately or masculinely. A number of the men I interviewed, even though some of them were fine high-performance athletes, referred to themselves and their gay teammates as "sissies." One man talked about the juxtaposition of fine athletic ability and markedly gay self-expression.

> In gay sports, the sports I play, there are some athletes that are absolutely superb. These people could have played on any state university team and they are in fine physical shape. So it's a very competitive sport, especially the North American Gay Volleyball Association, but those wonderful, superb athletes are the most outrageous screamers you've ever seen and they'll do it right there on the court.*

A very fashionable young man, who used to be a gymnast and a certified gymnastics coach, joined a gay baseball team. Although many of the men on the team were very good baseball players, many of them did not behave in the traditionally masculine manner of baseball players.

> In baseball this summer I've never seen so many nelly boys. There's a lot of nelly boys and they can be just amazing

---

*"Screamers" refers to "screaming queens," which is an expression for gay men who make a point of their gayness by behaving in blatantly effeminate ways—it often entails a lot of shrieking.

36

athletes. They may not have a masculine bone in their bodies but put a baseball bat in their hands and they'll show you how to play baseball. I think that surprises a lot of people—it surprised me. But I surprised a lot of people too. They expected this trendy little fag to not know what to do with a baseball bat; but, you know, I got up there and did a good job and I helped my team. . . . Everyone always associates sports with being a butch man and the idea of fags playing baseball . . . Playing baseball with gay people was really interesting; it was a lot of fun.

Commenting on the juxtaposition of fine athletic ability and sissy-like effeminate manners, a former college basketball player said:

I have friends who are effeminate, and athletically speaking, I know of some very good volleyball players, who are among the best in North America, who are very effeminate, drag-queen types, and that opened my eyes a long time ago. How could this person possibly be better than me when they have long hair, long finger nails, every time he gets a spike he screams, and then I realized that your level of masculinity or femininity really doesn't have a hell of a lot to do with your athletic ability.

It's important to note that these three examples referred to the experience that these men had with gay community sports. When gay men are involved in mainstream sports organizations, they usually do not feel free to express sissy sensibilities. The orthodox masculine leitmotif, although it is most severely expressed in violent team sports, reverberates throughout the athletic world, albeit in varying degrees.

Not surprisingly, it is the aesthetic sports that are the most gay sports. A gymnast I spoke to said that being a gymnast in high school made his peers suspect that he was gay. Figure skating is dominated by gay men. A former figure skater who is now a policeman told me:

Figure skating was called "fairy skating." Figure skating is very close to ballet; it's a feminine sport. I was a figure skater. Everyone automatically assumed you were gay if you were a figure skater. Straight men were so far in a minority in figure skating—I can remember sitting at the 1980 national men's championship, and of the eight senior men at the national level, seven of them were gay. And that's probably a fairly accurate projection of the numbers in figure skating. Eighty or ninety percent of the men in figure skating are gay. My suspicion is that it's because of the artistic component in figure skating. I've also heard that there are a lot more gay men in gymastics than there are in other sports. I don't know whether its overgeneralizing to say that gay men are attracted to a sport that involves some sort of artistic expression, but it seems to be that there are more gay gymnasts and figure skaters than football players.

Although figure skating is dominated by gay men on the ice, the rules and traditions of the sport belie that fact somewhat. The pairs competition is the only sport that requires the competitors to ape heterosexual relations—it is ironic indeed that the sport with the highest proportion of homosexual men employs the most blatantly heterosexual signs. Even in football men don't have to feign an interest in women in order to score points. The rules do not allow two men to skate the pairs event together. Most of the time, the men wear pseudo-masculine outfits—tight-fitting little military uniforms are de rigueur on the ice. But these uniforms are not without irony; invariably their masculinity is elegantly undermined by glittering accents in sequins and gold lamé.

Because most male figure skaters are gay, the sport can feel like home for gay men and boys. Nevertheless, there are at least shadows of the experience of estrangement in this sport. The inherently romantic heterosexual significance of the pairs competition is at odds with the proclivities of gay men and boys. And famous figure skaters try to keep their homosexuality a secret. Whereas most sports heroes like to feature their wives and children when the media does personal profiles, gay figure skaters hide their "significant others" from the press. So, hiding homosexuality and the sense of estrangement that comes with it is a feature of even the most homosexual (mainstream) sport.

* * *

By showing that homosexual men tend to gravitate to individual, nonviolent sports, I am not suggesting that there are no homosexual men and boys in violent team sports. There certainly are homosexual men who pursue these sports, David Kopay being a well-known case in point. In fact, that there are homosexual men in such sports, given the overwhelmingly orthodox and heterosexual significance of those sports, is very important; it speaks of the multifaceted nuances of homosexuality—nuances that for the rest of this book we will try to illuminate.

Sports for homosexual men is a place of estrangement. It is an orthodox masculine world that emphasizes the unusual relationship homosexuals have with our culture in general. But so far we have only documented the experience of that estrangement. The question remains: What is the deep source of this estrangement? What is homosexuality in the first place? And how does homosexual desire offer a special experience of sport? It is to these questions we will now turn.

III

Sexual Mythology

"But love is blind, and lovers cannot see
The pretty follies that themselves commit."
—William Shakespeare, *The Merchant of*
Venice

What is the difference between homosexuality and heterosexuality? Is it the simple physical fact that one involves sexual activity between males or females and the other between males *and* females? Or is there a psychically deeper distinction between them? Some men and boys who engage in objectively homosexual behavior find it to be a more or less simple physical sexual release. Perhaps it's a substitute for heterosexual sex; perhaps it's an experiment with homosexuality that fails to ring true with the erotic world of the experimenter. Whatever it might be, homosexuality emerges for them as inauthentic, failing to resonate with their deepest sense of themselves and their erotic desires. Others, however, find their objectively homosexual activity to be in harmony with themselves, an authentic realization of their erotic needs. Clearly, the difference between hetero- and homosexuality is more than physical; it involves the *meaning* one finds in one's physical sex and that of others. Even more fundamentally, it involves the nature of sexuality itself.

The following theory of sexuality, being an attempt to explain the *difference* between homosexuality and heterosexuality on the basis of lived experience, will in some ways be a departure from the predominant contemporary approaches to sexuality. The "liberal" attitude is to minimize differences, claiming that homo- and heterosexuality are really minor variations—gay people are basically no different from straight people. This is at odds with the lived experience of being gay. The difference between homosexuality and heterosexuality is one of contrasting interpretations of the cardinal myths of our culture, myths that become the subject of erotic experience.

EROS

Why is sex so important? Why do religion, medicine, law, and commerce lavish so much attention on it? The Christian Church, realizing the power of sex, has circumscribed it in deference to its spiritual concerns—limiting sex to marriage and procreation. Medicine has established scientific disciplines for the study and "treatment" of sex. The state, by means of the law, has developed vast legal documents to regulate acceptable and unacceptable sexual practices. Commerce has taken sex not only as a commodity in itself, but also as *the* enticement by which it transforms products into objects of desire.

Sex is a special interaction between mental and physical experience. The physical dimension of sex transforms the mental and the mental transforms the physical. Consider the difference between having sex and thinking about having sex. This can be illustrated by comparing the different experiences of just thinking about a scene you find sexually exciting and the same imagined scene accompanied by masturbation. The masturbatory experience is more intense, more involving, in some way more actual. When the physical and mental come together in sexual activity, they are intensely and pleasurably merged. This is a process in which the abstract nature of thinking becomes incarnate in actual physical experience.

The essence of thinking is to abstract and codify our experiences of things and relationships in order that they may be cognitively manipulated. Essentially, this is the function of language.

42

(Probably the most important issue of twentieth-century philosophy and literary criticism, the relation of thinking and language has been much written about. Not wanting to digress, I will say simply that language shapes thinking. It does not, however, have dominion over all experience.[1]) It is the nature of language to transcend particularity, to universalize, to leave our *personal* experience behind. This averages out our experience so that it loses its particular and unique quality. Language depersonalizes experience. The sexual incarnation of thought in physical experience is a supreme *re*personalization of experience. The power of sexuality is the intensely pleasurable, consummate union of thought and physical experience, the marriage of our mental and physical lives. It brings us down to earth from the ethereal world of ideas and images. It saves us from abstraction and reclaims the *particular* and *unique* nature of our experience. It is salvation from the oblivion of the individual in linguistic thought, and therefore an affirmation of self.

The root of the self is physical life, that is, being embodied, physical existence.[2] But the body has not fared well in Western culture. In some respects the body has been discounted, ignored, made a mere servant of the mind, soul, or spirit. The body as a source of knowledge has been trivialized. The philosopher David Michael Levin said:

> According to our tradition of metaphysics, the human body is not capable of thinking. Thinking takes place only in the "mind" and this "mind" is contingently located in the region of the head—which for that reason, is often not counted as part of the human "body." Our tradition is not easily liberated from this dualism, because it has been very deeply committed, for many centuries, to the Judeo-Christian ideal of asceticism and its path of renunciation.[3]

That dualism that privileges the mind over the body has become basic to our thinking. Our tradition makes it seem that the body has no place in thinking, that it offers us no knowledge. But as Merleau-Ponty has shown, this is not actually true; the body is at the center of knowledge, informing us in the most basic way. Merleau-Ponty says that our bodies constitute "a communication

43

with the world more ancient than thought."[4] This font of bodily knowledge is disguised by our tradition of privileging the mind. In some ways we live our lives as though we were disembodied. But in fact we do not really believe that: frequently, in order to confirm our thoughts, we use our bodies. Take, for example, the experience of the expression of sympathy. In listening to a friend's sad story, one can say and think many things, but those thoughts and words become much more concrete when accompanied by a physical embrace. That embrace, if sincere, is more than just a *sign* of sympathy; it is the *embodiment* of sympathy, an incarnation. The desire to embrace, or conversely to hit, in life's more intense moments shows the *truly* privileged place of bodily knowledge.*

Sexual acts offer some of the most intense forms of bodily knowledge. In sexual acts the body is aroused from its generally numb state, transforming psychic experience, giving that experience the potency, the *authenticity* of bodily, physical, carnal experience. Sexual incarnation is one of the most profound human experiences possible. This is the experience of ecstasy, which the *Oxford English Dictionary* defines as "an exalted state of feeling which engrosses the mind to the exclusion of thought; rapture, transport." Sexual incarnation is ecstatic because the fleeting, intangible world of thought, the world of ideas, desires, and myths, is transformed. The intangible is made actual in the moment. Most of life is lived in abstraction, in what Heidegger would call the everyday world, in which everything is averaged out, where nothing is particular. Ecstasy happens when averageness vanishes and our experience is consumed with incarnation, with the experience of being now, of being actual, of being embodied. The ecstasy of sexual incarnation is the domain of eros.

Eros is the subjective world of sexuality. It is the psycho-physical *form* that sexuality takes in personal experience. As such it

---

*There is good reason that the body has such a high position as a source of understanding. The body is the supreme hermeneutical instrument of ontology. As Heidegger has pointed out, an authentic appreciation of Being emerges only in the radically temporal context of Being-toward-death. But what he fails to point out is the role of the physical body in Being-toward-death—death, and therefore life, being intensely physical phenomena. The body is the announcer of the deepest truth of being-there, Dasein. That we would call upon the body to impress the truth is highly appropriate.

44

is a fundamental structure that people employ in their lives. The urge to eroticize arises from the need to make life actual, that is, to incarnate our abstracted mental life. *Eros* is the capacity to transpose mental experience into physical existence; when eroticized, our thoughts have the potential for actual existence in personal time. Eros is a form that embodies our thoughts and makes them tangible. *Sexual acts* are the actual working out of the erotic, the incarnation of eros. In sexual acts, the potential of eros is realized.

If eros is a form, what is its content? Eros may be better understood if we think of it metaphorically as a musical instrument, let's say, the piano. On the piano one can play a vast spectrum of music: sonatas, mazurkas, ballads, blues, honky-tonk, hymns, orchestral transcriptions, and free-form jazz. Eros is similarly open for a spectrum of expression. The variety of themes for erotic expression is infinite. By way of introduction to erotic instrumentation, consider one of the more popular themes, the eroticism of romance. There are many who believe that love between two people is most fully expressed sexually. The consummation of romantic relations is sexual. In the sexual relations of lovers, their feelings or thoughts about their romantic relationship become eroticized; they become embodied in sexual experience and thus tangible. Taking on this physical reality, romantic feelings become undeniable. The eroticization of romance is a confirmation of romance. The meaning one finds in one's relationship with one's lover, when eroticized, becomes incarnate in sexual experience. Made sexual, one's lover becomes part of one's own physical being. This is what is meant in the oft-repeated romantic phrase: "And we became one!" Erotic desire for another person is a desire literally to *have* that person, to *incorporate* that person into one's own being.

Eros individualizes the world. It plays on myths, language, and the common understandings that people have of the world. Sexual acts are once-in-a-lifetime, *actual,* physical experiences. As such, they cannot be generalized; they are absolutely individual, utterly down-to-earth. Therefore, it is impossible to say exactly what meaning people find in their sexual experience. The exact content of these experiences cannot be described because each is a unique union of thought and individual, physical experience.

45

However, when discussing sexuality, we can describe what kind of experience it is, the way it is structured in terms of the cultural contents that become the subject of eros.

So far, I have described *successful* sexual encounters, that is, encounters in which the erotic themes are consonant with the world of the person involved and the sexual techniques are appropriate and adequate for the consummation of those themes. Just as there is variety in the quality of piano performances, so too some sexual performances are more successful than others. Successful sex is by no means an all-or-nothing event. While elements of the erotic theme may be of only marginal interest, aspects of the sexual technique may be of virtuoso accomplishment. It may happen that the erotic material of a sexual encounter plays powerfully on the world of the participant while the sexual technique falls short of excellence. And occasionally, there are perfect performances in which the most profound matters of one's life are eroticized and consummated with sexual techniques of supreme accomplishment. These are rare and great moments in life.

It is in the interplay of eros and sexual techniques that sexuality has its forum. The spectrum of possible sexual techniques is endless, no doubt worthy of a lifetime of study. The Marquis de Sade was one of the more remarkable and prolific students and authors of sexual technique.[5] Eastern cultures have produced impressive manuals, the *Kama Sutra,* for example. Choice of sexual technique, of course, depends on the erotic content that is to be incarnate, and the temperaments, sexual experience, and imagination of the eroticists.

Eros is an instrument one plays to transform the mental and physical into significant actual events. The erotic content of sexual acts is fluid. Viewed objectively, a man may seem to have a fixed erotic interest, fellatio, for instance. But the erotic significance that fellatio may have for that man may well change through different times in his life and from encounter to encounter. Early in his career it may be the vehicle for the youthful exploration of homosexuality, of being homosexual. During that time it could be a sexual expression thoroughly imbued with the negative images he has of homosexuality as a dark force, an unacceptable, unmentionable world that could ruin him. When he "comes out," fellatio may become the sexual instrument of his gay liberation; no longer seeing himself as a "monstrous homosexual cocksucker," fellatio becomes the sexual expression of his authenticity and integrity as a gay man. With his lover, fellatio may be the erotic and sexual consummation of his love, the erotic integration of his lover into himself, a bond that will unite their futures. Seen objectively, this man's propensity for fellatio seems constant and repetitive. But when looked at subjectively, as the sexual working-out of erotic meaning, fellatio emerges as a fluid and variable experience for this man, dependent upon his sense of himself, his place in the world, his past, present, and future.

Eros may express many things, on many levels, simultaneously. It plays on myths, social contexts, and formal structures such as earnestness, irony, admiration, affection, and so on. Eros is intensely personal, operating both consciously and unconsciously, emerging out of the individual's past, present, and sense of his or her future. Homoeroticism (homosexual eroticism) plays on the myths of masculinity and femininity, homosexual and heterosexual, gay and straight. It involves the social context in which the homoeroticist finds himself: be it homosexual, heterosexual, gay, straight, supportive, hostile, ambiguous, or ambivalent.

The difference between homosexuality and heterosexuality lies in their variations of erotic meaning. It is not so much a matter of the *physical sex* of those involved in sexual encounters or desires as it is the *erotic meaning* that they find in their own physical sex and that of their partners, real or imagined. The meaning of physical sex lies in the world of gender. Because the significant difference between homosexuality and heterosexuality lies not in the objective fact of members of the same sex engaging in sexual activity or desires, but in subjective erotic variations on the themes of gender, it is gender that is at the heart of homosexual and heterosexual difference, and not physical sex.

GENDER

There is an important distinction between sex and gender. Sex is a physiological distinction that is drawn between male and female, whereas gender is a cultural distinction that divides power between men and women. There are four categories of sexual physiological distinction. Genetic sex, male or female, and phenotypic sex (that is, the manifested, observable structure), male or female. The genetic sex of an individual is determined by the presence or absence of the "Y" chromosome. If an individual has an "X" and a "Y" chromosome, he is genetically male. If she has two "X" chromosomes she is genetically female.[6] Judging genetic sex is possible only by the examination of DNA under an electron microscope—a procedure that is usually followed only when there are other chromosomal medical problems.

The phenotypic sex is physically determined by the action of certain hormones that are responsible for the development of internal and external genitalia and the secondary sex characteristics that appear at puberty (such as the development of facial hair in males and breast development in females). The action of androgen, the male sex hormone, brings about the development of male genitals; the absence of this hormone allows for the development of female genitalia. It is only in the eighth week of embryonic development that genitalia become distinguished as male or female—until that point, the phenotypic sex of the embryo is undifferentiated. Interestingly, the difference between male and female genitalia and physiologies in general is only one of emphasis. A penis is an elongated version of the clitoris, the scrotum is labia that have fused. The action of hormones affect the extent of genital development. Sometimes, at birth, it is difficult to tell whether a baby is phenotypically male or female. Doctors then decide whether the child will be regarded as a male or a female. It is a very important decision in a patriarchal culture, the application of a major distinction, one that determines the status and therefore possibilities an individual may have in his or her life. This absolute distinction drawn between men and women is made on the basis of a physical attribute as minor as the degree of genital development. A development that is the result of the level of activity of hormones—a level that can and frequently is adjusted by the administration of drugs.

Before continuing, some mention should be made of the role of reproduction in the construction of gender. Much has been written on this subject, so there is little point in going into details here. Although it is a fact that, generally speaking, women must carry a child to term for the reproduction of the species, there is no reason to believe that they must be tied to that role. The slogan of the women's liberation movement, "biology is not destiny," should no longer be debatable. The nobler history of humanity is the history of the ability of the human mind and of culture to overcome the dictates of biology and "nature" in the service of a better life, one that is not the mere slave of biological impulses and the "forces of nature." The quest for an egalitarian organization of society in which people choose how to organize child-rearing is just one example of our ability to organize life as we see fit. In actual practice, reproduction has only a small role in sexual relations between people. This is amply proved by the fact that for growing numbers of people in heterosexual relations, contraception is becoming the norm and pregnancy is often the unwanted outcome of heterosexual relations in which contraception either failed or was ignored. There can be no doubt that the use of sexuality goes well beyond a desire to reproduce.

In a culture that is dominated by gender, in which gender is like a class system, giving power to men and withholding it from women, all aspects of a person's life will be influenced by his or her gender. By peering at a baby's little genitals, an enormous decision is reached regarding its sex and future.[7] From that point, every effort is made by the child's family and society to develop a distinct application of masculine or feminine gender. Whereas sex is a physiological distinction, gender is a cultural distinction.[8] Sex is socially neutral, gender is not. Without gender, physical sex is a mere biological fact; outside of gender, sexual characteristics are no more significant than any other physical characteristic. Therefore, it is gender that makes physical sex meaningful in social, cultural, and sexual contexts.

The idea that there is a "natural" difference between men and women presupposes a dichotomy between these genders that would have to be universal, that is, present in all cultures throughout history, with variations being nothing more than anomalies. The sociologist R. W. Connell points out that the notion of dichotomous sexes is not universal. He refers to the work of fellow sociologists Suzanne Kessler and Wendy McKenna They argue that most research, both of a scientific and popular nature, works within a "cultural framework in which the 'natural attitude' is to take gender as strictly dichotomous and unchanging. What they call 'gender attribution,' the social process 'by which we construct our world of two genders,' is sustained despite the failure of human reality on almost any count to be simply dimorphic."[9] For instance, anthropological literature on *berdache,* North American Indian transvestites who were socially accepted as women, indicates that gender is not always assigned on the basis of the biological differences of male and female.[10] This indicates, moreover, that one can choose gender.

Connell, essentially arguing against biological determinism offers another important criticism of the notion that there is a "natural difference" between men and women. "The idea of natural difference is that of a passively suffered condition, like being subject to gravity. If human life were in its major internal structures—gender being one—so conditioned, human history would be inconceivable. For history depends on the transcendence of the natural through social practice."[11]

Gender, understood as a cultural phenomenon, is a mythic world that polarizes the sexes, giving them social and psychic significance and status. Myths have great power. According to Roland Barthes, myth is a type of speech.[12] It is a form of communication, a way of transmitting meaning that fuels the understanding people have of themselves and their culture. When a subject is treated mythically it has an aura; there is a sense that the way it is presented in myth is the way it has always been—the subjects of myths are timeless, eternal, and necessarily true.

Myths describe "nature." But anthropology has taught us that what is considered "natural" varies extensively from one culture to another.[13] When we say something is "natural," we are pretending that somehow it is the product of "Nature," which is a force greater than ourselves. But, in fact, to say something is natural is to make a judgment; what we are really saying when we say that a phenomenon is natural is that it fits our view of the world—a view that is the product of tradition.[14] Myths operate as received wisdom; they enjoy the power of being traditional ways of seeing things. Tradition has its own authority.[15] People bow to tradition. To question tradition is to have the wrong attitude toward it. The myth of gender, being traditional, brings with it the sense that the content of the myth is authoritative. Gender myth communicates the traditional division of power in our culture between males and females, making that division seem natural, ahistorical, universal, and necessarily the way things must be.

Gender myth exaggerates the minor physiological differences between male and female, transforming them into opposites. There is a metamorphosis in which relatively slight physical variation becomes an absolute distinction; these physical variations become the basis for the mythic hierarchical division of the world into men and women, commonly known as the "opposite sexes." People live their lives and understand each other in the context of the myth of gender. A multitude of gestures, physical attributes, and attitudes are interpreted in the light of masculine and feminine gender myth. Gender is a way of seeing things; it is a worldview, a *weltanschauung.* The physical characteristics of sex become mythic signs of gender.

Masculinity and femininity are interpretive contexts that assign value to gestures and attitudes that are in themselves valueless. These values are along a spectrum of power, with masculine being powerful and feminine powerless. When a man behaves in a way that is interpreted as masculine, he is placed in this spectrum of power. This power need not be actualized; in fact, it usually is not.[16] The power is mythic. For example, while in the gym working out with weights, a man may without good reason drop the weights to the floor so they make more noise than is necessary; simultaneously he will grunt. Because aggressive noise-making is a masculine gesture, such behavior in the weight room is meant to indicate a man's sense of his place in the myth. The interpretation of a gesture as masculine is an invocation of the mythic world of gender power; it endows that gesture with such power. Acknowledging or accepting the power that's been invoked by the interpretation of a gesture as masculine is a matter of faith in the gender myth. It's similar to a Catholic priest at the Eucharist claiming to invoke the power of God so that bread and wine become body and blood. Whether or not they actually become body and blood is beside the point; to those who care, the bread and wine have been changed: they are endowed with a new meaning.

The myth of gender creates and supports differences between males and females that consolidate men's power over women. Keeping in mind that the myth of masculinity and femininity is cultural and therefore the product of historical developments and subject to social change, it can be argued that this myth plays a role in the division of labor and the structure of power in our society.

> The central fact about this structure in the contemporary capitalist world is the subordination of women. This fact is massively documented, and has enormous ramifications—physical, mental, interpersonal, cultural—whose effects on the lives of women have been the major concerns of feminism. *One of the central facts about masculinity, then, is that men in general are advantaged by the subordination of women.* [17]

The gender categories of masculine and feminine are fundamental to the structure of patriarchal power and how it works. Men are in a position of power over women. This difference in mythic power is blatantly realized in the social sphere. Women are discouraged, in some cases prohibited, from competing with men in economic or professional life. In our culture and many others, they frequently act as unpaid servants and bear children who will perpetuate the *man's* lineage—children are usually given the paternal surname. The high incidence of men's violence against women in their homes and on the streets is now a well-documented fact. This violence is the most obvious social manifestation of mythic gender power.

Gender is a myth that justifies, expresses, and supports the power of men over women. As such, it is an important tool for giving men that hegemony. Remembering that Barthes said that myth is a form of speech that endows its subject with a sense of ahistorical universality and necessity,[18] we can see how the myth justifies hegemonic gender relations. The notion that the dominant and subordinate positions of men and women respectively are dependent upon social and historical influences is alien to the mythical understanding of masculinity and femininity. Until the blossoming of modern feminism, almost everyone in Western culture assumed that gender was somehow a fundamental feature of one's sex, that the power men have over women is natural and universal. Because it is the effect of myth to enshrine social relations in the false prestige of the "natural order of things," challenging the social order is seen as going against nature.[19] Certainly, this is a traditional accusation leveled against feminists demanding equality for women. Through the myth, gender is justified by being a "natural" aspect of the way things are.

An examination of the nature of power reveals the way that gender myth expresses and supports masculine and feminine power relations. Michel Foucault offers a comprehensive definition of power.

> Power must be understood in the first instance as the multiplicity of *force relations,* immanent in the sphere in which they operate and which constitute their own organization; as the *process* which, through ceaseless struggles and confrontations transforms, strengthens, or reverses them; as the *support* which these force relations find in one another, thus forming a chain or a system, or on the contrary, the disfunctions and contradictions which isolate them from one another; and lastly as the *strategies* in which they take effect, whose general design or institutional crystallization is embodied in the state apparatus, in the formulation of the law, in the various social hegemonies.[20]

Gender myth, while attempting to polarize the relations between men and women, allows for extensive interplay within those relations, which indicates that the respective dominant and subordinate positions of men and women constitute a "multiplicity of *force relations.*" The "battle of the sexes," that is, the fact that masculinity and femininity are expressed and played off one another, thereby realizing their power relations, is the *process* that "transforms, strengthens, or reverses" those relations. The complementarity of masculinity and femininity, strength and weakness, dominance and submission, function as the *"support* which these force relations find in one another." And finally, the institutionalizations of patriarchal hegemony and privilege in law, medicine, religion, commerce, sport, and so on, clearly function as the *"strategies"* through which the force relations of masculinity and femininity "take effect."

The gender myth involves three related axes: physical sex (male/female), sociocultural status (man/woman), and signs of gender (masculine/feminine).

As discussed earlier, *physical sex* is a matter of being male or female, that is, having the "X" or "Y" chromosome and the phenotypic results of it: male or female genitalia and secondary sex characteristics.

Sociocultural status is what it means to be a man or a woman in our culture. The gender order is hierarchical and divided into two. Men are superior to women. This is the birthright of men and exists independently of any individual merit. Being a man automatically places one on the positive side of power. This status is changing. Men's birthright is being challenged by women and the superior status of men is slowly being eroded. Although it is changing in practice, remnants of this classlike system remain in people's thinking. Certainly at a conscious level, many are attempting to dismantle the superior position of men; there are now laws prohibiting discrimination against women. Subconsciously, though, even in enlightened circles, women are still often understood as inferior to men by both men and women. The reasons for this are deeply psychic, emanating out of the fundamental sense that one has of one's own position in a patriarchal world.

The *signs of gender* are various gestures—by which I mean assorted body deportments, clothing customs, hair styles, and complex behaviors such as "being a football player"—that indicate the forcefulness or significance that one's gender is supposed to take. The mythic division of power is expressed and secured through the complex relationship between the spectrum of masculinity and femininity and the use of it by men and women. At one end of the spectrum, a man behaving in a way that is interpreted as masculine is powerful; at the other end, a woman inter-

54

preted as feminine is not powerful.[21] In a rigidly gendered society, men would be completely masculine and women completely feminine. The world is not so simple. Some women do not embrace the enervated life of femininity entirely and some men do not take up a purely masculine one. Men, however, can exert considerable power over women by using masculinity. Women complement that power by being subordinate in femininity.

From infancy, one's family and society work very hard to convince one of one's place in the fundamental sexist division of power in our society; this is the process of learning one's gender. The ways in which gender are learned are well known and therefore need only a passing reference here.[22] Boys and girls are usually given respectively masculine and feminine names; as they learn those names they simultaneously learn whether they are boys or girls. Mother says to her child, "Bobby's a big boy," or "Cynthia is a sweet little girl." The physical treatment of little boys is rough and aggressive compared to that of little girls. Boys wear clothes designed for activity; girls' little dresses are delicate and inhibit active behavior. And so on. Most people grow up with a strong sense of where they belong in the gender order. One day I was playing with the three-year-old son of a friend of mine. He wanted to know why I wear an earring. "It makes you look like a girl," he said. He was surprised that I would do something that would make me look like a girl. Although he was too young to read, he was fully aware of a sign of gender (an earring). Moreover, he saw it as a contradiction for a man to wear feminine paraphernalia. That episode illustrates that at a very young age, a child knows not only the signs of gender, but also the importance of adhering to the gender that one has been assigned. It also indicates a basic intuition that gender is fluid, that is, that it is possible for a male to dress or behave as a woman.

Gender is deeply personal. One's relation to gender is a matter of one's relation to power. The fundamental meaning of being a man or being a woman in our culture lies in their relative mythic powers. Gender is a kind of prison. It is difficult to think about another person without thinking of his or her gender. For example, if you meet a person briefly you may well forget most everything about them; it is very unlikely, however, that you will forget whether they were a man or a woman. We are usually aware of

the gender of the person with whom we are having sex; it's difficult to conceive of sexual relations in which gender would have
no place in the experience. Because gender is fundamentally a
matter of power, knowing a person's gender is essentially a matter of knowing their status within the myth of gender power. This
is a way of knowing that emanates out of one's earliest infantile
adjustments to the mythic patriarchal discourse of power. This
discourse has been thousands of years in the making and operates
like a language that imbues our thinking or being in a way that
is quite similar to the profound influence of ancient Greek metaphysics.[23] Our earliest cultural experience of ourselves and others
has been mediated by the language, the discourse of patriarchy.
As long as we continue to see the world through the gender myth,
as divided into men and women, we will continue to see a relative
patriarchal status for each.

It is essential to point out that this interpretation can be conscious or subconscious. For the most part, it is *subconscious.* Almost all men and women dress, cut their hair, and carry
themselves in such a way that their gender is obvious. Those who
present themselves in a convincingly androgynous way make
most others uneasy. The fact that in English and many other
languages, it is difficult to refer to someone without using a masculine or feminine pronoun, illustrates the way in which gender
imbues our language and therefore culture. The tendency to interpret people and their behavior in light of the myth of gender
remains, for the most part, in the subconscious mind because it
is a fundamental, accepted, and largely unquestioned way of seeing things. Although in the 1970s, feminism did draw elements of
this thinking from the depths of the subconscious, making them
explicit and open to criticism, such "consciousness-raising" is no
longer fashionable.

The mythical interpretation of gender emerges from the individual's personal experience as it confronts culture. *Culture* is
the world of meaning or significance in which one finds oneself.[24]
For the most part we don't choose it; we are, as Heidegger would
say, "thrown" into it. In any culture there are many "languages."
Of course, tongues such as English, French, and Swahili are languages. Born and educated in Pakistani culture, one will probably
understand and speak Urdu. One's experience will be filtered

through the grammar, vocabulary, and literature of Urdu. Although the language is common to all who speak it, depending on one's experience and creativity, one is able to fashion unique statements with it. Myths are languages also. Just as the Urdu tongue subconsciously guides one's thinking and therefore experience, so too gender myth filters experience without our being aware of it for the most part. The culture that imparts the myth of gender offers its standard language of gender, its signs of gender. Depending on one's experience and creativity, one is able to use that culture, to employ those myths and their signs in one's own way.

Just as the myth affects the thinking of people, so too people affect the nature of the myth. Different people have encountered our culture and its gender myth in different ways. This means there is great variability in the notions people have of gender. Gender may be a major concern or a minor one. Some may see the myth as an authentic view of the social difference between male and female; others may see the myth as the tool of the patriarchal oppression of women. Some dismiss the myth; others cherish it.

Anthropology has shown us that the gestures that constitute masculine and feminine gender vary significantly from culture to culture.[25] This illustrates that nothing is inherently masculine or feminine; rather, masculinity and femininity are dependent on cultural conventions. The masculine and feminine constitution of gender varies not only from culture to culture, but also from group to group within a culture and from person to person within a group. The signs of gender are profoundly influenced by other cultural factors such as class and ethnicity. What may be seen as masculine by one class may be considered effeminate by another. Interpretations of gender are idiosyncratic in the extreme. Nevertheless, there is some basic agreement on the nature of masculinity and femininity in North American and British culture.

It's illuminating to see how the dictionaries define "masculine," "feminine," and related words. A number of important themes emerge. Power is the distinguishing feature of masculinity, whereas lack of power is the distinguishing feature of femininity. The *Oxford English Dictionary* (OED) defines "masculine" as "having the appropriate excellences of the male sex; manly, virile, vigorous, powerful." The OED defines "femi-

nine" as "the characteristics of, peculiar or proper to a woman."
"Woman" is defined not only as "an adult female human being,"
but also "with allusion to qualities generally attributed to the
female sex, . . . their position of inferiority or subjection." Interestingly, whereas "masculine" is defined in terms of "excellences,"
the OED offers a depreciative use of "feminine," which is "womanish, effeminate." It is in this depreciative use that the powerlessness that is associated with femininity is borne out. *Webster's
Third New International Dictionary of the English Language*
(1976) defines "effeminate" as "lacking manly strength of purpose; exhibiting weakness." *The Dictionary of Contemporary
American Usage* (Random House, 1957) says that "effeminate" "is
a term of contempt, applied to actions or qualities in a man that
would be fitting in a woman." The OED defines "effeminate" as
"to make womanish or unmanly; to enervate; to grow weak, lan-
guish." Four of the OED definitions of "enervate" make explicit
the dearth of power that our concept of feminine indicates. "1.
Wanting in strength of character; spiritless, unmanly, effeminate.
2. Wanting in bodily strength or physical power. 3. To weaken
mentally or morally; to destroy the capacity for vigorous effort of
intellect or will. 4. To render ineffectual."

It is important to note that the dictionaries suggest that although masculinity and femininity are seen as attributes of
males and females respectively, they are not *necessarily* attrib-
utable to those respective sexes. These definitions leave open the
possibility for masculine women and feminine men. *The Dictionary of Contemporary American Usage* says that "Masculine
applies to the qualities that properly characterize men as compared to women. If applied to a woman, it suggests something
incongruous with her femininity (Large shoulders gave her a
masculine appearance) or conveys a compliment (She had a logical, masculine mind)."

Masculinity is seen as superior to femininity.* It is more so-

---

*There are feminist arguments that try to claim respectability for femininity by
affirming the positive traits that are attributed to it and downplaying the negative.
It is only by adoption of a masculine standard, they say, that physical strength,
aggressiveness, and so on are seen as superior and that "feminine" attributes are
seen as inferior. These arguments usually amount to a dangerous form of "essen-
tialism" positing women as biologically predisposed to care and nurture. This is
not only unfounded biologically, psychologically, anthropologically, and sociolog-

cially acceptable for a woman to be masculine than for a man to be feminine because it is more acceptable to take power than it is to relinquish it.[26] Because in patriarchal culture it is generally accepted that it is better to be powerful than weak, masculine things are usually seen to be superior to feminine things.

By reference to the myth of gender, one can interpret the behavior of others in the context of the spectrum of power between men and women. One can invite interpretations of one's own actions within these mythic contexts by behaving in ways that play on the myth of gender. One's clothes, carriage, and body all become signs of gender. The characteristics of male and female physical sex become signs of gender. It is in the context of gender myth that muscles have masculine significance and breasts feminine. The importance of the phallus lies in its mythic significance as the organ of masculinity, the sign of men's power.

Eros, you will remember, is the human capacity to transform the mental and physical. It is the form that makes possible the incarnation of mental experience. Sexually speaking, the myth of gender exists as a mental phenomenon until it undergoes the metamorphosis of our erotic capacity. Eroticized, gender becomes more than an idea, not just some abstract myth, and has the potential of becoming part of one's actual personal experience. The eroticization of gender, "worked out" in sexual acts, is the incarnation of gender in one's *own* time. Thus temporalized, it is the experience of ecstasy.[27] Since gender is a myth of power, its eroticization is the ecstatic incarnation of mythic power. The meaning of gender, as we have seen, is the assignation of power to men and the denial of the same for women. When gender is the subject of eros, the patriarchal power of men or the lack of that power of women becomes incarnate in the life of the eroticist.

In patriarchal culture the eroticization of gender is the eroticization of power as it is divided between men and women on the

---

ically, it is also oppressive to women, keeping them in their traditional labor. The superiority of masculinity consists not in ethical superiority, by any means. The superiority of masculinity lies in its (unethical) ability to subjugate others. Males and females are inherently neither inferior nor superior, only the myth of gender makes it so.

basis of their sociocultural status, a black and white distinction. So, if the object of one's erotic desire is a man, then the sexual experience is the incarnation of that positive masculine power. Likewise, if the object of one's erotic desire is a woman, one incarnates that lack of power in the sexual act. The eroticization of gender is a way of making its mythic power (or lack thereof) subjectively real; mythic gender power is materialized in physical experience. Eros, then, brings myths to life; it is the actualization of gender myth in personal lives.

The eroticization of gender involves not only the incarnation of one's partner's gender but also one's own gender. We always bring to erotic experience our sense of our place in the gender myth; eros cannot be objective. Erotic experience, therefore, is also the incarnation of the relationship of one's gender to the other. If in the erotic imagination there are two men involved, since the very soul of the meaning of manhood is the mythic power men have and women don't, then the incarnation is of two positive mythic powers and the interplay between them. If there is a man and a woman, then it is the interplay between the myths of the dominant power of men and subordinate power of women that is incarnate.

Herein lies the fundamental distinction between homosexuality and heterosexuality. What distinguishes homo- from heterosexuality is the erotic interest that one has in the sex of one's partner. Because this involves the *meaning* of physical sex, it's an erotic interest in gender power. Male and female body parts derive their erotic significance from the gender myth. The pleasure that many find in sucking cocks is not merely a matter of wrapping one's lips around human tissue made erect by its engorgement with blood. The excitement lies in the ecstasy of sexual contact with the ultimate sign of manhood, the power of patriarchy, the quintessential presencing of the myth of gender power, which is the phallus.

The meaning of gender lies in the division of mythic power as it is given to men or withheld from women. Homosexuality involves the eroticization of basically *similar* power as it has been apportioned on the basis of the *sociocultural status* of men in patriarchal culture. (This does not mean that there cannot be considerable interplay of different powers between men through the variable *signs of gender* or other kinds of power such as race, class, or wealth.) Heterosexuality, on the other hand, is the eroticization of the power men have over women, the eroticization of the basically subordinate position of women in patriarchal culture; it is the eroticization of power *difference.* That's why some feminist women refuse to have sex with men—they realize that nonpatriarchal sexual relations with men are difficult in the extreme, if not altogether impossible.

This conception of sexuality can lead to misunderstandings—misunderstandings that come about as the result of reducing the domain of eros to only one sphere, that is, gender relations. In sexual relations between people, many themes can be eroticized. It must be stressed at this point that I am describing only one theme of eroticism, gender. But there is no limit to possible erotic themes. The various manifestations of gender power are not the only texts for eros. Class, race, violence, love, hate, procreation, respect, danger, and impropriety are all potential erotic texts that can become sexually incarnate in tandem with gender.

The very being of one's partner—by which I mean the primordial existential self that is prior to, more profound and authentic than, any cultural categories such as gender, class, or race that are applied to that self—can be the subject of sexuality. The sexual experience of another's being, certainly, is the most profound and intimate relationship possible between two people. In that experience, the being of another is incorporated in one's own being. Such an experience is the *incarnation* of the meaning of life itself. It delves deep into the psyche, going beyond the mythic power relations of gender. But because gender is so basic to our world, to the sense we have of ourselves and each other, such nongendered eroticism is very difficult, if not impossible, at this point in the development of our culture.[28] Such eroticism is impossible not only because of the overwhelming importance we place on gender, but also (and this is a more fundamental issue than this volume can concern itself with) because our history over the last two thousand years or so has been one of turning away from being.[29]

It's probably true that there are at least elements of genderless eroticism in some people's sexual experience. In that regard, the physical sex of one's partner is unimportant. Usually, although it may not be the primary theme of an erotic experience, because gender is fundamental to our thinking, the sociocultural status of gender (that is, manhood or womanhood) is an essential background for the successful eroticization of other (coexisting) themes. Most people are aware of, and care a great deal about, whether they are having sex with a man or a woman and organize their sexual affairs accordingly.

Now, in light of the concept of eros and sexuality I have just set out, we should refine our notion of homo- and heterosexuality. Our concern is with the *meaning* of erotic desire as it shows itself in its attraction to gender. Sometimes consciously and at other times in a deeply subconscious way, people understand themselves and everyone else in the mythic context of gender, a cultural creation. And so their erotic desire for others is in that context. The desire that a man has for another man, or a woman for another woman, is the play of homoeroticism in the myth of gender; the desire that men and women have for each other is the play of heteroeroticism. These are the forms that people use for the incarnation of the power of gender. One's homo- or heteroerotic desires are fundamental expressions of one's personal relation to power in the gender myth. Eros tells tales.

The notion that homoeroticism is a matter of the interplay of similar power is not new. In the *Symposium,* Plato has Pausanias deliver a speech on two forms of Eros, one being superior to the other. "This Eros (the common whose worshipers love women as well as youths, and with those they love, love the body more than the soul) is the offspring of the goddess who is far younger than the other, and owes its existence to a union of the male and female. But the other Eros is the offspring of the heavenly goddess in whose birth the female has no part but only the male. . . . Those who are inspired by this love turn to the male because they love that which by nature possesses more power and a larger share of mind."[30] Plato sees power as one of the essential features of being male—attraction to males is an attraction to power. This attraction is only from the point of view of men, since no consideration is given to the view of women.

In the eroticization of gender, one reads one's partner and oneself through the gender myth. This involves the *sociocultural* interpretation of the basic status of being a man or a woman. Bu this black and white distinction of positive and negative power can be modified or amplified through complementary interpretations of the *signs of gender.* The signs of masculinity and femininity are the instruments of nuance in the erotic interpretation of gender. In the eroticization of gender, *against the backdrop of manhood or womanhood,* people play with the signs of gender, manipulating their erotic meaning in a profound and personal experience of the vicissitudes of mythic power.

People use the signs of gender to customize the basic division of gender (the sociocultural status of being a man or a woman) to their unique erotic tastes. Involved in a heteroerotic experience, a man may prefer to narrow the gap of his mythic power over his partner by finding in her some signs of masculine gender such as muscles, an aggressive attitude, or short, "mannish" hair. Another man in a heteroerotic experience may want to emphasize the mythic power gap by behaving in a brutish, masculine way, keeping himself unshaved, perhaps even unwashed. Meanwhile, he looks for exaggerated signs of femininity in his partner: perhaps exotically teased hair, heavy makeup, large breasts, slender, unmuscular arms, and a submissive disposition. A woman involved in a heteroerotic affair may wish to de-emphasize as much as possible the mythic division of power between herself and her lover by refraining from wearing makeup, wearing more tailored clothes, and taking charge of the affair. She seeks out feminine signs in her partner such as a malleable disposition, consideration for her feelings and needs, an unmuscular build. Another woman in a heteroerotic relationship may want to emphasize the difference in mythic power between herself and her man. She wants a "man who will make her feel like a woman." In his strong muscular arms he will whisk her delicate body away into some paradise where "opposites attract." And so the story goes.

ORTHODOXY: THE HETEROSEXUAL MYTH

Intimately related to the myth of gender is the myth of heterosexuality. According to the myth, heterosexual relations are the "natural" arena for the sexual play of mythic gender power. Hetero-sexuality is the erotic arrangement for the incarnation of the mythic power difference between men and women. Heteroeroti-cism, by definition, is an erotic interest in gender different from one's own. Gender is a division that is considered complementary as a balancing between two essentially different beings: man and woman, strong and weak, hard and soft, rational and emotional. This "balancing," as feminism has shown us, is nothing more than a cover-up, a concealment of male supremacy, which, as Anthony Wilden has said, is "the biggest and most deeply rooted form of organized bullying in the history of human culture."[31] Heteroeroticism is the—often deeply subconscious—incarnation of those relations. The heterosexual *myth* is, as Barthes would say, a "speech" on the interplay of the different mythic powers of men and women that gives heterosexuality the false appearance of being "natural," ahistorical, universal timelessness, when, in fact, heterosexuality is a cultural creation.

The mythic difference of power between men and women is incarnate in heteroerotic sex. Remember the four elements of Foucault's conception of power: force relations, process, support, and strategies. Since gender in our culture is foremost a mythic, patriarchal division of power, heteroeroticism is fundamentally the erotic incarnation of the interplay of the "force relations" of gender.*

The "process" by which the force relations of gender are "transformed, strengthened, or reversed" consists in the interac-tion between men and women. This process can be manifested in a variety of ways. Heteroeroticism employs signs of power in the service of the differentiation of power. The "missionary position," which consists of pinning a prostrate woman and pushing a penis into her vagina, is a sign of the mythic power of men. Being on top of a woman signifies domination, and the thrusting of the penis, itself a well-established icon of masculinity even when not "in action," by its penetrations, signifies masculine power. It is both a technique for the sexual working-out of an erotic theme

---

*The following short review of power in heteroerotic sexual relations is not in-tended to be comprehensive. It is offered as an *illustration* of the machinations of mythic power in heteroeroticism.

and a sign of the theme itself. Until recently, the "missionary position" was the standard of "respectable" heterosexual coitus; variations on it were not only considered improper but were also frequently punishable by law. In the movies, even in "liberal" films, heterosexual sex is still most often portrayed in the missionary position.

The violent rape of women is the ultimate consummation of the violence inherent in the myth of gender. The most masculine thing that a man can do is to fuck a woman violently against her will. It is in this act that the mythic power difference between men and women is most clearly realized. It is the debasement of a woman, wherein she is not only made subordinate and brutalized, but is also reduced to a mere object over which the man may run roughshod in his pursuit of the erotic incarnation of his mythic, masculine power. In our culture, the most feminine thing a woman can do is submit.

One of the "supports" that the force relations of gender find in one another is the relative physical strength of men and women. We live in a society that encourages men and boys to be active and develop larger, more muscular bodies than women and girls. Because this kind of sexism is pervasive, most women are physically weaker than most men.[32] This "support," that is, relative strength and weakness, can easily become an erotic element in heterosexual sexual relations. Obviously, the spectrum of relative physical strengths of men and women allows for considerable latitude in this erotic dimension. So much so that the physical strength of a woman could overwhelm that of a man in such a way that eroticism would lie in the subversion of the mythic power of men. This is generally considered rather "kinky," what many psychologists and sociologists like to call "deviant sexuality."

Finally, one of the "strategies" of gender power is the institutionalized arrangement for heterosexual sexual relations, namely marriage and the nuclear family. This is a man's castle in which, traditionally, he has conjugal rights over his wife and, it's becoming increasingly acknowledged, his children.* In some

---

*Admittedly, incestuous sexual relations between a father and his children are not considered legitimate in our culture, at least on the surface. However, it is a practice that continues in secret and whose secrecy is made possible by the organization of the nuclear family, whose affairs are conducted in private under the

jurisdictions the concept of a man raping his wife does not exist. Traditionally, the state has been reluctant to interfere in familial disputes because such interference constitutes an abrogation of patriarchal autonomy. Only when a man's abuse of his authority in his home becomes so severe that death or at least serious injury may ensue will the state sometimes move in and offer protection to women and children. The right of a man not to be bothered by the state in his home is usually referred to as his right to privacy. This facade of nonregulation is just a smoke screen for the preservation of the patriarchal status quo—it is, after all, virtually only heterosexual men who draw up legislation and control the operations of the police and other major social agencies. Women, being financially dependent on men and having most of the responsibility for children, often see little recourse except to grit their teeth and bear the abuse. Many see it as the fate of women, a destiny over which they have no control. (Recently, though, some governments have taken a more interventionist approach and established special programs to protect women and children.) Of course, not all men abuse their conjugal privileges. Nevertheless, the fact remains that a pervasive heterosexual institution exists, which, if a man chooses, can offer him considerable immunity for his sexual use of power over women.[33]

Heteroeroticism is that place where individual men and women can have a personal experience of the fundamental division of power in our culture. For a man to eroticize his relationship with a woman is to personally incarnate his patriarchal birthright. For a woman to eroticize her relationship with a man is to personally incarnate her subordinate position in patriarchal culture. Sigmund Freud believed that heterosexuality is the most fully developed sexuality. Reflecting patriarchal culture, his belief is an accurate assessment of the intrinsic sexual ramifications of orthodoxy in the gender myth. A man who has accepted

---

authority of men. Foucault points out that incest is an innate aspect of family life; it is "an obsession and an attraction, a dreadful secret and an indispensible pivot." (1976, p. 109) It is true that the authority of men in the nuclear family is diminishing as the liberation of women increases; that there are substantial remnants of patriarchy in most familial settings, however, is undeniable. For empirical research and a detailed discussion of violence against women and children, see Connie Guberman and Margie Wolfe, eds., *No Safe Place: Violence Against Women and Children* (Toronto: The Women's Press, 1985).

his orthodox position in the gender myth and fully incorporated it into his sense of himself, feels, often in a deeply subconscious way, his mythic superiority over women, which is to say, he appreciates the difference between men and women, will incarnate that difference, in sexual acts, not because he has to but because he wants to. It is this lust for the incarnation of mythic power difference that fires the engines of men who want women. The signs of those differences, be they ruby-red lipstick, curvaceous hips, or voluptuous breasts, stimulate heteroerotic men. Such signs give them erections, making rigid the organ that secures the mythic conquest. Heteroeroticism, confirming as it does the relative dominant and subordinate positions of men and women in the gender myth, is the *orthodox* eroticization of the myth.

Some heterosexual men talk of a fear of sex with women. In a deep way, they understand the meaning of sex with women; they know intuitively the power relations that will be incarnate there. This might be called "performance anxiety." But the source of that anxiety probably concerns more than the technical ability to have sex; it likely involves the significant chasm that the myth of gender has created between men and women and the role that the power difference between them will play in the sexual encounter. Men may be afraid of revealing the sinister nature of their desire to eroticize gender difference, that is, their power over women.

Some might argue that they are the hapless victims, just as much as women, of a gender myth that is oppressive. Connell said that this is nothing more than an abdication of responsibility.

> Conventional [orthodox] masculinity is, to an extent, hegemonic masculinity in bad faith. Men enjoy patriarchal power, but accept it as if it were given them by an external force, by nature or convention or even by women themselves, rather than by an active subordination of women going on here and now. They do not care to take responsibility for the actions which give them power. . . . The power relations of the society become a constitutive principle of personality dynamics through being adopted as a personal project, whether acknowledged or not. . . . The subordination of women and the marginalization of

homosexual and effeminate men are sustained neither by chance nor by the mechanical reproduction of a social system, but by the commitments implicit in conventional and hegemonic masculinity and the strategies pursued in the attempt to realize them.[34]

One of the most pleasurable realizations of orthodox masculinity is having sex with women. It is an important symbolic, psychic, and physical "strategy" that "realizes" in personal lives orthodox gender power. It is the realization of their deep desires that makes some men afraid. Sloughing off responsibility for this lust for power by accusing society of imposing it upon them is one way of feeling better and avoiding blame.

Another way of avoiding the true significance of gendered eroticism is to candy-coat it with "love." "Because I love you, I can fuck you." In an attempt to cover up the meaning of their sexual activity, some will even call it "making love." It is no coincidence that women are traditionally more concerned about "love" than men;[35] it is they who are being subordinated in the sexual act, so it is women who need to be mollified by love. Queen Victoria encouraged her daughter to lie back and "think of England" while her husband did what he would. Love, like patriotism, can conceal the meaning of sex as it draws on the myth of gender.

As I said earlier, by employing the *signs of gender,* men and women can modify or exaggerate their mythic status according to their erotic taste. But these constitute *variations* on the erotic themes of mythic power, not *transformations* of the *sociocultural* apportionment of power between men and women. Even if a woman plays the part of "Ilsa, She Wolf of the SS," sadistically abusing and dominating the man with whom she is having sex, her basic sociocultural status of being a woman and his of being a man remain intact. Essential to that ironic erotic scene is the difference in the sociocultural status of the participants. Only if they were unaware *and* didn't care whether the other was a man or woman would they truly subvert the gender order in that sexual scene.

One's erotic preference for a man or a woman may not be a conscious theme of an erotic encounter. People become so accustomed to their homo- or heteroerotic lives that the gender of their partner *seems* to disappear as an erotic theme. But this does not mean that gender no longer plays an important role in erotic life. Gender becomes a fundamental structure for eros, eroticized at a deep subconscious level, while at the conscious level other themes, such as love, hate, class, status, accessibility (that is, the excitement of having sex with someone who had appeared inaccessible), and so on, are at the fore of the erotic imagination.

So, in heteroeroticism, the power difference between men and women remains basic to the experience regardless of the variable eroticism of masculine and feminine signs. Heteroeroticism is the "natural" form that sexuality will take in patriarchal culture because it so deeply expresses the fundamental division of mythic power, which is the very heart of gender in patriarchal culture. Heteroerotic desire constitutes a profound, for the most part subconscious, psychic acceptance of patriarchal culture as it is handed down, an embracing of the orthodox reading of the myth of gender and the finding of personal meaning in it.

THE HOMOEROTIC PARADOX

Erotic desire focused on specific genders expresses one's personal response to power in the myth. Not everybody wants to eroticize the *hetero*geneity of gender power; some want to eroticize *homo*geneity. Homoeroticism, I suggest, emerges out of an unusual sense of one's relation to the gender myth. This sense is a deep psychic intuition about one's place in the gender order; it informs gestures and desires but remains, for the most part, beneath the surface of conscious experience. The erotic desire that men have for other men discloses that sense; it is an erotic expression of one's interpretation of oneself and others in the gender myth. Since the gender myth is foremost a myth about the power difference between men and women, in homoeroticism a very important part of the gender myth is obviously missing: namely, the erotic desire for the incarnation of the *different* mythic powers of men and women. Homoeroticism is the incarnation of the manly aspects of the gender myth but not within the context of the domination of women.*

Homoeroticism deals with the basic mythic understanding of oneself and one's partners being men (or boys). The erotic desire for other men is, of course, an issue of gender. Homoeroticism is the incarnation of affinity within the gender myth. *It is the eroticization of basic gender equality, whereas heteroeroticism is the incarnation of basic gender inequality.* This is not to say that power has no place in homoerotic desire. On the contrary, it is a special paradoxical relationship with gender power that is the very heart of homoeroticism. Also, while equal sociocultural status (man/man) is the basis of homoeroticism, the manipulation of the signs of gender (masculine/feminine) is the mutable world in which masculine power is augmented and diminished within the context of equality. Masculinity and femininity, as signs of modulating power in gender myth, are the instruments of homoerotic fancy.**

Most people do not engage in homoerotic sexuality out of a noble commitment to equality. The inclination to homoeroticism usually emerges out of a deep psychic intuitive sense rather than an overtly conscious ethical or ideological attitude. There are, however, feminist women who claim they pursue lesbian eroticism because they find the inequality implicit in heterosexual relations too offensive.

The attraction to masculine or feminine gender in one's sexual partner is a deep psychic expression, within the context of the myth of gender, of one's sense of oneself and one's partner. Some men feel comfortable in sexual relations with women, others do not. Some men are at home in sexual relations with men. Still others feel comfortable with both men and women. The level of

---

*It is essential to keep in mind that I am talking about *eroticism*. Men who are homosexual can be just as sexist and misogynist in their attitudes toward women as their heterosexual counterparts, but not in their homoerotic experience because women are simply not involved. Generally speaking, homosexual men do not take advantage of patriarchal power in their erotic/emotional relations with women. Those who do, I will argue in the section on "De-emphasis" in Chapter Four, do so for fundamentally different reasons than heterosexual men.
**Some homoerotic examples of these modulating signs of power will be discussed in Chapter Five.

70

comfort, I suggest, indicates how well the orthodoxy of the gender myth resonates with one's sense of one's own position in the myth. Feeling comfortable with his mythic dominance over women, consciously or subconsciously, a man will find sexual relations with them to be in harmony with his sense of his relative position of domination. Being uncomfortable with or having no interest in the incarnation of his mythic power over women through sexual acts indicates at least some dissonance between orthodoxy in the myth of gender and a man's sense of himself, or of women for that matter. It should be reemphasized here that sexuality is the union of the mental and physical; it is the meeting place of myths and individuals in which the myth is incorporated into the individual's being. For this to be a satisfying experience, the myth must suit the individual.

By definition, homoeroticism emerges out of the gender myth—a man could not eroticize men if there weren't such a mythic category. Gender is fundamentally a patriarchal heterosexual distinction: the orthodox erotic incarnation of gender is, as I have shown, heteroerotic—the erotic confirmation of difference. The essence of manhood lies in its *difference* from womanhood; the eroticization of gender *affinity* violates the preeminence of difference and therefore manhood. Homosexual acts are the incarnation of that violation. Because homoerotic desire focuses on manhood but ignores the sexual acts that bring about the erotic incarnation of manhood (difference), preferring sexual acts that violate manhood, homoeroticism reflects a paradoxical sense of what it means to be a man. *Because it both embraces and violates masculinity, homoeroticism is paradoxical eroticism.* A homosexual man is a paradoxical man.

The original Greek meaning of the word "paradox" *(paradoxon)* means something unexpected or contrary to received opinion.[36] The Greek prefix "para" also means "alongside, past, or beyond" (OED). This is to be contrasted with the word "orthodox," which the OED defines as "Holding right or correct opinions, i.e., such as are currently accepted as correct or in accordance with some recognized standard." (In our case the standard is the implicit heteroeroticism of the gender myth.) The prefix "ortho" is from the Greek meaning "straight" or "right." The Greek *doxa* means opinion or notion, the related verb, *dokéo,* means "seem."

In Latin, the word *"doceo"* means teach. Although there is no etymological connection between *doceo* (teach) and *dokéo* (seem), there is an obvious semantic similarity: which is the sense that the seemingness of things is handed down or taught. Certainly, heterosexual relations are orthodox; they are the incarnation of the accepted opinion or seemingness of gender as it is handed down through our culture. Homosexuality is paradoxical in that it exists alongside the received tradition of gender and its common eroticization. So the homoerotic paradox is twofold. It is a paradox by being outside the orthodox erotic interpretation of gender myths. It is also a paradox in the stricter sense of being a self-contradiction; homoerotic desire both reveres and violates masculinity.

Rather than being an essential "type," that is, the product of consistent genetic or social determination, the paradoxical man is one who finds himself on a special frontier of interpretation. Being paradoxical is in some respects like being an existentialist or a Christian; a paradoxical man is one who understands the myths of our culture in a special way. But the paradox is unlike a philosophical or religious point of view, in that rather than being the offspring of conscious reason or faith, it is a knowledge that emanates from a deep subconscious psychic intuition. This intuition is an interpretation, a historical and individual response to the myth of gender; it constitutes a special relationship of the individual with the myth of gender and therefore with his or her culture. For most paradoxical men, this intuition stems from their earliest memories; it is probably coincident with their first awareness of the masculine power that they are meant to accept as their destiny. It is an intuition that emerges from the disharmony between gender power and a deep sense of self.

A fundamental question arises, "What is this self that is interacting with gender myth?" At the deepest level, this is the existential, primordial, embodied human being who *uses* culture.[37] This primordial human being is *not* the *creation* of culture as many philosophers, social scientists, and literary critics often suggest. The human being, at birth, is thrown into a culture that it must use to live a social life. The culture becomes a mode of self-understanding and action for the human being. Culture, although crucial to human life as we know it, conceals the primordial nature of human beings. Culture averages out the unique self-disclosiveness of human beings into banal cultural categories, such as gender.

Human beings "make do" with the cultural categories they have been given; this is the interaction they have with culture. Different human beings will use the categories in different ways. One sublimates one's being in various cultural powers (gender, race, class, and so on) by appropriating those powers. This appropriation of culture takes place deep in the psyche at the level of the subconscious. For the most part, it is in the subconscious that the struggle between primordial human being and culture takes place. This struggle constitutes the personality.

Human beings are fundamentally free. As the French existentialist philosopher Jean-Paul Sartre said, "freedom is identical with my existence."[38] Choice is fundamental to human being. "To be is to choose oneself."[39] According to existential psychology, the personality is the cumulative result of the choices each human being makes. Sartre's famous phrase, "we are condemned to be free," emphasizes that we must live with the consequences of our choices. Human beings choose their relationship with gender myth. These are profound choices made in the subconscious from the time of infancy as each human being confronts and is given little choice but to understand itself and its relation to others through the myth of gender. That one's place in gender is a matter of choice is evidenced by the fact that some people have homoerotic desire, that is, the desire for the erotic incarnation of the paradoxical subversion of gender power. In our culture, *tremendous* pressure is placed on people to pursue orthodox lives and orthodox eroticism. That some, seemingly against all odds, prefer to say no to orthodoxy, to violate and subvert that orthodoxy, attests to the freedom of choice.

Paradoxy is a dimension in a *spectrum* of psychic intuitions of the relationship between human beings and the myth of gender. It falls somewhere in the middle between a total acceptance of masculine power and a total rejection of it. It is, as I have said, a paradoxical mingling of acceptance and rejection. Whereas complete acceptance is orthodoxy, complete rejection might be called "antidoxy"; this is expressed in transsexualism.[40] The spectrum is as follows:

Antidoxy   Paradoxy   Orthodoxy

The struggle between primordial human being and culture is a lifelong development. Consequently, there is fluidity in the intuitions of each human being and his relationship with the gender myth. Orthodoxy, paradoxy, and antidoxy form a spectrum of deep psychic intuitive understanding human beings have of the relationship between their being and the type of power they have appropriated in the gender myth. At a deep psychic level, the paradoxical interpretation of oneself in gender is both a rejection and an acceptance of one's place in the myth. (It's crucial to keep in mind that paradoxy and antidoxy are degrees of rejection of one's *place* in gender and not a rejection of gender itself.) To explain why people choose different places in the spectrum of orthodoxy, paradoxy, and antidoxy would be to explain the difference between primordial human beings. Since it is a matter of choice and every human being is unique, I believe it would be impossible to make any transcendental claims about such difference. Only deep existential psychoanalysis with individuals would have any hope of shedding light on why *they* made the choices *they* did from infancy.

Myths circulate in our culture unevenly. One's understanding, and therefore interpretation, of myths is dependent on a host of social, economic, and regional factors. Most importantly, one's interpretation of gender myth is the dynamic result of one's *unique* history of experience with the myth from infancy, a history that for most is probably a complex mingling of apprehension and misapprehension of the meaning of gender. That history is further complicated by the developing experience of an emotional being-with others: mothers, fathers, sisters, brothers, peers, and so on. One's interpretation of gender myth may modulate through different periods of one's life, day to day and from moment to moment. Some men live for many years with an orthodox interpretation of themselves in the gender myth. They have satisfying sexual relations with women, get married, and have families. But as time progresses they begin to see the possibility of another interpretation of themselves and the myth, a paradoxical interpretation. With this new interpretation of the myth comes the desire to bring it to life in homosexual experience.

Before coming out, many homosexual men and boys find homoeroticism difficult to reconcile with their sense of themselves as men. The *paradoxical* interpretation of gender that is implicit in homoerotic desire makes acceptance of that desire difficult to fathom. Having grown up as a boy, immersed in orthodox culture, the homosexual youth understands himself on the manly side of the gender myth. But he has a nagging sense that something is odd, that he is different from his peers. This is the youthful intuition of the gender paradox. Coming out as a gay man is the acceptance of the paradox.

Paradoxical masculinity is not a total rejection of the power given men in the myth—it constitutes a paradoxical relationship with that power. As *men,* homosexual men are accorded and may, in fact, take advantage of the power and prestige of patriarchy. But being *paradoxical men,* at a deep psychic level their desire for masculinity is also a desire to undermine masculine power. (Their sense of the paradox may or may not lead them to a more thorough rejection of patriarchy in their lives.[41])

Having orthodox or paradoxical intuitions of oneself is not a matter of having some sort of essence, one intuition being the polar opposite of the other; these are not black and white distinctions. They are interpretive domains through which one sees oneself in gender culture. Orthodoxy and paradoxy are, in fact, intimately related. It is that intimate relationship that strikes fear in the hearts of some men. Paradoxical desire is a desire for the company of men, masculine contact. But the desire for male company is also felt by men whose intuitions are ostensibly orthodox. One of the strange paradoxes of orthodox gender relations is that women, whose gender *difference* makes them indispensable for the orthodox erotic celebration of masculinity, are unequal to men and therefore traditionally marginalized from the rest of men's lives. Orthodoxy likes segregation; that's why the vast majority of sports are segregated, especially the really masculine ones such as football, hockey, boxing, rugby, and so on. Most men prefer to do business with other men—this fact makes it notoriously difficult for women to break into traditionally male-dominated occupations. *Within* orthodoxy, affinity between men is a cherished experience. Locker rooms are places where orthodox men like to hang around naked, talking and joking with each other. They enjoy touching and pushing against each other playing contact sports, or at least watching other men doing so. But these are also *paradoxical* pleasures. Always lurking in masculine camaraderie is a fear that something could go amiss, that the ostensible orthodoxy of a man's world might turn out to be paradoxical. Hidden in the orthodox relations between men is the potential of the homoerotic paradox. For some that is frightening, for others it's exciting, and for still others it's both.

The gender paradox offers freedom in the myth of gender. But this is not freedom *from* gender; it is the freedom of latitude *within* the world of gender. To be free of gender would be to live a social and erotic life, to see oneself and others, without the filter of gender. The paradox is not such a dramatic departure from our culture; it continues to operate within the web of meaning of the gender myth. Nevertheless, within that web, paradoxy encourages a freedom of expression that is generally discouraged by orthodoxy.* For some, freedom itself is fearful. But perhaps even more frightening is that homoerotic desire, an appetite for the incarnation of the gender paradox, is a hunger for the violation of masculinity.

The violation of masculinity is fearful because it exposes the frailty of masculine power. The gender paradox illuminates the mythical basis of men's power, making it apparent that the justification of such power in "nature" is spurious.** It shows that "the emperor has no clothes." When the mythical power of men is shown for what it is, the gendered order of our culture and the gendered power of individuals in it begins to crumble. And that

---

*This freedom is evident not only in the lives of individual men but is also institutionalized in gay culture. Various expressions of that freedom will be discussed in Chapter Seven.

**This is currently being reworked culturally so that homosexuality is seen as just as masculine as heterosexuality, thus maintaining the mythic gender order. There are many gay men who have been able to come out of the closet by thinking that homosexuality poses no threat to their masculinity. This is a covering-over of the truth of the mythic basis of homosexuality, which is the paradox. I will pursue this point further in Chapters Four and Five.

can lead to a trepidation called homophobia. Homophobia, being a fear of masculine violation, is also a fear of exposure. The fear of exposure is the fear of the loss of patriarchal power. And that is the heart of homophobia—the fear of the loss of power.

Homophobia goes hand in hand with the homoerotic paradox. Of course it does; in a culture that maintains as one of its most important myths an oppressive power difference between men and women, the violation of that power and its promise of freedom is going to be disturbing. Homophobia is not limited to red-necked heterosexual men. Most homosexual men labor under this fear for years. In large measure, it is the fear of the loss of power that keeps many "in the closet"—and the resentment felt by many gay men toward those gay men who, relinquishing the dictates of orthodox masculinity, behave effeminately also originates in that fear of a loss of gender power.

Homosexual men also fear the homophobia of others. Not wanting to see the gender myth violated, there are many who make a point of discouraging homosexual men (and women) from being themselves. The vast discrimination, hatred, and violence leveled against homosexual people is a well-known and much-documented fact that there is no need to reiterate here. But a few words about a myth that has helped perpetrate homophobia may increase our understanding of the way homophobia is experienced. Bolstering the orthodoxy of heterosexuality, that is, preserving the power difference between men and women, is a subsidiary myth that silences the voice of the paradox, conceals it, by making it appear as a dark, mysterious force. This is the myth of the "homosexual monster."

The homosexual monster myth paints a dismal picture of homosexuality, one that has worked its way through the culture and has been enshrined not only in a multitude of sociocultural institutions such as religion, medicine, law, and athletics, but also in the minds of most people. A monster is "a person of inhuman and horrible cruelty or wickedness." It's also "an animal or plant deviating in one or more of its parts from the normal type; specifically an animal born with some congenital malformation; a misshapen birth; an abortion" (OED). Marginal and ugly, homosexuality is to be avoided and heterosexuality pursued. The monster plays no small part in the experience of estrangement. Consequently, many who know the desirability of the paradox will pursue orthodox lives.

Knowledge of the monster myth does not emerge from the experience of homoeroticism itself. Sir John Betjeman, a Poet Laureate of Great Britain, wrote a poem called "Narcissus"; it describes how the vision of the homosexual monster works its disturbing way into the mind of a little boy. This poem discerns the early experience of homosexuality as a mysterious, sinister force. Blissfully happy in his childhood, delighting in his friendship and sexual relations with his boyfriend Bobby, the narrator tells us how he became acquainted with the terrible vision of the homosexual monster. His boyhood affair with Bobby was innocent and trouble-free until his mother told him how "unwholesome" it was. The homosexual monster is so terrible, so loathsome that Mother cannot describe it. It is unspeakable. "My Mother wouldn't tell me why she hated / The things we did, and why they pained her so. / She said a fate far worse than death awaited / People who did the things we didn't know."[42]

Boys come to know they are encountering a terrible monster without really knowing what the monster is. "Oh tell me, Mother, what I mustn't do— / Then, Bobby, I can play again with you."[43] They know it's a disgusting monster, but they don't know why. The monstrosity of the monster lies in its ignominious reputation, shrouded in secrecy. Fear of a lurking monster characterizes the experience of homophobia. Homosexuality is always other, something unknown, something best kept at a distance. The monster myth, by so distancing homosexuality, makes the intimate relationship of orthodox and paradox seem to be less so. This myth discourages the paradoxical desire for the violation of masculinity from working its way into orthodox lives, thus keeping the gender myth safe and sound.

It is ironic that homosexuality be cast in the monster mold since it is heterosexuality that eroticizes the most truly monstrous dimension of gender, that is, the subordination of women. Patriarchal power is erotically actualized and confirmed in heterosexual acts. The homosexual monster myth diverts attention from that deep psychosexual oppression of women. This is a mythical version of Orwellian "newspeak"; the myth passes injustice off as justice and makes the just unjust. The eroticization of inequality (heterosexuality) is accorded an ethically superior status, while the eroticization of equality (homosexuality) is made ugly and morally reprehensible. But such ethical lying is no doubt essential to the perpetuation of a social order bent on keeping women down.

If we understand the mythic power difference between men and women and the ways in which difference (heterosexuality) and affinity (homosexuality) are eroticized, and if we believe that social relations characterized by equality are ethically superior to those based on inequality, then we are compelled to see homosexuality as the nobler erotic desire. But because homosexuality is not a rejection of an oppressive myth but rather an option *within* the myth of gender difference, homosexuality also perpetuates that unjust myth and therefore shares in the patriarchal oppressiveness of gender.

IV

Gay

Sensibility

"And one trembles to be so understood and, at last,
To understand, as if to know became
The fatality of seeing things too well."

—Wallace Stevens

"Victor is gay." "Steve is homosexual." "Alex is a fag." "Peter's queer." What do we mean when we say these things about people? You might say, "It means that Steve scores six on the Kinsey scale." Which would mean that since puberty, he has had sex only with other men. But this is merely an objective account of the sex of the people with whom he had engaged in sexual activity. It tells us very little about Steve as a person. Most or us, when we describe someone as gay, homosexual, queer, or a fag, want to convey more about that person than the meager fact that some percentage of his sexual encounters have been with members of the same sex. We are trying to assert something about his personality, about the way he lives his life, about the subjective meaning he finds in his life, both sexual and otherwise. Many say that a homosexual person is one who has a homosexual or gay "identity." But the notion of a gay identity is limiting. Many men who are perfectly comfortable with their homosexuality, who enjoy being gay, also live their lives in non-gay contexts. Homosexuality, in our culture, rather than forming an identity, is best understood as an unusual way of looking at the world, a paradoxical mode of being in the world. The paradox presents a special sensibility through which some men understand themselves and the world they live in. It is a sensibility that they can employ at various times, depending on the personal and social circumstances. A homosexual man is not just someone who has had a certain number of objectively homosexual experiences. Nor is he someone whose life can be understood primarily through his homosexuality. He is a man whose paradoxical intuitions of the myth of gender have given him a special sensibility.

In the first chapter, I drew a distinction between objective and subjective homosexuality. *Objective homosexuality* is merely a matter of two persons of the same sex engaging in sexual activity. Objective homosexuality describes observable, physical behavior. *Subjective homosexuality,* on the other hand, refers to the psychic dimension of sexual experience. This psychic dimension was explored in Chapter Three, where I suggested that it is the domain of eros. So, subjective homosexuality is the psychic world of homoeroticism. It's possible for two men to engage in objectively homosexual behavior and not experience it as homoerotic. This is often the case in boys' schools, prisons, the military, and other exclusively male environments where men engage in homosexual acts without finding it homosexually significant; they don't think of themselves as homosexual and often don't consider their *objectively* homosexual behavior as a homoerotic expression. It is just a substitute for sex with women.[1] This is not to say that there aren't men in prisons and the military who experience a homoerotic dimension in their sex with other prisoners, soldiers, or sailors. The point is, the act does not *necessarily* define the individual's psychic experience.

Homoeroticism lies in the individual's paradoxical interpretation of the myth of gender. We have seen that one of the effects of being paradoxical, of being gay, is estrangement. Gay men are estranged from the culture from which they themselves have emerged. Knowing they are different, feeling estranged from a culture that is in many ways their home, how do homosexual or gay men see themselves and go about their lives?

THE SOCIAL CONSTRUCTION OF HOMOSEXUALITY

The concept of homoeroticism as a paradoxical interpretation of myths is drawn from the experience of *living in the world* of gender and sexual myths. In other words, it's a concept that emerges from the point of view of the individual. Most recent research on sexuality has not taken this perspective—it looks from above. Michel Foucault is probably the most influential voice on the theory of sexuality since Freud. Foucault is interested in the big picture, that is, the historical, cultural forces that have shaped our sexual world. Basic to this historical approach to sexuality is the notion that particular sexualities (such as homosexuality or heterosexuality), or indeed sexuality itself, are not transcendental or universal human features. Jeffrey Weeks points out that the meaning of sexual practices varies from culture to culture and therefore should be seen as a social construct and not a "natural" human proclivity.

> In different cultures (and at different historical moments or conjunctures within the same culture) very different meanings are given to same sex activity both by society at large and by the individual participants. The physical acts might be similar, but the social construction of meanings around them are profoundly different . . . [and] the various possibilities of . . . homosexual behaviors, which seem from historical evidence to be a permanent and ineradicable aspect of human sexual possibilities, are variously constructed in different cultures as an aspect of wider gender and sexual regulation.[2]

In our culture, homosexual relations constitute a betrayal of masculinity. Because masculinity is vitally important to the organization of our society, to the mythic division of power between men and women, homosexual practice is *dis*couraged. But in other cultures it is actively *en*couraged, which proves that the meaning people find in sexual activity depends on their cultural setting. Illustrating the importance of cultural context to understanding of sexual practices, Gilbert Herd, in his book *Guardians of the Flutes,* describes how in the Sambia tribe of the Highlands of New Guinea, homosexual practice among young men is the acceptable venue through which they associate themselves with their culture's myth of masculinity.

Seven-to-ten-year-old Sambia boys are taken from their mothers when first initiated to the male cult, and thereafter experience the most powerful and seductive homosexual fellatio activities. For some ten to fifteen years, they engage in these practices on a daily basis, first as fellator, and then as fellated. Elders teach that semen is absolutely vital; it should be consumed daily since the creation of biological maleness and the maintenance of masculinity depend on it. Hence from middle childhood until puberty, boys should perform fellatio on older youths.

Near puberty the same initiates become dominant youths. Ritual helps remake their social and erotic identity, the bachelors becoming the fellated partners for a new crop of ritual novices. And at the same time, youths and boys alike must absolutely avoid women, on pain of punishment. For not only must homoeroticism be hidden from women but females are also believed to be contaminating—their menstrual blood polluting, and worse, lethal. This dual pattern—prescribed homosexual activities and avoidance of women—persists until marriage. So all casual heterosexual relationships, intrigues, and even casual conversations among boys and girls are blocked, and forbidden.

Whereas homosexual practices begin with initiation, they become far more than a ceremony. All boys are forcibly initiated. They scarcely have choice. For long afterwards, ritualized homosexuality becomes the centre of their existence.[3]

In *our* culture, there has been a great polarizing momentum in sexuality over the last hundred years or so. This polarization of homosexual and heterosexual and, more recently, gay and straight is mythical and doesn't represent the way people actually live their lives. The way people live and interpret their sexual lives is, in fact, quite convoluted. Notions of bipolar sexuality, however, have worked their way into our culture. By their mythic status they have an influence on people's lives, but not to the point of controlling them.

These sexual myths are not timeless; they have a genesis and their history can be traced. Michel Foucault says that exclusive sexualities emerged during a period in history in which the lives of people were being regulated by the creation of sexual categories. Until that time there were no homosexuals, only homosexual acts. He says that the ultimate power held over people until the eighteenth century was the threat of death. A new power that emerged at this time was power over life. This power is social in nature and has the effect of ordering life through the structures that create reality. This structuring of reality Foucault calls "discourse," which is the complex of historical, social, cultural, and linguistic settings that shape our sense of the world and, therefore, our possibilities in it. "What occurred in the eighteenth century in some Western countries, an event bound up with the development of capitalism, was . . . nothing less than the entry of life into history."[4] Previously, it was the fear of being killed that kept people in line. In the eighteenth century, sexual activity became an effective *locus* for control over the body and human reproduction; consequently, it is an effective means of regulation of entire populations. "Sex was a means of access both to the life of the body and the life of the species."[5] The result is that sex has replaced the threat of death and has become the center of power for the regulation of life. So, by the creation of sexual categories such as homosexual, heterosexual, pedophile, and transvestite, people's lives become confined to those categories and regulated in the service of social order.

With the advent of the Industrial Revolution came a need to regulate many aspects of life. High productivity in highly organized business bureaucracies required a degree of social discipline that was much greater than that of precapitalist societies.[6] The regulation of sex involved the creation of an importance for sexuality. "This would not only assure a high level of reproductive activity but also provide socially available rewards unlimited by natural resources, rewards that promote conforming behaviour in sectors of social life far more important than the sexual."[7] Max Weber argued that a Protestant ethic of organization and discipline—an ascetic sense that all human activity was significant and the appropriate object of moral discipline—developed with capitalism.[8] People would extend this discipline to every aspect of their lives including their sexuality.

Since the eighteenth century, the norm has been a powerful force in the regulation of sex, restricting "normal" sexuality to heterosexuality and the family.[9] Sexuality outside of this norm became deviant sexuality and the object of severe public regulation. The authority of the norm was reinforced by the medical and psychiatric professions and by the enforcement of laws dealing with "perversions"; these replaced the authority of the church in the regulation of sexual behavior. For example, the Labouchere Amendment to the Criminal Law Amendment Act (Great Britain, 1885) made all homosexual activities, that is, acts of "gross indecency," illegal and punishable by up to two years of hard labor. The case of Oscar Wilde was a famous example of the application of this law. Although it would be incorrect to say that this regulation of homosexual behavior through the law and medicine was a simple effect of the development of capitalism, it is correct to suggest that it was intricately linked to the complex of social changes that were emerging at that time.[10]

The early development of capitalism coincided with the triumph of positive science. The entire world was being categorized and quantified—the development of systems of classification was very much in the intellectual vogue. Carolus Linnaeus's delineation of species is one of the best known classifications of the period. His work is a reflection of the scientific desire to reduce the variety of the world to a uniform and universally valid system. This is an intellectual tendency that can be traced back to the Enlightenment quest for universal knowledge.[11]

Just as botany attempted to classify and thereby reduce the variety of botanical phenomena, so too there was later a scientific trend toward the classification and therefore reduction in the variety of human sexual behaviors. Emil Kraepelin published his *Textbook of Psychiatry* in 1883; this contained a comprehensive classification system for "mental disturbance." Richard von

Krafft-Ebing published an encyclopedia of "sexual disorders," *Psychopathia Sexualis,* in 1886. In the nineteenth century, a new imperialism was enthroned—scientific imperialism. Scientific imperialism posits that nature can, and perhaps should, be dominated and controlled by man [sic].[12] One technique for control is conceptual, involving scientific schemes for organizing phenomena. The development of classification systems is one such scheme. Scientific imperialism, and its preoccupation with delineation and classification, continues to dominate much of our thinking, thereby setting limits to thought and experience.

The word "homosexual" is a product of the vogue for scientific classification. It was first coined in its German form, *homosexualitat,* by Dr. Karoly Maria Benkert in 1869. It came into popular usage in American medical books and journals in the 1890s and became part of standard American usage in the 1920s; its first appearance in *The New York Times* was 1926. Interestingly, the word "heterosexual" was introduced in medical literature *after* "homosexual," rather by default.[13] Until the late nineteenth century, there were no words denoting these two sexualities; indeed, the notion of polarized homo- and heterosexualities didn't exist. They are creations of modern science. Foucault described this creation in the following famous passage.

> The nineteenth-century homosexual became a personage, a past, a case history, and a childhood, in addition to being a type of life, a life form, and a morphology, with an indiscreet anatomy and possibly mysterious physiology. Nothing that went into his total composition was unaffected by his sexuality. It was everywhere present in him: at the root of all his actions because it was their insidious and indefinitely active principle; written immodestly on his face and body because it was a secret that always gave itself away. It was consubstantial with him, less as a habitual sin than as a singular nature. We must not forget that the psychological, psychiatric, medical category of homosexuality was constituted from the moment that it was characterized— Westphal's famous article of 1870 on "contrary sexual sensations" can stand as its date of birth—less by a type of sexual relations than by a certain quality of sexual sensibil-

ity, a certain way of inverting the masculine and feminine in oneself. Homosexuality appeared as one of the forms of sexuality when it was transposed from the practice of sodomy onto a kind of interior androgyny, a hermaphrodism of the soul. The sodomite had been a temporary aberration; the homosexual was now a species.[14]

This new species was not discovered; it was created. The "homosexual" and "heterosexual" are concepts that exist in our culture as myths of sexuality. These are ways of thinking that have emerged in a particular historical and cultural setting; like other myths, they both reflect and create the culture of which they are part. They influence the understanding that people have of themselves and each other. What is revolutionary in these new nineteenth-century myths is the idea that a person's sexuality constitutes an all-encompassing definition. What were once disparate sexual acts became the expressions of an essential being. What developed in the nineteenth century were mythical homosexuals and heterosexuals. One of them was monstrous and the other was virtuous. Their monstrosity and virtue came out of their very being. The horror of homosexuality lay not so much in homosexual acts as it did in the depravity of the creature that would perpetrate such acts. Someone who practiced homosexuality, then, would be seen as a creature worthy of hatred or pity, and in need of help, punishment, or both.

Realizing that sexuality is not a natural, transcendent, and universal phenomenon, that it is instead a cultural creation, Foucault developed a history of sexuality that tries to account for the organization of our culture's sexual world. He has tried to explain the social forces that create our concepts of heterosexuality and homosexuality, of normal and abnormal sexualities. Exclusive homo- and hetero-sexualities developed over the last two centuries as a form of social control, stigmatizing homosexuality and thus encouraging the population to live circumscribed heterosexual lives.

The fact that sexual categories have a social status is borne out by the sundry literatures of religion, medicine, and law. The Roman Catholic Church has published statements on the purity of marriage as the only legitimate venue for sexual expression. It has also made statements on the sinfulness of homosexuality: in 1986, the Congregation for the Doctrine of the Faith, best known for the Inquisition, published a pastoral letter entitled "The Pastoral Care of Homosexual Persons," in which homosexuality is regarded as "an objective disorder" and a "behavior to which no one has any conceivable right."[15] Christian fundamentalists like Jimmy Swaggart and Jerry Falwell are well known for their rants against homosexuality and raves for marriage and the "traditional" family.[16] Medicine, of course, has dedicated much effort to the study and treatment of sexuality. The scientific papers and monographs on homosexuality fill hundreds of feet of library shelf space. Laws have been passed making homosexual acts between consenting adults illegal. Some more tolerant jurisdictions have passed laws forbidding discrimination on the basis of "sexual orientation," which effectively grounds the concept of sexual orientation in the law. The social status of the categories of homo- and heterosexuality is undeniable.

In the mid-twentieth century, the homosexual species or creature was given a new conceptual framework. It was suggested that people are actors playing socially constructed roles. Some sociologists, known as "symbolic interactionists," have suggested that the category of the homosexual has come to dominate the lives of people who see themselves as homosexual. The homosexual category, they say, exercises control over individuals through the "homosexual role."[17] In 1968 Mary McIntosh wrote an influential article, "The Homosexual Role"; in it she says that this role emerged primarily as an aspect of social control. The technique for the assignation or acquisition of the homosexual role is a process called "labeling," in which some individuals come to be seen both by society and themselves as deviants.

The practice of the social labeling of persons as deviant operates in two ways as a mechanism of social control. In the first place it helps to provide a clear-cut, publicized, and recognizable threshold between permissible and impermissible behavior. This means that people cannot so easily drift into deviant behavior. Their first moves in a deviant direction immediately raise the question of a total move into a deviant role with all the sanctions that this is likely to elicit. Second, the labeling serves to segregate the deviants from the others and this means that their deviant practices and their self-justifications for these practices are contained within a relatively narrow group. The creation of a specialized, despised, and punished role of homosexual keeps the bulk of society pure in rather the same way that the similar treatment of some kinds of criminals helps keep society law-abiding.[18]

Role theory has become a dominant notion in both the academic psychological literature and popular thinking.[19] "Role-playing" is jargon that emanates from a particular psychological school of thought. It is jargon that the general public and many scholars have taken up quite uncritically. But the theory of roles is seriously flawed in at least four respects.

Role theory assumes that there is a distinct sexual role that influences the behavior of people. William DuBay said, "What makes a person homosexual? Whatever it is it is not sex. It is the role."[20] This way of thinking is the result of a basic epistemological error, the "fallacy of false cause." Certain behaviors are observed; by a process of reduction and abstraction, elements in the behavior are found to be similar and a category for the behavior is decided upon (homosexual); on the basis of that abstraction a homosexual role is posited; this role is then credited with being the source of the behavior. A technique for the conceptualization of behavior (the concept of roles) has been mistakenly credited as being the source of the behavior. It is the behavior of people that creates the role, *not* the other way around.

The psychological theory that attempts to explain how roles are adopted by individuals is a simplistic social-learning theory in which people are more or less passive recipients of a homosexual identity and social behavior.[21] This shallow behavior theory ignores the choices, sometimes anguishing, that people make when confronted with the problems of sexuality and social behavior. "Once a particular conception such as 'the homosexual' becomes part of an existing social order, the members of that social order start to act in terms of that conception."[22] Such a mechanical relationship between social order and individual consciousness and actions is not convincing. There is no simple causal relationship between the emergence of social categories and the thoughts and actions of people. The determinism inherent in that notion would suggest a consistency of homosexual behavior and identity through society that simply does not exist. Some researchers have suggested that there are probably as many homosexual "roles" as there are homosexual people and prefer to talk about homosexualities rather than homosexuality.[23]

Role theory fails to take into account what in this book I call the "fluidity" of homosexuality, which is that some people pass in and out of homosexual or gay contexts moment to moment, situation to situation, day to day, and through different periods in their lives. Eilert Frerichs, a gay Christian minister I interviewed, explained the experience of moving from setting to setting where homosexuality is more featured at some times than it is at others.

> I don't go 'round advertising, consciously at any rate, that I'm gay and that everything I do is because I'm gay, no, not at all. Being gay is a part of my experience on the same level, or of equal importance, to my having been raised in Germany and having a third culture. All human beings live in a whole variety of cultures all the time and move with relative ease (at least the healthy person) from one culture to another. It's a sign of integration and personal wholeness that one can do so. And so I, too, move in a whole lot of cultures with relative ease, there's the academic environment, there's the political, social policy, religious, gay, etc. At different times in one's life, dictated to some degree by circumstances, and by needs, one's own and other people's, that certain culture becomes more prominent for a certain period of time. But it doesn't have to be so exclusively—no, I've always said that I don't want to be a "professional gay man."
>
> I think a lot of people would accuse me of copping out, certainly the gay politicals in the late 70s would accuse me of copping out. They like to make black and white distinctions; that's not the way my life experience leads me to describe what I am doing.

And so there is fluidity as one passes from situation to situation, gearing one's behavior accordingly.

Although fluidity entails the sense one has of oneself in various contexts, it also describes the experience of passing as straight, an everyday experience for gay men. This fluidity is not a matter of rapidly changing roles with all the attendant changes in psychic orientation. Any serious method actor would be "burned out" in one day if he had to accomplish the extensive changes in role that are part of the day-to-day life of gay men. (Certainly, if roles were being played, the portrayals would not be just "technical"; they would involve immense psychic backgrounds and require highly developed skills of "method acting" in the tradition of Stanislavsky.) Another aspect of the fluidity of homosexuality is the enormous diversity of people that can be included in that group. The variety of styles and ways of life among homosexual men is vast. There are clones (that is, men who wear mustaches, blue jeans, short hair, construction boots—they look uncannily similar, hence the term "clone"), drag queens, body builders, academics, preppies, punks, GUPPIES (gay urban professionals), earnest Marxists, flippant bar flies, classical musicians and rock musicians. Homosexual men may live sexually promiscuous, monogamous, or celibate lives. They may prefer to live in the country, the gay ghetto, the suburbs, in the fashionable or unfashionable parts of great cities. Role theory cannot account for such diversity.

Finally, role theory is reductionist. In order that a distinct sexual role can be isolated, the complexities of human thinking and behavior must be so simplified that they no longer resemble real life. For the convenience of categories and ease of intellectual manipulation, phenomena are hopelessly reduced. Reductionism is endemic to positive science—commonly known just as "science"—which forms the intellectual basis for the behaviorist psychology that is the foundation of role theory. Positive science works by analysis, dividing the world into components and investigating them. Components are further divided into subcomponents that can be divided into subsubcomponents. The greatest accuracy is said to be achieved when a component can be reduced no further. By a process of reduction and isolation variability is minimized, contradiction is resolved, and accuracy is supposedly achieved. Contemporary physics, the science that all others attempt to emulate, has recently argued that this analytical division of the world into components fails to comprehend the whole. Reality is not just the totality of parts—parts interact with each other in such a way that true understanding is only possible when reality is grasped as a whole. Attempting to understand the meaning of homosexuality by reducing its experience among men to an isolated role or identity is symptomatic of simplistic positive science.

The pervasive notion in the literature on the psychology and sociology of homosexuality has been that homosexual people establish an identity between the homosexual category or role and themselves—this is called "gay identity." It's certainly true that many people see themselves in the light of a homosexual category. Knowing the paradox, they have felt the effects of homophobia and their estrangement from orthodox culture. But does this constitute an *identity?*

Many people will talk about their identity. They will speak of their national identity, ethnic identity, gay identity, and so on. But I wonder if they mean what they say. The problem of identity is at least as old as Western civilization and its philosophy. Heidegger traces the question of identity back to the Ancient Greek philosopher Parmenides, who was born around 515 B.C. Heidegger says that human beings have a fundamental, primordial, intuitive understanding of their identity—we understand who we are just by the experience of living and thinking. Our identities lie in each of our own primordial human being.[24] Foucault, Derrida, and a host of other fashionable thinkers have forgotten that people have this profound intuitive sense of self. Caught up in the study of our culture, they have got carried away with its structures and forgotten that there are human beings in it whose identity in their own existence is not in question. This is not to say that categories like "homosexual" don't exist—obviously they do. The point is that people don't find their *identity* in them. Identity lies in primordial human being; cultural categories are only modes of understanding and action that are variously appropriated and relinquished by human beings. The homosexual or gay categories are ways that people think of themselves and others in certain social spheres. These are ways of interpreting oneself in certain situations.

The emergence over the last century of exclusive "sexualities," that is, the notion that a person is either homosexual or heterosexual, has emphasized the difference between orthodox and paradoxical interpretation, mythically polarizing these into opposite essential types, but these types are not reproduced in real life. Homosexuality is a world of understanding that emerges from a paradoxical reading drawn from a spectrum of interpretation of the myths of gender. Men and women will understand themselves in the light of that understanding at different times and under a multitude of circumstances; cultural categories do act upon people, but people also resist and manipulate categories. This is the freedom of humanity.

While it is often useful to speak of gay identity in, for example, political contexts—one's "gay identity" expresses one's allegiance to a positive, political way of thinking about homosexuality—it is more accurate to say that homosexuality is experienced by individual human beings as a paradox that has given some of those people a special sensibility, an exceptional way of understanding themselves and the culture in which they live, a distinctive mode of being in the world. "Gay identity" is one aspect of that sensibility.

THE TRIAD OF GAY SENSIBILITY

For those who have a personal acquaintance with the paradox and its estranging effect, there are three possible responses to the situation in which they find themselves. The first is to de-emphasize or ignore the paradox. The second is to live with it ironically. The third is to attempt to change the authority of the myths that are responsible for the paradox in the first place; this is the goal of gay liberation and feminism. I think that most gay men today employ combinations of all three. These responses constitute gay approaches to the world, what I will call "the triad of gay sensibility." This triad is a flexible mode of being in the world, a mode that emerges from one's experiences of the paradox and estrangement, allowing one to survive and sometimes transcend those experiences.

Gay sensibility is not just a way of thinking about, perceiving, interpreting, or understanding the world in which the paradoxical find themselves, although it is that too. Gay sensibility should be understood more widely as a *mode* of being in the world, a whole bearing or deportment by which homosexual men live their lives. As a mode, this sensibility is a way that some human beings take up or appropriate their culture. The triad of gay sensibility is effective in the "artistic" realm, shaping the way homosexual men read, write, paint, dance, compose music, and so on. But this sensibility goes beyond the elite compass of the arts. Gay sensibility can bear on most every aspect of a man's life, including the way in which he plays sports, builds and displays his body, desires other men or indeed women, and engages in sex.

The effects of this sensibility and the emphases within the triad vary from situation to situation and through different periods of one's life. Gay sensibility is a fluid mode; it doesn't bear on all situations. One man, a professor, told me, "When I'm in a lecture room, I'm not aware of being gay, or advancing a gay viewpoint. When I'm teaching Wordsworth, I try to express his point of view, or Shakespeare's or whatever. And I think whether I'm gay or not is beside the point there." This is an experience common to many gay men: their lives are lived in various contexts, not all of which draw on their gay sensibility.

Gay men contextualize their experiences. They apply culturally received categories of homosexuality at different times and under different circumstances. Consequently, it is possible for a gay man to go to a gymnasium, be completely involved in the athleticism of his workout, and experience that time as being simply athletic, devoid of sexuality as far as he is concerned. Another day, he may go to the same gymnasium, find the same men there, doing much the same exercises as they were previously; this time, however, he is aware of the experience as a gay experience. He may find the situation erotic; he may find it ironic; he may decide that he is with other gay men only and experience his workout in a gay fraternal context. The gay context depends on the man's interpretation. One's sense of oneself is also dependent upon personal interpretation. A man who is a runner may enter the Boston Marathon, an event that he considers very important to himself athletically. His concerns involve his strategic pace, what his time might be, or how physically painful the experience will be. Here, his sense of himself is that of a runner. The same man could enter the Boston Marathon another year and having decided to wear a singlet with a large pink triangle emblazoned with the word "GAY," he sees himself as a *gay* runner and his participation in this race as an expression of his pride in being gay.

An important feature of the fluidity of gay sensibility is the prevalence of an individual's paradoxical (that is, homosexual) interpretation of gender and sexual myths. For some, there is considerable flux in their interpretation of these myths. Consequently, some men may have no, or at least relatively shallow, intuitions of themselves as paradoxical; they may live genuinely *orthodox* lives for many years, discovering a new interpretation of themselves in the myths of gender and sexuality at later points in their lives, launching themselves on homosexual careers at that time. Others may understand themselves *paradoxically* for many years and gradually come to see a space for themselves in the orthodox world of gender and sexual relations. And there are men who are vaguely aware of the intimate relationship between orthodoxy and paradoxy, whose intuitive feel for one erotic incarnation of gender does not exclude the possible allure of the other. For these men, lurking in the shadow of the orthodox is always the erotic potential of the paradox and vice versa. For many, especially after adolescence, the waxing and waning of their paradoxical intuitions and therefore preference for sexual and close emotional relations with members of the same sex remains within fairly narrow bounds and feels more or less consistent for most of their lives. Naturally, one's sensibility works in concert with one's interpretive relationship to myths and sense of estrangement. The experience of coming out, for example, is the experience of a heightened awareness and acceptance of paradox that leads to a new sensibility (change), a substantially different way of being oneself and understanding one's place in the world.

There has been a tendency in the gay liberation movement to dismiss the fluidity between homo- and heterosexuality as a kind of inauthenticity. It's said that those who have erotic interest in both men and women are vacillating; they aren't facing the facts of their own lives—the assumption here is that people are either homosexual or heterosexual and that orientation is more or less fixed. It is true that some who oscillate between homo- and hetero-sexuality do so because they are afraid of the anathematic status of homosexuality; they are shrinking back from estrangement. This homophobia is not only a fear of estrangement, but is also for men a fear of losing orthodox masculine "respectability," that is, a loss of power. For numbers of men, estrangement and the loss of mythic masculine power seem so horrible that they take what opportunities they can to avoid seeing themselves in a homosex-ual light, denying homosexuality and attempting to live orthodox lives; this is usually known as living in "the closet." Others, how-ever, have a *genuine* sense of themselves in the light of both para- and orthodox interpretations at different times in their lives or even in the company of different people. The play of the triad of gay sensibilities, then, will depend on these modulations of para-doxical or orthodox interpretations of oneself in gender and sex-ual myths.

De-Emphasis

De-emphasis is a mode of being paradoxical or homosexual that downplays the role of the paradox in one's life. This can be a homophobic strategy; fearing the loss of masculine status and power, knowing the potency of estrangement, or mystified by the secrecy of the monster myth, some homosexual men will try to de-emphasize their association with it. As a homophobic strategy, de-emphasis is the sensibility of the closet. But the sensibility of de-emphasis is not limited to the closeted mode of being homosex-ual. The historical development of the homosexual category has made homosexuality out to be an all-pervasive influence over the lives of homosexual people. Foucault points out that "nothing that went into his [the homosexual's] total composition was unaffected by his sexuality. It was everywhere present in him: at the root of all his actions because it was their insidious and indefinitely active principle. . . . It was consubstantial with him, less as a habitual sin than as a singular nature."[25] But few who are homosexual believe that. One's paradoxical mode coexists with a host of other appropriations of culture. What Foucault is describing is the *myth* of the homosexual monster as a devouring force. Because this myth has insinuated itself most effectively in our culture, homosexual men will often attempt to combat the myth by the sensibility of de-emphasis. Whether or not such a strategy is in fact a closet sensibility or is a genuine attempt to authentically represent oneself in the full complexity of psychosocial life rather than simplistically in the context of one, often reified, sexual category, needs to be judged case by case. The truth in most instances is probably a mingling of both.

There are homosexual men who have personal knowledge of themselves as paradoxical, many of whom will have had homosexual experience—men who, wishing to live orthodox lives, resent having this knowledge and experience. Their feeling of estrangement is intense and they will make a concerted effort to dim it by denying their personal knowledge of paradox and its sexual expression. Viewing homosexuality from an orthodox perspective, some may join in the chorus of homophobia and think of homosexuality in malicious, pejorative terms. By doing so, they associate themselves with orthodoxy, eclipsing, at least partially, their estrangement.

I remember being in grades nine and ten and making a point of calling other effeminate boys in my class "fags." (As Harold, in Mart Crowley's *The Boys in the Band,* said: "Now there's the pot calling the kettle beige.") There was one occasion in the cafeteria where I remember giving the boys at my table a speech on the disgusting lives of "homos" and pointing out one boy on the other side of the cafeteria as the embodiment of that depravity. "Imagine," I said, "he puts guys' dicks in his mouth!" That I knew as a fact, since I had had sex with the boy a number of times. By giving such hate-filled, name-calling speeches, I was attempting to appear more orthodox in the eyes of my peers. I was conjuring up the myth of the homosexual monster, hoping to distance myself from it, if not all together successfully in my own eyes, at least in the eyes of my friends. I had swallowed the myth so completely, I saw homosexuality as so irredeemably horrid, that the monstrosity of homosexuality discolored my own desire for it. Because I saw lurking in our passion the ugliness of the monster myth, I hated the same boy with whom I had so often had the pleasure of sex, a boy who, in fact, I continued to desire even as I called him a "fag."

In much of gay liberation literature, that hateful attitude among homosexual men and boys is known as "self-oppression."[26] By appropriating the monster myth and seeing themselves and others in its grip, homosexual men and boys, whose erotic desire, after all, undermines the power of orthodoxy, reinstate that power and give a hand to its patriarchal oppressiveness. It is often said that self-oppression manifests itself in self-hatred. Although it certainly *is* hatred, whether or not it is directed at the self is debatable. Rather than being the hatred of *oneself,* this hatred is often of the *myth* of the monstrous homosexual. This hateful attitude toward homosexuality expresses the resentment that is felt by many who have grown up estranged in a culture that should be their home. It's important to remember that in the early experience of homosexuality, in which one is faced with an ugly future of being marginalized and monstrous, one's sense of the paradox is almost inevitably shrouded in secrecy and solitude. Unaware of other opinions on the status of homosexuality, all but the most rigorously independent-thinking people will be inclined to accept the myths as true. Being different, alone, and surrounded by the cruel orthodox notion of monstrous homosexuality, one would naturally hate the myths that are so demeaning and estranging. This hatred, then, is the expression of the need *not* to establish an identity between monstrous homosexuality and oneself.

Although I think it's true that many hate the *myth* of homosexuality and deplore its association with themselves, it is also true that some do establish an association between homosexuality and themselves in which their contempt for homosexuality surfaces as contempt for their paradoxical intuition, which is then virtually a hatred of *self.* This is indeed a perturbing situation, one that drives some miserable men to desperation, culminating in the need for psychotherapy, or religious escape, and in the most distressing cases, suicide.

Many men, uncomfortable with the monstrous sense they have of their homoerotic desire, will attempt to de-emphasize its place in their lives. Some will do this by trying to avoid homosexuality altogether; one of a number of strategies for that is to immerse oneself in sport. One man I interviewed was an avid athlete all through high school and college, which he attended on a basketball scholarship. He said that in retrospect he realized that he used sport as way to avoid homosexuality.

> The old myth was if you were an athlete you weren't supposed to have sex because it ruined your athletic performance, so I went right along with it. I thought, "this is a great out." I didn't realize it at the time. Looking back on it now, I realize that was what I was doing, I was looking for an out. The coaches, of course, were saying, "No sex, no sex, no sex, don't fool around with women." I bought it hook, line, and sinker.

It was convenient for him to accept the idea that sex and sports don't mix. It got him off both the heterosexual and homosexual hook. Dedicated athletes expend an enormous amount of time and energy in their sports; that, combined with school responsibilities, makes it possible for them to avoid both heterosexual relationships with women and doing anything about their desire for men. A commitment to sport allows one to maintain a seeming orthodox status both for oneself and one's family and peers.

A commitment to sport coupled with the wish to de-emphasize one's homosexuality needn't make for a life of total homoerotic abstinence, however. The sporting life can be an excellent way of de-emphasizing the paradox while still finding erotic pleasure in other men. When John Argue (who became a varsity swimmer), was in high school, he found some escape from the homosexual monster via his athletic involvement. The monster myth had shaped his understanding of homosexuality, making acceptance of himself as homosexual seem to him impossible. So he transformed his homosexual desires for men into more acceptable sporting relations. He said,

> I've been attracted to guys all my life, certainly by the time I was fifteen. But I just repressed or expressed it in different ways. One of the ways was by being a jock. I kept myself in good shape. Being a good swimmer enabled me to participate at camp equally with the other boys. I was conscious of my attraction to guys, but expressed it in a heterosexual, goodhearted jock way and that was my release.

He found summer camp to be especially satisfying. Many of the guys at camp would put their arms around each other and touch each other; it was an accepted expression of affection "among the guys." For John there was emotional and erotic satisfaction in being with these boys in that kind of situation. "Sometimes, we would sleep together. You'd be on a camping trip and your sleeping bag would get wet, you'd be 'forced' to share a sleeping bag with some other, hopefully, handsome guy. I don't think I ever deliberately got my sleeping bag wet! But sometimes it just happened." When he went to university he became the "athletic stick" for his year, that is, he was responsible for organizing his class for the intramural athletic program. Under his leadership, his year won.

> So, I became a well-known jock around the university. . . . That was a very happy time because I was at the center of things. Sexually, however, I was quite frustrated because I was with all those sexy guys to whom I was quite attracted, but I hadn't yet resolved my homosexuality. While I knew by this time that, yes, I am a homosexual, I still didn't know what I was going to do about it. I dealt with homosexuality at this time by putting it aside. I got some satisfaction by being with the guys.

John Goodwin, who was an internationally competitive oarsman on the Canadian national team, more or less unconsciously decided to shelve his homosexuality as he became involved in sports. His early homosexual experiences with a closeted older man and a boy who turned out to be "straight" made him see homosexuality in a negative light, so he stopped having sex with men and boys. He developed a new circle of friends, athletes. With these boys, he pursued platonic relationships. In fact, his distaste for homosexuality had become so great that even though sexual opportunities with these boys presented themselves, he wouldn't follow through. As an athlete he was able to sublimate explicit homosexual desire while still appreciating the implicit homoeroticism of being with other male athletes. He said:

I was meeting all these really wonderful people, boys, who were my friends. And it was sufficient to have them as friends. Some of them I was really sexually attracted to. . . . One friend, who was on my rowing team, I got a huge crush on the first night when we became pals. I met him over at the high-school yard and there was a whole gang of us, and he wanted to change his pants—we were going swimming—so he was going over to this other guy's house to get his cutoffs and he came over to me and said come on over, and the two of us went to this guy's place, and we got to know each other, and I also got to sit on this guy's bed while my friend took off all his clothes and put on his cutoffs. It's a great way to meet somebody, I remember that. Very hot as he undressed. Anyhow, we became very close friends.

It was very seductive, but at this point I was kind of determined I wasn't going to fall for anybody and go through all that shit. He ended up inviting me to stay over at his place one night, which I thought was nice, and we were lying on our stomachs, watching TV, and he had this trick where he would just put his leg over my side and his arm 'round me while we watched TV; meanwhile, I would try and remain conscious . . . I know the first time he did it I was so surprised because that gesture was such an obvious "let's-have-sex" gesture. It was the sort of thing that [before] I would automatically have had sex. But that's what I'd just been through, so when he did it I kind of froze up. We didn't have sex. We always ended up getting in a knot. Whenever

he came to my place we slept entwined together in various
positions, but we just didn't have sex. I had a lot of friend-
ships in high school very similar to that. We always seemed
to end up in each other's beds, sleeping together. But I
wasn't having sex, because I was afraid to; I thought I had
a lot to lose by having sex with these guys.

In his new circle of athletic friends he was able to avoid homosexuality. He was even able to get physically very close to the boys
without endowing the experience with the mythical significance
of homosexuality. When he became a national athlete, he developed an intimate, but platonic, relationship with one of his teammates. They were like a couple: they did everything together; they
always sat together on buses and planes; they would bunk next to
each other; they would socialize together. John said that no one
else on the crew formed couples in the way that he and his friend
did—nevertheless, they were comfortable with their arrangement. For John, it was a homosexual affair without the homosexuality. His friend eventually got married and had children.

Throughout his career as a high-performance athlete, John
abstained from homosexual sexual entanglements. By immersing himself in the involving world of high-performance sports, he
was able to avoid homosexuality. For six years, rowing overwhelmed his life; it consumed all his time and attention. He didn't
go into sports with the intention of shelving his sexuality—but it
turned out to be convenient. By being in sports he was able to have
close male friends without kindling the dark fires of his homosexuality. It was an arrangement, however, that couldn't last. A few
weeks after the last race of his competitive career, the world
rowing championships in Holland, he retired from the sport and
came out of his closet.

Pursuing athletics can be a way of casting oneself as "acceptable" in orthodox culture. One can feel better about oneself by
being a good athlete, thereby proving that one can fulfill the orthodox expectations of men. One can also find approval among
one's peers. Tom Waddell was a United States Olympic decathlete
(at the age of thirty, he placed sixth at the 1968 Olympics) and the
founder of the international Gay Games, which have been held
quadrenially since 1982. He recalled why, knowing the homosex-

ual monster myth as a young man and wanting to avoid its negative impact, he involved himself in athletics. He said: "I liked who I was. I liked how I felt. I didn't want any of that to change. But I didn't want to be this bizarre social and physical outcast. I wanted to be liked. I wanted to have lots of friends, and I realized the way I was going to do that was not through my intellectual capacity—because I didn't feel any of that at the time—but through an athletic capacity, and that came easily to me."[27]

Athletics allows paradoxical men and boys to make themselves acceptable to the orthodox world on orthodox terms by displaying traditionally masculine orthodox signs, that is, successful athletic performance. Whether this is a good strategy is questionable. If a homosexual man gains acceptance by appearing as orthodox as his truly orthodox peers, by de-emphasizing his paradoxical intuitions, in fact, by concealing them behind a facade of orthodoxy, I doubt whether his acceptance means much, since it is based on the deceitful use of orthodox signs. Certainly one is likely to be fooling *oneself* by such a strategy. Friendship doesn't amount to much if it's based on misrepresentation.

Irony

The second tendency in the triad of gay sensibility is to see the world ironically. *Irony* is a way of approaching the world, a sensibility, which comes quite naturally to many gay men. The experience of being homosexual in our culture is fundamentally an ironic experience. In one form of irony there is an interplay between two contradictory phenomena: appearance and reality, which in our case are orthodoxy and paradoxy respectively. In this form, contradiction can be resolved; appearance can give way to reality. That kind of ironic interplay is basic to the experience of virtually all homosexual men. That which seems to be the case actually turns out not to be; this is the experience of being taken for heterosexual when one is, in fact, homosexual. For instance, a good wrestler, because of his muscular build and athletic ability, may be seen as orthodox when in fact his understanding of himself and of his wrestling is quite paradoxical. Intentionally or unintentionally, homosexual men are often thought of as heterosexual; when this is actively pursued by them it is known as "passing." Passing predisposes homosexual men to an awareness of the irony implicit in their lives. But another, perhaps deeper, gay ironic sensibility emerges from the duality inherent in the paradox itself. It is to that duality we shall first turn.

It's not uncommon to hear gay men at parties, in gay bars, on the streets of gay neighborhoods, or in the repartee of members of gay sports clubs, calling each other "fags." When asked to describe himself, one man I interviewed said, "Faggot has a nice ring to it." It's become popular among gay men to refer to gay bars as "fag bars." One man I interviewed called his gay volleyball league "fag volleyball."

The conscientious use of the word "fag" by gay men underscores the ironic meaning of homosexuality.* The truth of being homosexual in our culture is double-edged; it's a matter of being paradoxical in an orthodox culture, of being gay in a mostly straight world. The paradoxical interpretation of the myths of sexuality and gender does not do away with orthodoxy in the minds of homosexual men. They know the orthodox world; it is a world in which they grew up and in which most continue to live a significant part of their lives. Structurally, moreover, the paradox emerges out of orthodoxy itself; the paradoxical erotic desire for men would be impossible without the orthodox construction of masculine gender. Paradoxy, therefore, is always intimately associated with orthodoxy in the lives of homosexual men and boys. That is the irony of homosexuality.

Homosexuality involves not only a *different interpretation* of myths, it also involves an *awareness* that the interpretation is different. Gay men using the word "fag" are obviously giving it a different interpretation (a paradoxical interpretation); they do not sincerely intend the hateful significance of the word (which

---

*I believe that there are important parallels between the gay ironic appropriation of pejorative language and the appropriation that other oppressed groups, like blacks, make of language. It may well be that irony is intrinsic to the experience of many forms of oppression and also to sowing the seeds of liberation. I am not suggesting that irony is the exclusive preserve of gay men. It is, however, a highly developed sense among them. The ironic fact that the paradox is often hidden, that it goes undetected, heightens the irony of gay sensibility. Blacks are seldom mistaken for whites; gay men are frequently mistaken for straight men.

is the orthodox interpretation). But also, they are not unaware of its traditionally hateful meaning. When gay men call each other "fags," they are commenting on the orthodox attitude toward homosexuality by confronting it ironically. This ironic use of the word conveys both the orthodox and paradoxical understandings of homosexuality, reminding us that contempt is the traditional perspective on homosexuality.

Ironic vision is especially well suited to being gay. According to the German philosopher Schlegel, "Irony is the form of paradox"; and "Paradox is the *conditio sine qua non* of irony, its soul, its source, and its principle. . . . Irony is the analysis [as opposed to synthesis] of thesis and antithesis."[28] Paradox contradicts the received way of seeing things. (In dialectical terms, the orthodox interpretation of the myths of gender and sexuality is the thesis, and the paradoxical interpretation is the antithesis that has emerged out of the thesis itself.*) The gay sensibility that analyzes or appreciates the relationship between orthodox and paradox is irony. Irony is the most penetrating interpretation of what it is to be gay.

Estrangement distances gay men from conventional myths; this is a detachment that allows the gay sensibility to unfold the world ironically. Detachment allows one to be less a participant in orthodox culture and more an observer—the position of the observer is a traditional ironic stance. "Straight" or orthodox people, who see themselves in their gender and sexual relations as "natural," are less inclined to see through the myths than those whose lives are outside of "nature." Kierkegaard says that irony does not present itself in nature to those who are themselves very natural or naive.[29] In our culture, homosexuality is unnatural. Therefore, those who see themselves in a homosexual context, estranged from "nature," are often less committed to the "natural" order and are able, and in many cases willing, to see through this "natural" deceit. The "straight" world loses its "natural" patina in the light of gay irony.

Gay irony is a positive destructive force that exposes the "natu-

---

*A gay Marxist might say that just as capitalism contains the seeds of its own destruction, so too the orthodoxy of patriarchy will be the source of its own eventual demise.

ralness" of orthodox myths. This, for example, is the experience of coming out, of having a special ironic insight into the myths of gender and sexuality. Coming out is an interpretive experience; it's a process in which a truer meaning is seen beneath a false. The "naturalness" of heterosexuality is revealed as a socially constructed form of erotic power-mongering. (The monster myth, by discouraging the homosexual alternative, helps keep that power-mongering going, thereby maintaining the patriarchal heterosexual status quo.) Having believed that the homosexual monster myth somehow described oneself, one decides that it doesn't. In coming out, the status quo is undermined: the assumption that everyone is heterosexual is undone; the grip of the monster is loosened. By changing one's mind the world is changed; they're wrong and you're right.

Now, the great strength of irony lies not just in its power to negate false appearances. Irony, while destroying appearance, maintains appearance *as appearance*. As Alan Rodway says, "Irony is not merely a matter of seeing a 'true' meaning beneath a 'false,' but of seeing a double exposure . . . on one plate."[30] Even though we see the false as false, it is presented as true. In irony, then, there is a coexistence of truth and falsehood. The false does not fall away when truth is revealed; a dramatic tension is maintained. And here is an important truth about the meaning of gay men's lives: things are not only *other* than what they seem to be, but they also *seem* to be other than what they are. When a gay man comes out, he sees through orthodox myths, but this doesn't mean that those myths have vanished; they are, after all, the paradoxical source of his desire. Irony appreciates the new interpretation of myths in the face of orthodoxy.

Irony is a kind of eloquence. As the historian of rhetoric Wayne Booth said, "Perhaps no other form of human communication does so much with so much speed and economy."[31] It is in this elegant economy that the true genius of irony lies. Through irony, the most complex truths can be immediately grasped. The *analysis* of irony is complex and laborious, whereas the *practice* of irony, while commanding a profound and intricate view, proceeds with the ease and grace of a highly accomplished violinist whose technique has become so transparent that we are aware only of the music it produces. Irony becomes an instinctive way of thinking for many gay men. Because it is a structure that is inherent in the experience of being gay, irony is often used in an unself-conscious way. Like the rules of grammar, which in many ways unconsciously shape our ability to think and speak, irony often proceeds unnoticed *as* irony, all the while reaping its ironic effect.

I have often been struck by the seeming ironic instincts of many gay men. Young men with little education from small towns or the country can arrive in the gay neighborhoods of big cities and in short order understand a sophisticated way of thinking that they probably would not have encountered in their families or among hometown nongay peers. For instance, many will quickly come to understand the complex ironic significance of drag, and they are often prodigious in their understanding and employment of camp sensibility, the essence of which is irony. This special ability is an intuitive feel, a talent, for ironic apprehension, the gift of growing up paradoxical in an orthodox world.

Irony appreciates contradiction. Gay irony destroys the inauthenticity of the orthodox world, setting the ironist free. Having destroyed the facade of orthodoxy, irony takes up the task of reconstruction; a new authentic, ironic edifice is raised. This new structure will express the gay ironist's *paradoxical* intuitions. Think again about the gay use of the word "fag." On the first level it is a pejorative word. On a higher level, however, understood ironically, the orthodox worldview in which the pejorative sense of the word "fag" originates is both *dismissed* as being inauthentic and *maintained* as the wellspring for an authentic appreciation of homosexuality—keep in mind that the paradox emerges out of orthodoxy. The gay use of the word "fag" expresses the triumph of a gay interpretation of the orthodox world.

Irony is not for the faint of heart. An ironic disposition requires a measure of courage because it means that the myths of orthodoxy, the often cherished beliefs of our culture, are overturned in favor of new and unfamiliar ground. With the freedom of irony comes uncertainty. Unlike the sensibility that de-emphasizes homosexuality and the experience of being different, irony confronts being different, taking it as the inspiration for a new interpretation of oneself and the world. Some homosexual men find irony uncomfortable. The product of the history of Western civilization, enshrined in religion, medicine, and law, orthodoxy pervades social institutions such as the family and sports. To undermine orthodoxy ironically is to take as mere surface what most people consider eternal verities. For those who are not brave, irony may be an intolerable confrontation with truth and uncertainty. The philosopher Schlegel said: "Irony is duty." The duty of gay irony lies in the uncovering of those myths that obscure a genuine appreciation of paradoxical intuitions. Irony, therefore, is the authentic engagement with homosexuality in our culture.

But an ironic disposition can be a dangerous one. A deeply ironic temperament may cast one into an endless free-fall of ironic destruction, leaving one with nothing. Conrad writes in *Under Western Eyes,* "Remember, Razumov, that women, children and revolutionists hate irony, which is the negation of all saving instincts, of all faith, of all devotion, of all actions." The German philosopher Hegel was aware of this dark side of irony when he defined it as "infinite, absolute negativity." The ironist's temptation is to see *everything* ironically, falling into an impoverished nihilism.

But the paradoxical intuition that is at the heart of homosexuality and the gay ironic sensibility does not suggest that the world is absurd, essentially meaningless. On the contrary, it is the intuition that the orthodox conception of the world of gender and sexual relations is inauthentic for those with paradoxical intuitions and that there is another, more authentic view. This is a form of irony that Wayne Booth calls "stable." Here, there is not a sense of an endless succession of ironic destruction; rather, there is a move to a more solid ground. Gay irony is a *positive* destructive force.

With gay irony, one is performing on the high wire. Having destroyed orthodoxy, one has moved to a superior (paradoxical) abode. This feeling of superiority, of looking down from on high, can be dangerous. For when the ironist is at his most lofty—like Icarus coming closest to the heat of the sun—he is most likely to plummet and become the victim of his own irony. The gay product of ironic reconstruction often turns out to be a new orthodoxy, as prone as the old to ironic destruction. There are signs of this new orthodoxy and its consequent ironic destruction in the gay liberation movement. A runner I interviewed commented on that orthodoxy:

What I was feeling, after coming out, was that there seemed to be a political correctness in being gay and it was like, hey wait, I didn't give up a set of rigid restrictions or proscriptions [Roman Catholicism] in my life to replace it with something else. I will do a critical analysis of what's right for me. I had a hard time with what I saw as, at times, running down monogamy, or running down certain types of relationships as being destructive to me. Some people will choose a lifestyle that replicates heterosexuality or is seen in terms of living in the suburbs with a white picket fence and a dog and all that. They may have done that because it's a comfortable model for them and they may not have done the analysis, but then again they may have done the analysis and figured out that that's what they want. Even if they haven't, if they are happy that way, fine.

For a period, gay magazines such as the *Body Politic* advocated a "politically correct" homosexuality that was promiscuous and rigorously opposed to people choosing sexual/emotional partners on the basis of race, looks, or age.* There were policies regarding what machinations of sexual desire were considered appropriate for the classified advertisements of the magazine. But as time went on, the *Body Politic* came to realize that they were dictating an orthodoxy. Gay ironic sensibility was eventually triumphant: being "politically incorrect" came to be "politically correct." At a large party held at the offices of the *Body Politic,* people who had paid the admission fee had stamped on the back of their hands, "PI (Politically Incorrect)." This, of course, signified their ironic acceptability at the party.

---

*Interestingly, this advocacy of nondiscrimination didn't include sex, since that would undermine the whole point of a division between homo- and heterosexuality. So the gay liberation movement at that point was, in a very deep way, unapologetically sexist. This is in itself quite ironic, because the advocates of nondiscrimination considered themselves avid feminists, opposed to all forms of discrimination on the basis of sex or gender.

* * *

So far, I have looked at the gay ironic sensibility as the medium through which gay men reflect upon themselves and their place in the world. This sensibility also influences the way gay men present themselves. The social and cultural context in which gay men find themselves is always a concern: if they are in an orthodox or a straight setting, whether or not they let their homosexuality be known or at what volume it is to be heard is an issue that needs to be addressed. There are perhaps "neutral" settings where one's personal life is not supposed to be an issue. In jurisdictions where there are laws prohibiting discrimination on the basis of sexual orientation, one's use of public services, rights to employment, shelter, and so on are supposed to be "neutral" territories. But gay men know that such "neutrality" is often superficial. Our culture is pervaded by orthodox myths of gender and sexuality—regardless of laws, these myths form the cultural context for human relations. Because being gay is substantially different from being straight, when a gay man is in a straight setting, as a matter of tact or even social survival he must present himself carefully. Some gay men are comfortable playing along with orthodoxy and, in varying degrees, depending on the situation, passing themselves off as straight—not mentioning that they have male lovers, for instance. Most gay youths, generally unaware of any other option and feeling the poignant adolescent need to be acceptable to their peers, will behave in as orthodox a fashion as possible. Because in most of our society there is an assumption that everyone is heterosexual, many gay men pass as straight more by default than intention. And there are gay men who feel distinctly uncomfortable when people think they are straight; they will avoid situations where that will be the case, correct false impressions where they have an opportunity, and behave in ways that make it clear that they are gay.

A professor told me:

I think with a great many of my friends and colleagues—I may be kidding myself—but I think they don't know. A friend of mine who got married had had a long and active [homo]sexual life, and he was my best friend for maybe six or seven years, and it wasn't until he had read a letter that I was writing to [my lover] that he realized that I was gay too. And some of my students who have come out after they stopped being my students were shocked to discover that I was also gay. So, yes, I know I [pass]. When I think of some of the much younger people I know, in their thirties, also teachers, some of them, they also like to pass. There's a doctor who is terrified of being found out. He comes here to my house to meet his lover whom he lives with, but he doesn't want to be seen on the street with him, which I think is very extreme. They arrive here separately, just in case someone sees them together.

Whereas a man who teaches in a public school said:

I'd like to be in a position of never having to pass—applying for a job . . . if I feel there's any danger that I'll be in a situation where I'll be uncomfortable, I avoid it. It's very open in the school where I work that I'm gay and I wouldn't have it any other way. I have no energy to spend on hiding, making up stories. I'm beyond that . . . so there're no games. I want people to know that I'm gay, because if they don't, then it's not an honest relationship.

Passing intensifies the irony of being gay in a straight world, of appearing to be straight when one is in fact gay. In the orthodox world it is generally assumed that everyone is heterosexual. Especially in one's youth, this assumption is particularly pervasive. Immersed in orthodox culture, many homosexual boys grow up believing themselves to be heterosexual; their family and friends think they are heterosexual; they will be members, at least ostensibly, of what I earlier referred to as "the boys-wanting-girls club" and will go out on dates with girls; they may even plan to get married, some going on to do so. Because of this assumption homosexual boys learn to behave in an orthodox fashion, all the while harboring paradoxical interpretations. The experience, for example, of being on a double date and desiring the other boy rather than one's girlfriend is not uncommon for gay boys. The early experience of homosexuality is also the experience of hiding it, the irony of appearing to be what one is not. Said another man I interviewed:

> I think that before I came out, and I mean telling my friends openly and explicitly this is what it is, which occurred in my last year of university, that for a while it was a little bit of a buzz to play the double agent, so to speak.

This is a strategic irony that serves the useful purpose of shielding oneself from stigma. The "buzz" that this man describes is the feeling you get when you hide. It's a bit like the feeling of playing the game hide-and-seek. Under the cover of a bush, you see the seeker, commonly known as "it," run past in a futile attempt to discover you. Suddenly you notice that under the veranda, right next to you, another hider is hiding. The two of you can barely suppress the giggles as you share the joy of hiding while "it" seeks in vain.

Passing is an experience that predominates in the lives of homosexual youths; as one comes out of the closet, its role in life can diminish.

> When I was a teenager I definitely passed as straight. As far as I know I did. Nobody told me otherwise. As an adult, I never tried to pass as straight. If people ask me, I'm pretty up-front.

This man is in a privileged situation: he doesn't need to pass at work, where he is a social worker in a liberal-thinking agency, or with his family, who know that both he and his brother are gay and have accepted the fact, or socially, since most of his friends are gay and those who aren't are his friends because homosexuality is not a problem for them.

Obviously, it's much easier to live openly gay lives now than it was thirty or forty years ago. The deeply bifurcated homosexual life, the cautious division of one's life into public and private, has lost some of its necessity. Although hiding homosexuality no longer has the utter importance it once did, it still influences the lives of gay men. Many of us grew up in the age when homosexuality was "the love that dare not speak its name." That background should not be forgotten. A retired man said:

If I had been thirty years younger perhaps [my life] would be more a unity. Perhaps people who have come out in the seventies and eighties, their lives are more of a unified pattern. Because they don't have to hide as much. Since I have social and financial security, what would have worried me in the fifties does not worry me now. I don't really mind if the people across the hall know that I'm homosexual and I don't mind if the hall porter downstairs sees my friends and takes it for granted that they are homosexual. I think it's right and proper, whereas I think perhaps twenty to thirty years ago I would have found this uncomfortable.

Fluidity, as I have said before, is basic to gay sensibility—context is everything. Many men can live openly gay lives at home and among their friends but find it necessary to cover up at work.

There have been occasions where I have put on a very good act. I was a truck driver for a while, so it was a matter of survival because I knew that if I raised the issue with those people, they couldn't deal with it. If I tried to help them deal with it, I wouldn't have been of much help because we were functioning on different levels, so I just avoided it. And the way they might have had to deal with it might have been to punch me in the face.

Often, taking advantage of the assumption that everyone is heterosexual, one is able to pass simply by keeping quiet about one's homosexuality.

A man who is very active in a gay volleyball league pointed out that his work and personal lives are different.

The one situation is work, of course, where I always have to [pass]. At work with me it's all business anyway. So I don't know if I'm passing for being straight or passing for being a competent businessman, but I just put myself in that mode of thought. I've never been in a social situation other than work [where it was necessary to pass] and in the last six years I've never been anything other than what I am, gay.

A former competitive swimmer who is now a salesperson for a large firm said that he passes at work because he sees no other option.

> The nature of my work demands that I pass. You tend to be a chameleon. You're having to blend in with the woodwork. I don't think I'm sacrificing any personal values but you are basically being aware of who you are with, your environment, and you have to blend in. It may be convincing, it may not be. Some people say that it is. I don't really go out of my way to do so. . . . I suppose there are times when I consciously put up this front and yes, I think I've got a pretty pat routine I can do under certain circumstances, and I think I can pull it off fairly well. But only when I have to.

Walking in the streets can be dangerous for gay men. "Queer-bashing" is a phenomenon most gay men know about.

> I did get punched in the gut and rolled into a big pile of garbage. I was with [a gay friend, Peter]. I was walking down the street in the middle of the sidewalk with Peter and these two guys were coming at us and one of them was walking straight for me and I thought, Okay, I'll split to the left, but he just kept walking straight toward me, with glazed eyes. So I kept walking, and when I was right on the curb the guy walked up to me. . . . I had no air in my lungs, I was completely flat, lying in a pile of garbage, and Peter said, "Hey, what are you doing," and this guy whopped Peter in the head and sliced his ear and it was bleeding all over. It was very strange. That's the only scene I've ever had. Other than name-calling. I think everybody experiences people driving by—hicks from the suburbs yelling "faggot."
>
> It makes me want to fight, to roll somebody in the garbage. It makes me mad that they are narrow-minded. It really irks me that people take their fun driving around the town yelling "faggot." It really irritates me because they are out of reach. It doesn't hurt me in the way that I wish I wasn't gay. I don't go home crying. Some people do.

Some gay men will modify their behavior, will pass as straight, in order to avoid violence on the streets. This experience of going about undetected has obvious ironic implications.

With the assumption that everyone is heterosexual, gay men will frequently pass as straight by default. John Van Druten, in his play *Bell, Book and Candle* (1950) writes about three homosexuals, cast metaphorically as witches. One of them, called Queenie, expresses her amazement at the blindness of people.

> He'd never suspect, darling. Not in a million years. No matter *what* I did. Honestly, it's amazing the way people don't. Why, they just don't believe there *are* such things. I sit in the subway sometimes, or in buses, and look at the people next to me, and I think: What would you say if I told you I was a witch? And I know they'd never believe it. And I giggle and giggle to myself.[32]

We live in a world dominated by orthodoxy. Consequently, there are many, both gay and straight, who insist on behaving in orthodox ways and seeing orthodoxy in each other. The rower John Goodwin was, when I interviewed him, the director of a public art gallery.

> If someone thinks I'm straight, they just chose that, because that's the convention they are comfortable with. Professionally, people want me to be straight, but they know I'm gay, but for the convenience of accomplishing what we do, it's better for me to be straight. Especially for the gay people who are there. I've been at conferences where everything happens straight—all the men chat with the women and hug them and tease them and the men all shake hands and it's proper and the conversation never gets off-color. And then after dinner, I go to the fag bar for some sanity and walk in there, and five of the guys who've been doing all that all day are on the dance floor, doing poppers and dancing like maniacs, and they come over and start talking to me in a completely different tone in this other completely familiar [gay] way and I say, "How can you people fuck around like this, back and forth, I would be just so ex-

hausted after running two systems like that simultaneously."

The attitude of his gay colleagues is a conscious decision to see appearance rather than reality. It is a deliberate ironic play, on their part, in the interest of maintaining ties with an orthodox world.

Many people prefer to operate in primarily orthodox contexts. In this case, I am using the word "orthodox" in the sense of a general frame of mind, an overall conservative disposition. Making it known that one is gay can lead to ostracization, not necessarily because of homophobia, but because being gay is a matter of being unorthodox—one will be suspected of tending not to see things from the "right" point of view. There are many people who sincerely have no interest in what their peers, colleagues, superiors, and subordinates do in bed or with whom they do it. They have a great interest, however, in their fellows' desire and ability to "fit in." By making it known that one is gay, one is making it clear that one thinks there is a different legitimate interpretation of the fundamental myths of our culture. This constitutes a basic rejection of conservatism, of the status quo. Hiding homosexuality, on the other hand, *even if it is known that one is hiding,* indicates that one either agrees with the status quo or at least defers to it. Some homosexual men will go to great lengths to prove their dedication to orthodoxy. Those who are members of the church will argue vehemently against the ordination of homosexual men and lesbians to the ministry or priesthood. Homosexual politicians will block antidiscrimination legislation, and homosexual police and military personnel will assist or even initiate homosexual witch-hunts within their organizations. Homosexual businessmen and professionals will engage in scandal-mongering. All to show their affinity with orthodoxy. It's in this way the implications of homosexuality often go beyond the sexual arena.

Men are encouraged to display their orthodox sexuality and therefore commitment to the status quo by the exhibition of blatantly heterosexual behaviors, such as bringing their wives to important social functions, taking out family memberships in clubs, and displaying their orthodox masculinity in aggressive sports. Paul de Man is reputed to have said that "irony has its roots in the 'covering up of the scandalous.' "[33] For those who prefer to cover their "scandalous" homosexuality in the guise of orthodoxy, passing is an ironic experience.

It's often said that men who make their homosexuality known in orthodox society are tactless. There is some truth in this, because implicit in making one's homosexuality known is an unwillingness to go along with the status quo, which is then seen as a criticism of orthodoxy. Uninvited criticism is not tactful. This is why there are so few openly gay men in high-profile positions. To allow an openly gay person in an important position is to give credibility to an unorthodox, indeed paradoxical, reading of the fundamental myths. Consequently, it is only the most liberal institutions (some art galleries, ballet companies, and avant-garde schools) that will give high-profile positions to openly gay men. This is basically a homophobic version of provincialism, of not trusting people who are different.

That there are homosexual men in hiding on major league baseball teams, as the stars of the National Hockey League, or as the bright lights of national Olympic teams is not a great concern to sports officials or the public. By keeping their homosexuality a secret, they are endorsing the significance of their sports as orthodox masculine heterosexual and patriarchal institutions. What is intolerable is if they make it known that they are gay, because this would expose the mythic relationship of masculinity and sports. If a star athlete can be gay, then obviously these sports are not the high expressions of orthodox masculinity they are normally thought to be. If famous athletes don't keep quiet about their homosexuality, the major appeal of sports as the arena of masculinity will be destroyed. As the sportswriter in Patricia Nell Warren's novel *The Front Runner* commented on the average sports spectator: "He pays five bucks to see the pure blooded American boy run the mile. He doesn't pay to see no fairies."[34] This is why, after he came out, David Kopay was prevented from having any further employment in professional sports. Thus far, it has been impossible to be openly gay and at the top of the sports world.

Orthodoxy can be signified in many ways: having and flaunting a wife and children, playing sports, watching and talking about sports, wearing certain styles of clothing, speaking in a masculine fashion, maintaining an inflexible deportment (body language)—the list is endless.[35] For a gay man to be successful in straight settings he must play a careful game in which the chief skill is the clever manipulation of orthodox signs, indicating the degree of his (at least apparent) affinity with traditional sensibilities. Generally speaking, it is no longer necessary to keep homosexuality a deep dark secret; the issue now is how open one should be about it. The degree of openness depends on the situation. Some straight situations demand more adherence to orthodoxy than others. The ability to read these situations and render the appropriate degree of openness is essential for gay men who want to maintain contact with the orthodox world. Irony helps gay men to survive or perhaps even transcend the mire of orthodoxy.

Because there is an assumption in our society that everyone is heterosexual, passing can be subtle. One may simply not draw attention to homosexuality; gay men who want to maintain their contact with the orthodox world will often do so by carefully not saying things.

> I suppose there are occasions when I'm not going to go out of my way to say that I'm gay, sitting on a bus, for example, bouncing through northern Ontario. My chameleonlike quality would come into effect every now and again.

John Goodwin said that when he was younger, people often thought he was straight.

> I don't know if I did anything to assert that I was straight, so that people would assume I was straight, I think I was very quiet. I remember actually that question [whether he had girlfriends] often came up. Everybody had to know who had a girlfriend. I always said "I don't have girlfriends." And then there'd be a long pause—you were supposed to explain *why* you didn't have a girlfriend or when you last broke up with a girlfriend, but I didn't say anything.

Because he was a rower, people would assume he was straight.

> I think I just look like any other oarsmen, we just look all the same. I was at the regatta this summer, and I was look-

ing at all the crews and they just all looked the same. You could never spot a gay person among any of the crews, just no way. You'd *wish* that they were all gay, but you can't tell. Even when I came out, I used to run into people who I knew in gay bars, but they didn't know I was gay, because I didn't know them well enough to tell them when I came out. They were always quite surprised.

Because of the pervasive assumption that everyone is heterosexual, people will take the resulting appearance to be the reality. As a result of being taken for straight, gay men are sensitive to the interplay of appearance and reality. While the experience of duplicity, of being a chameleon, which comes with passing may well be unattractive to gay men, something that they avoid as much as possible, it is, nevertheless, a fact of life.

Change

Homo- and hetero-sexualities, as Foucault pointed out, are socially created categories that regulate human lives. Religion, medicine, law, and sports have played an important role in that regulation. Under the auspices of these institutions, homosexuality was made mythically monstrous and estranging. The monster myth has met with increasing resistance from the estranged. In the hope of removing the stigma of homosexuality, the homosexual liberation movement was born in Europe about one hundred years ago.[36]

The contemporary gay liberation movement has focused on a range of issues and taken many tacks in its war on the monster myth. The movement is well known for its protest marches, acts of civil disobedience, legislative lobbying for gay rights, AIDS action, "gay pride" events like the Gay Games, and its very active publishing of books and periodicals. One of the crucial spheres of influence has been language. The promulgation of the word "gay" is one of the better known and effective campaigns. The word "homosexual" is the creation of nineteenth-century medicine and was seen by the gay liberation movement as emphasizing the notion of illness and clinical treatment. In a largely successful attempt to wrest homosexuality from the sciences, the word "gay" has replaced "homosexual" in much of popular discourse. Generally, someone who uses the word "gay" is expressing a positive, or at least sympathetic, attitude toward homosexuality and the overall aims of gay liberation. Those who have little affinity with gay liberation, or who prefer to encourage the power of the homosexual monster myth, are reluctant to use the word "gay."

Gay liberation is the political manifestation of the third tendency in the triad of gay sensibility, *change*. The gay ironic sensibility, because it maintains the tension between orthodoxy and paradoxy (a fact of homosexual life), is the authentic analysis or appreciation of being homosexual in our culture. The sensibility of change, on the other hand, does not preserve that duality; it is a revolutionary mode, one that approachs the world assertively, seeing what is in terms of what should be. Whereas irony is the analysis of thesis and antithesis, change is the sensibility of synthesis. That is to say, there is a positive movement away from the status quo.

As one acknowledges the paradox and chooses not to de-emphasize it, the desire emerges to develop a new relationship to sexual myths. This is a matter of seeing one's place in the world in a new light, a legitimate one. The heterosexual myth bestows legitimacy only on those who embrace and practice, both erotically and otherwise, the orthodoxy of gender difference. Complementing that orthodoxy, the homosexual monster myth intensifies the illegitimacy of the paradox. To accept the paradox, one must unseat the superlegitimacy of heterosexuality and legitimize homosexuality.

One *becomes* gay, in the "modern" political sense, through the sensibility of change. Being homosexual is the expression of a deep paradoxical, psychic relationship to the myths of gender. Becoming gay, one cultivates a positive attitude to the paradox by asserting one's legitimacy in thought, word, and deed. Originally, this is a personal acceptance of oneself as a paradoxical man. But for many, that personal sense of legitimacy inspires a desire for public expression.

The monster myth drove homosexuality into secrecy. Barry Adam points out that "both women and gay people have long been taught to 'know their place,' to keep silent before their 'superiors,' and to believe themselves unworthy of the rights and privileges of men and of heterosexuals."[37] In response to such abnegation, the sensibility of change breaks the monstrous conspiracy of silence. When one begins to see that one is just as legitimate (if not more so) as the heterosexual adherents of orthodoxy, one ceases to see any reason for keeping one's life quiet and private; good things, after all, should be shared. And so the sensibility of change entails a public assertion of gay legitimacy, of gay pride.

In athletics the sensibility of change can be seen at work in gay culture. Gay community sports clubs express the desire to change the myth of athletics as an orthodox pursuit. In gay community sports, lesbians and gay men are not only athletes; they are *gay* athletes whose paradoxical intuitions have lead them to a different way of being in the world of gender. Gay sports express the pride one takes in the paradox. When gay men are openly gay in mainstream sports, thereby refusing to hide under the ostensible orthodoxy of sports, they publicly demonstrate their pride in their own legitimacy as paradoxical men.*

The assertion of legitimacy is one thrust of the sensibility of change. But there is another movement within this sensibility that is more powerful both in its historical breadth and in the depth of change it implies. To assert the legitimacy of homosexuality doesn't challenge, at least immediately, those underlying myths of gender upon which homosexual desire is based. But deep within the sensibility of change, indeed emanating from the paradox itself, is the radical possibility of the eventual disintegration of gender. This is an expansive, historical possibility, a potential for change that does not lie so much with individuals as it does in the long-term historical discourse of gender.

The homosexual paradox is a historical response to the pervasiveness of orthodoxy in the gender myth. It is a deep psychic option that men and women can take to extricate themselves from some of the more oppressive aspects of gender, namely the intensification of gender difference via the heterosexual myth. But this option, as I have said earlier, continues to operate *within* the myth of gender; it is not opting *out* of gender. The paradox,

---

*Because the last chapter of this book explores the impact of gay sensibilities on athletic culture, I am only briefly introducing the phenomenon here.

and gay life as we know it now, are only "moments" in the historical development of the power dynamics of gender myth. But if
these moments become elongated—that is, if the paradox is allowed to flourish in the positive light of the sensibility of change—
an option even more iconoclastic than paradox could appear. I
suspect that for this to happen, the full significance of the paradox must be realized over a lengthy period of time, just as the full
significance of orthodoxy has.

A more profound change that may eventually emerge would
be the end of the *doxa* (that is, the seemingness or tradition) of
the myth of gender itself. This was one of the high hopes of the
early gay liberation movement. Dennis Altman in 1971 foresaw
the "end of the homosexual." "Once everyone is free to express his
or her latent sexualities, boundaries between the homosexual and
the heterosexual should fade into irrelevance, and false parti-
tions in the flow of desire give way to personal fulfillment."[38] The
gay liberation movement at that time did not truly understand the
deeply patriarchal source of sexual desire in our culture and
failed therefore to see the difficulty, if not impossibility, of individuals at this time in history escaping from it.

We live immersed in a culture of patriarchy—the wish to
break away from it is not sufficient for actually doing so. Erotic
desire is a complex phenomenon that develops out of each individual's appropriations of the culture in which he finds himself:
it is deeply dependent upon one's earliest readings of that culture
and ongoing adaptations to it. Divorcing oneself from one's psychic past is not easy. Even if it were possible to abolish the past,
one is still faced with life in an overwhelmingly gendered, patriarchal culture. So, escape at this time is not tenable.

But if young people grow up with the positive possibilities of
paradoxical culture rather than with the pervasiveness of orthodox culture, as is now the case, a gradual erosion of the edifice of
orthodox masculinity may come about. Over many generations,
each made more free by the positive destructive force of the paradox, gender culture could eventually dissolve. It is in this long-
term, historical way that the paradox could genuinely undermine
patriarchy. I am not suggesting that the paradox can single-hand-
edly bring about such an important liberating destruction of a
mythic world that has oppressed people for centuries. Without a

doubt, a host of social, cultural, and economic factors must be involved. But the erotic potential of the paradox could well contribute to such an evolution.

When we say that a man is gay, homosexual, or a fag, we are commenting on much more than what he does in bed or with whom, although we are certainly speaking of that too. These words convey a vast realm of experience, ways of being in the world that can, but needn't always, affect virtually every aspect of a man's life. Being homosexual in our culture is a fluid experience that depends not only on the amplitude of one's paradoxical intuitions, but also on the complex interplay of the triadic sensibilities of de-emphasis, irony, and change as they emerge from the special experience of being paradoxical in an orthodox world, forming for each man his sense of the past, present, and future.

V

Jocks

and

Paradox

"A wondrously supple athlete was leading me about in the night."

—Genet, *The Thief's Journal*

There is a sexual connotation to [jocks]; a big butch guy, muscular, not too muscular, but with an athletic build. Always in a jock strap. Overtly masculine. Goes out with the boys. They are sexy without even knowing it, although some of them know it. They may not even be all that attractive but they have something about them, a certain *je ne sais quoi.* They have a certain sexual aura.*

Athletic imagery abounds in gay pornography. A regular monthly pornographic magazine[1] entitled *Jock* boasts over half-a-million readers.[2] There are pornographic magazines, often published in conjunction with videos, with titles like *The Jogger, HARDball, Pumping, Knockout, GymNasty, Lockerroom Fever, Jock Itch,* and as a play on the Olympic Games, *Skin Games. Basket Practice* has a picture on the cover of a young man throwing a basketball while another cups the thrower's genitals

---

*Said one of the men I interviewed.

in his hand. ("Basket" is gay slang for the outline male genitals form when pressed against tight pants.) A quartet of jock magazines are advertised as: "Handy, dandy picture books you can keep with you all the time for a quick look whenever you'd like a quick 'lift.'" The first commercial homoerotic film was probably *The Cyclist,* produced in 1949.[3] Films and videos exploiting the homoerotic aura of athletes have proliferated since that time. *Spokes* was advertised with the following copy: "Cycling through the backwoods is what *Spokes* is all about . . . when seven guys wind up in an abandoned barn, all hell breaks lose." (See Fig. 1.) Similar videos are: *Spring Training, Games,* which has spliced into it nonpornographic, actual footage from the 1982 Gay Games, *Track Meet, Down for the Count, The Idol, Jock Dreams, Wrestling Meat, The Young Olympians, Jock Empire, The Last Surfer, These Bases Are Loaded, Tough Competition, Winner's Circle, Triple Workout,* and *The Other Side of Aspen II,* which exploits the homoerotic potential of a ski resort. The advertisement for the latter video looks like a homoeroticized ad for a ski resort. (See Fig. 2.) *Lifeguard* is a video promoting and illustrating safe-sex techniques; it was produced with the help of Dr. Robert Bolan, President of the San Francisco AIDS Foundation.

Sometimes, pornographers will use athletic titles even though the material doesn't actually employ athletic iconography; one such video producer is Jock Athletics Co., which does not include in its catalog any titles with athletic themes. Often amusing is pornography that exploits the world of athletics for its erotic potential but, because of the apparent lack of experience the producers have with sports, gets things wrong. In *JR.,* Vol. 1, April 1964, there is a photo of a boxer who has just come out of the showers. The caption reads "After punching the bag for a while, Sam Delany (at left) tones himself with a brisk shower." Although showers are a pleasant way to end a workout, their toning effects are nil. (See Fig. 3.)

In the last twenty years, the gay pornography industry has grown enormously and produced a proliferation of male homoerotic images. Out of this has developed a range of specialized homoerotic "types" that pornographic videos and magazines champion. *Drummer,* for instance, features mature, hirsute men with rugged, sadomasochistic proclivities. At the other end of the spectrum is *Stars,* a magazine featuring the "softer" eroticism of hairless teenage boys. Somewhere in the middle is athletic homoeroticism. What all these magazines have in common is the marketing of homoerotic masculinity, from its first bud *(Stars)* to its seasoned extreme *(Drummer).** In producing and cultivating these homoerotic images, the pornography industry has followed and reinforced these masculine dimensions of the erotic imagination of those homosexual men who like pornography. It has not, as some have argued, created that erotic desire. Homoerotic desire is an erotic expression of the personal paradoxical reading of the myths of gender. Erotic fantasizing with pornography is a way of exploring that desire. There is not a simple causal relationship between a pornographic icon and a successful homoerotic fantasy. To get a feel for the way that pornography works, it would be useful to do a quick phenomenological reflection on the sexual experience of fantasizing with pornography. Leafing through a magazine, the fantasizer will see many images that have potential as fantasy material. He may see some that inspire his imagination sufficiently so that the excitement of erotic incarnation becomes a distinct possibility. The fantasizer *interacts* with the images he sees, both endowing those images with and drawing from them elements of his own erotic world. He brings to a two-dimensional, sometimes black-and-white picture his multi-dimensional and colorful psychic background, filling that picture with the world of his erotic desire. As he masturbates, the picture comes to life and with his imagination takes on the actuality of sexual experience. The use of pornography is a kind of sexual *explication de texte* in which "the text" is the synthesis of the pornographic icon *and* the psychic world of the fantasizer.

Because of the role of one's own psychic world in pornographic sexual experience, one is not restricted to the precise, shall we say objective, content of the pornographic icon. One does, however, use that content. Pornographic icons represent worlds of homoe-

---

*It should be noted that the pornography industry has ignored some minorities in its choice of erotic imagery. *Drummer,* which is a gay-owned and -operated magazine, which is to say that it is guided by gay liberation ideology, has published issues eroticizing minorities that are frequently absent in most other porn, such as the disabled.

rotic desire as they emanate from the spectrum of deep psychic interpretations men have given the myth of gender, most especially in its various paradoxical masculine machinations. By its delineation of homoerotic types, pornography has probably contributed to the refinement of homoerotic taste, but it does so by appealing to desires that vibrate without it. Pornographic images are produced because they sell; they would not exist if they had no resonance with the world of the viewer. Because pornography is bought by men who have a basic desire for the images portrayed in it, it can be seen as representing that desire. And so, we will look at pornography in this chapter as it represents the paradoxical reading of the myths of gender that surface in homoerotic desire.

ATHLETIC ALLURE

What is the gay fascination with athletes and their muscles? To begin with, this homoerotic appeal is the eroticization of masculinity. A masculine body is a hard, muscular, athletic body. Masculinity is power in the gender myth. By recalling Foucault's concept of power, we can see how the athletic body embodies it. For Foucault power is: (1) a multiplicity of force relations; (2) a process that transforms, strengthens, or reverses those relations; (3) the support that those force relations find in one another; and (4) the strategies that these relations employ.[4] In our culture men are accorded mythic power and women are not; this constitutes the force relations (1) of the gender myth. Athletics, as "the practice of physical exercises by which muscular strength is called into play and increased" (OED), by putting muscles behind the myth, offers strength to those relations (2). That men traditionally should have muscles and women should not, that is, that men are athletes and women are spectators,[5] is one of the supports that these force relations find in one another (3). Athletic competitions and the displays of muscled athletic bodies at sports spectacles, on the beach, in the gym, and so on, are among the strategies that the force relations of gender employ (4). So the athletic body is an embodiment of masculinity and, as such, a vehicle of masculine significance in the gender myth.

The heart of homoeroticism is the eroticization of masculinity. Most gay men are attracted to masculinity. Said one of the men I interviewed:

I'm finding that with men, I'm not particularly interested in effeminate men. The reason I'm attracted to a man is I'm attracted to masculinity; so are many men, if you just look at any gay magazine.

Another said:

Meeting another gay man and holding and kissing him, it was so much better than with a woman, and I don't know why. Now, I find men's bodies much more attractive. I'm attracted to tall, slim, hard bodies, not a round, soft one. There's got to be more to it than that, but I don't know exactly what it is. The maleness of it, somehow, is attractive. I don't find myself attracted to women at all. Likewise, I don't really find myself attracted to effeminate men. I really like a strong man. As far as friends go, I'm equally comfortable with a football player as with someone who is really frou-frou, or whatever.

When I asked one man what he thought of masculinity, he said:

I love it! Gosh. Well, it means having a deep voice. I know I don't care for effeminacy in men, but I think that's just a matter of taste. I certainly know some effeminate men whom I am delighted to spend time with and who are wonderfully amusing and cheerful and so on, but I am obviously more attracted to masculine men. By which I mean the image of hairy-chested and self-reliant. People who can do things, people who aren't afraid. Competence.

And another said:

I can't imagine our sexual life if masculinity faded away. If there were no working-class heroes with utility belts and hard hats, or the muscular types that come out of the gyms—whatever part of masculinity you get off on. I can't think of gay sexuality without it.

Yet another:

[Masculinity is] delicious. I think it's—the word "strength" comes into it. You can't see the word "strength" without thinking a little bit about musculature.

Pointing out that what he finds erotically attractive is not always what he finds desirable in his real life, a wrestler said:

I'm a victim of my culture. I tend to be attracted to almost hypermasculine men, although they haven't always been the people with whom I've gone out or been lovers, but that tends to be the sexual stereotype that turns me on. [What is it about that that captivates you?] Strength and power in a *physical* sense. That comes from my experience with sports, from my fantasizing about sports. The image definitely comes from there.

Quentin Crisp said that one's partner in homoerotic encounters "is a phallus garlanded with fantasies, chiefly of masculinity."[6]

Although it would be quite wrong to say that all homosexual men are attracted to a certain type of man, that is, attracted to the same degree of masculine expression, masculinity *is* the source of homoerotic desire. The desire for male bodies, after all, is an attraction to the physical sign of masculinity. Those who are erotically interested in men are interested in the erotic experience of the interplay of their own gender with that of another man. But the signs of gender, the immensely variable expressions of masculine and feminine gestures, allow for the play of nuance in erotic gender relations. These nuances are intensifications and diminutions of the basic distribution of power between men and women in the gender myth. The signs of masculinity are played at different levels, rather like the dynamics of volume in music. Some homoerotic contexts are fortissimo expressions of masculine power, exploiting the most extreme dimensions of mythic masculinity. Other contexts are pianissimo erotic explorations of our masculine myths—a number of the men I interviewed were erotically interested in only very subtle expressions of masculinity in their male sexual partners. The homoerotic world of athletes can be understood as masculinity at a mezzo forte level.

The athlete is just one among many masculine homoerotic images, such as the construction worker, policeman, soldier, sailor, and prison guard. All these professions involve the exercise of masculine power. The power of masculinity can be felt in real life, being held at knife point by a street tough, for example. Or this power can be mythically present, such as thinking that the man with whom you are having sex is a hockey player. The most intense masculinity is power surfacing as aggression, the most radical expression of which is violence. As an expression and exercise of masculine power, athletics is stylized aggression, with the more masculine sports being the more aggressively violent ones. The homoerotic appeal of athletics is a soft variation on the same themes of power that are explicit in more obviously brutal, violent, masculine eroticism.

Genet, a master of homoerotic writing, frequently describes the eroticism of extreme masculine power. In *Funeral Rites,* for example, he writes of a sixteen-year-old French boy, Riton, who is raped by German soldiers as they flee Paris at the end of the occupation in the Second World War. The context is an erotic mingling of masculine revenge and murder. Riton is in love with one of his buggering soldiers, Erik, who senses that he is about to be killed.

In passing through all his flesh, the memory of the executioner obliged Erik to greater humility toward the child. All his excitement receded. The executioner's hideous but hard face and sovereign build and stature, which he could see in his mind's eye, must be feeling freer, either the thought of them gave him greater pride in buggering Riton and caused him to beat and torture him so as to be surer of his freedom and his own strength and then to take revenge for having been weak, or else he had remained humiliated by past shame and finished his job with greater movements and reached the goal in a state of brotherly anguish. Riton, surprised at the respite of love, wanted to murmur a few very mild words of reproach, but the vigour of the movements gave him the full awareness that great voluptuaries always retain in love. He said, almost sobbingly:

"You won't have me! No, you won't have me!" and at the same time impaled himself with a leap. . . .

The whole member entered in, and Riton's behind touched Erik's warm belly. The joy of both of them was great . . .

Riton murmured: "I now have the impression that I love you more than before." Erik did not understand.

No tenderness could have been expressed, for as their love was not recognized by the world, they could not feel its natural effects. Only language could have informed them that they actually loved each other. We know how they spoke to each other at the beginning. Seeing that neither understood the other and that all their phrases were useless, they finally contented themselves with grunts. This evening, for the first time in ten days, they are going to speak and to envelope their language in the most shameless passion. A happiness that was too intense made the soldier groan. With both hands clinging, one to the ear, the other to the hair, he wrenched the kid's head from the steel axis that was getting even harder.

"Stop."

Then he drew to him the mouth that pressed eagerly to his in the darkness. Riton's lips were still parted, retaining the shape and caliber of Erik's prick. The mouths crushed against each other, linked as by a hyphen, by the rod of emptiness, a rootless member that lived alone and went from one palate to the other. The evening was marvelous. The stars were calm. One imagined that the trees were alive, that France was awakening, and more intensely in the distance, above, that the Reich was watching. Riton woke up. Erik was sad. He was already thinking of far away Germany, of the fact that his life was in danger, of how to save his skin. Riton buttoned his fly in a corner, then quietly picked up the machine gun. He fired a shot. Erik collapsed, rolled down the slope of the roof, and fell flat.[7]

Genet's work reveals the most extreme machinations of masculine homoeroticism, which is the erotic realization of power wherein the ultimate orgasm is murder and death. In this passion, the climax was not the usual sort—Erik stops Riton from bringing him to a fellated orgasm—rather, their masculine passion is culminated when Riton kills his lover/rapist with a machine gun. This homoeroticism is an incarnation of the mythic power that is awarded men in the gender myth. It is the meaning of the myth experienced at the outer limit of possibility.

Before placing athletic homoeroticism within the larger dynamic flux of homoeroticism, especially in relation to its fortissimo expression as found in Genet, we should take a moment to consider the similarities and differences between the exercise of power in homoeroticism and its somewhat analogous heteroerotic corollary that culminates in the rape and violent death of women. In that erotic world, the thrill lies in the magnification of mythic masculine power over feminine powerlessness; it's the excitement that the strong find in overwhelming the weak. This is the crucial difference between homo- and heteroeroticism; it is the difference between eroticizing the play of power between mythic equals (homo) and the eroticization of the power that the despotic have over their subordinates (hetero). Although both homo- and heteroeroticism trade in power, the difference in the experience of these powers is significant. To take an athletic metaphor, the pleasure derived from the homoerotic play of power is like the pleasure found in wrestling an opponent of roughly equivalent strength and ability, whereas manly heteroerotic experience is like the pleasure of wrestling someone who is powerless and incapable of overthrowing one. This is not to say that there is no homoerotic pleasure in being overpowered—in this chapter, a great deal of attention will be paid, in fact, to that pleasure and its considerable ironic significance—but because homoeroticism finds its home in the equal gender status of men, the homoerotic context is quite different from the heteroerotic one whose essence is the mythic superiority of men over women.

The popular liberal attitude toward sexuality tolerates homo-sexuality because it sees homo- and heteroeroticism as being es-sentially the same. Sex is *just* sex; one's preference for masculine or feminine gender in one's partner is a "lifestyle" concern. As they say, "Different strokes for different folks." This tolerance is the product of the remarkably uncritical liberal attitude that is expressed succinctly in "I'm okay; you're okay." This liberal stance reveals a shallow understanding of eroticism, one that does not take into account the meaning of gender and the working of eros. The difference between homo- and heteroeroticism is deep and very important; it involves two different readings of the gender myth. Heteroeroticism is the incarnation of the mythic power that men have over women; homoeroticism is the paradox-ical incarnation of the equal power of men. It is because hetero-eroticism is based on power *difference* that it is a highly problematic eroticism, one that involves the monumental exploi-tation of women, often culminating in terrible violence against them—so much so that women routinely fear for their safety, both on the streets and in their homes; and this fear is not only of strange men but also of their own husbands and lovers.

The equality of homoeroticism is demonstrated by the relative absence of intimidation and violence in the openly sexual envi-ronments of parks, bathhouses, and backrooms. Men forcing themselves on each other in these settings is very rare, almost unheard of. Sex is not generally bought or sold at the baths; the exchange of money is not required to legitimize the acts or bal-ance the power relations between people. There have been few heterosexual equivalents of these facilities. The power differ-ences between men and women simply do not allow women to put themselves in such a vulnerable position—rape would be almost inevitable.

The canvas upon which homoerotic desire is painted is equality in the gender myth; within that context of equality, ho-moeroticism plays on the vicissitudes of mythic masculine power and it does so at different dynamic levels. Athletic homo-eroticism has much in common with the masculine homoerotic world of Genet. It plays on the same erotic themes of power, ag-gression, and, at times, violence, but it does so more quietly, as though from a distance. In some important ways, athletics is a

134

stylized expression of masculine power that, in its strictly sporting context, is more socially acceptable than beating people up or murdering them. It is legitimate to break someone's legs in a football game, to smash an opponent's teeth in hockey, or to knock unconscious a boxer during a match. It's admirable to tear up the water at a swim meet, exploiting one's aggressive capabilities, thereby putting oneself through an outstanding experience of excruciating pain. This world of power, violence, and pain is the masculine world of athletics.* Most men in their homoerotic encounters don't want to go to the extremes of Genet's characters. Masculine power is made more palatable by its stylization in athletics. Not only is athletics a more socially acceptable venue for masculinity, its eroticization is much less dangerous than toying with guns.

Homoeroticism usually consists of a highly complex blend of the mythic machinations of masculinity, femininity, and, ultimately, irony. The homoerotic desire for athletes is a paradox; it is at once a reverence for and a violation of masculinity. It presents us with the ideal form of the homoerotic paradox, which is an attraction to masculinity that simultaneously undermines the object of attraction. As we shall see, anal penetration constitutes the deepest violation of masculinity in our culture, but the elemental erotic desire for other men, especially other *masculine* (athletic) men, also violates masculinity. The quintessential masculine erotic desire is that which powerful men have for weak women because it is there that the mythic positions of dominance and subordination, the fundamental dimensions of gender, are most present. For a man to desire a man, especially an athlete who may exhibit similar if not greater physical strength, is to undermine the myth of opposite power that has developed through gender.

---

*Thinking that women can be active and excel in sports, the reader may object to this connection between masculinity and athletics. But athletic women *are* more masculine than their nonathletic sisters. In the myth of gender, a feminine woman is not strong or vigorous (except where it is in the interest of men, such as cleaning houses, bearing children, and working in the fields when there aren't enough men). Women who are athletes renounce their inferior status and lay claim to power; this is why there is so much resistance to women in sport, why they were excluded from the Olympics for many years, and why they still represent only 25 percent of the athletes at the Olympics.

THE MEANING OF FUCKING

Before looking at the meaning of anal penetration, I should point out that cultural meaning is by no means the only dimension in the experience. Most gay and homosexual men who have learned to relax their anal sphincters in deference to the probes and thrusts of an erect penis have discovered that the experience can be one of overwhelming physical pleasure, an ecstatic carnal experience that can take one's breath away. Likewise, the intense tangible gratification to be derived from being the "active" partner in such sexual relations recommends itself in and of itself. But these fervid physical pleasures are not without their cultural contexts, and although in the experience one may be so physically involved that the entire world may seem to have disappeared, the fact is, it hasn't. The following is an exploration of the deep and often subconscious meaning of fucking as it has been constructed in our culture.

The words "anal penetration" are intended to describe an objectively observable event, but this "objectivity" effectively de-emphasizes the significance of that event, concealing the meaning of the act. It is a term that is out of sync with lived experience. At the height of passion, no one gasps, "Oh yeah, yeah, anally penetrate me, anally penetrate me." In the Western world, "fucking" means a great deal. In the Hebrew religion, the god Yahweh was so sacred that his name was never to be uttered. Likewise, the penile penetrations of various human orifices are best left unmentioned or at least referred to more obliquely with medical expressions like "coitus" and "sexual intercourse," or with more mushy ones like "making love." "Fucking" is the name of one of our most sacred acts, which is the ecstatic sexual experience in which the myths of gender and sexuality become incarnate in one moment, or perhaps series of moments, in the lives of the participants.* Ecstasy is the experience of: this is it; this is *the*

---

*Fucking is so important that it should be kept a secret, be practiced only by adults behind closed doors. Children must not witness this act. Some governments see it as so important that it must never be accurately depicted, and if it is, those depictions should be seized and burned. The censorship of fucking is a testament to its authentic moment that cannot be deprived of being exactly what it is, which is present, unique, and unsurpassable. Ecstasy is abandonment. The erotic ecstasy of fucking is the experience of being abandoned to the incarnation of myth in one's life; this is the most "actual" the myth can become. Fucking is sacred because it is the metamorphosis of myths as concrete experience. Just as the Holy Eucharist is a ritual that makes the myth of God present, so, too, fucking is the act that realizes myths of gender.** As is usually the case with sacred words, they become profane expressions when used out of their contexts. "Fuck" is employed as a profanity in nonsexual discourse, for example, "There's never a fucking cab when you want one." The following use of the word is not profane because I am using it as a direct reference to the profound act that it names.

That the expression "getting fucked" has a nonsexual, profane use is significant. In this sense, "getting fucked" means to be abused, to be taken advantage of. Someone who believes he has not been dealt with fairly by, say, a referee in a hockey game, might be heard to say that he was "fucked over by the ref." When a person wants to dismiss another forcefully, he may say "get fucked," "fuck off," or "go fuck yourself." Such uses of the word, although not intended to convey erotic meaning, originate in a perspicacious understanding of its culturally created erotic meaning, which is that being fucked is a denigration. That sense of denigration comes from heterosexual discourse where the person who gets fucked is a woman, a man's mythic inferior.[8] It is that meaning that is conveyed in the not uncommon melodramatic (and very sexist) phrase: "I want a man that will make me feel like a woman!" Fucking is that act in which the power relations between men and women are embodied. The profane, and nonsexual, use of "getting fucked" reveals the true meaning of the sexual act of getting fucked in our culture.

There are different ways of looking at fucking. It is a rich

---

sacredness. Further indicating its eminence, it is fucking and not procreation that seals the marriage contract.
**I am not saying that fucking is the only technique for sexual experience; the variety of techniques is probably infinite. Fucking, however, does have a special status in our culture.

experience that cannot be reduced to "primary qualities." It can however, be considered from different angles that disclose its various dimensions. The dimension of fucking that is of interest to us here is that which involves the myths of gender (which is, of course, the defining feature of homoeroticism) and therefore power. We must keep in mind that there are other aspects, but from the point of view of power, there are basically three positions: assertive, receptive, and reciprocal.

Assertive fucking is the act of fucking someone. This is known as the "active role" in which the traditional perspective is that of entering another human being; it is masculine; it is the position of superiority. Fucking someone is traditionally a sign of mastery over them; the penis becomes the weapon that guarantees submission. In wars, rape is a traditional occupation of the victors, a sign of their conquest.[9] This is a tradition that even crosses some cultures. The Ancient Egyptians, when victorious in battle, had a "ceremonial custom of buggering defeated troops, thereby asserting sexual and political mastery over them."[10] The homosexuality of the Ancient Greeks was pedophilic. The older man, being superior by virtue of his age, was, upon entering the anus of the youth, imparting symbolically his learning and manliness. It was quite unacceptable for a mature man to be the willing recipient of another man's penis, because this would be placing himself in a position of inferiority to another man.

Receptive fucking is getting fucked, being entered; it is the experience of being subordinated; it is feminine. In John Boorman's film *Deliverance,* one of the men is raped by a hillbilly. He loses his masculine bravado and is ashamed. He asks his friends not to tell anyone what has happened, acknowledging that in the act his masculinity was undermined. Norman Mailer is arguably the preeminent macho American novelist of our century. In his novel, *Ancient Evenings,* one of the major male characters, Meni, gets fucked by a male god. Of this act, Meni says "The last of my pride was gone." "For I have never known more shame than in the days that followed. . . . I was not like other men, although I fell more of a woman."[11]

Reciprocal fucking is a union in which two join together as equals with a common purpose. In some respects, reciprocal fucking represents the ideals of feminism and some elements of gay liberation; it is an attempt to change the myths of gender. John Fox wrote a novel about a homosexual teenager in the throes of his first sexual experiences. His first lover, who is two years older and portrayed as a closeted, more old-fashioned homosexual man, has fucked him but refuses to be fucked himself. "He himself never got fucked and didn't want to. I think he thought that getting fucked up the ass meant *getting fucked up the ass,* if you know what I mean. Also, I felt he was treating me like a girl in a way since only he did the fucking. . . . 'Getting fucked' isn't *getting fucked,* it's fucking *both* of you at the same time, if you do it right, if you see what I mean."[12] Reciprocity is very much at work in situations where each of the fuckers willingly assumes both assertive and receptive positions.

"Real men," that is, men who fulfill the masculine requirements of the myth of gender, are assertive with both men and women because assertiveness is basic to the myth of masculinity. Men who are not assertive are failures in the myth. Men who are receptive are worse than failures, they have betrayed their dominant position and made themselves "like women." For a man to be like a woman in our culture is considered contemptible because it is a step down; the greatest insult one can give a man is that he is like a woman. Getting fucked, therefore, is the deepest violation of masculinity in our culture. Enjoying being fucked is the acceptance of that violation, it is the ecstatic sexual experience in which the violation of masculinity becomes incarnate.

There is a video entitled *Take It Like a Man,* in which the featured activity is anal fucking (a not unusual preoccupation of gay pornography). The sexual activity takes place while voice-overs enhance the action. (It is also not unusual in pornography to dub some, if not all, of the "actors' " dialogue, since their dramatic talent is often more visual than verbal.) The speaking is short, clipped, and of a masculine, deep-voiced nature. While one fellow is being fucked, the voice says: "Give it to him; give it to him good. Fuck him like he's never been fucked before." Presenting the ecstasy of the incarnation of homoerotic desire, the irony here is intense and very serious. Understanding the meaning of "it" is crucial. In the first place, "it" is the fucker's cock. The word "cock" refers to the masculine symbolism of the phallus, embodied in the penis. When the fucker is giving his cock to the fuckee, he is giving his embodied masculinity to his catamite. The man who is getting fucked is entered by the embodied masculinity of the fucker in a clear overwhelming of his own masculinity. In this act his own cock is rendered insignificant, or at most tangential, as he is overwhelmed anally by the masculine force of his partner. "It," then, is not only the embodied manhood of the cock—"it" is also the *event* wherein the masculinity of one man is paradoxically undermined.

The verb "give" does not have the sense of a gift, like a birthday gift, but rather the aggressive connotation implicit in expressions like "let him have it," which usually precede some act of violence. There is an interesting irony here in "giving," because with this sense of giving usually goes the giving of an unwanted gift—a bullet shot straight to the heart, for instance—but for the man who is experiencing the ecstasy of homoerotic paradox in the act of being fucked, this gift is, in fact, much desired. Surely this is the gift impassioned lovers give each other. Here is an intimacy with profound implications. With each thrust of the cock, the myth of masculinity literally penetrates bodies, while bodies appropriate the myth; in their ecstasy, the men become paradoxically one with the myth. In being fucked willingly, one opens oneself to the embodied, mythic, masculine probes of another man; a space is opened for the incarnation of paradoxical desire, the authentic consummation of one's own place in the preeminent myth of our culture. Fucking another man can be experienced as merely an egocentric violation of another's masculinity, acting as a confirmation of one's own (orthodox?)* masculinity. But it can also be an experience of sublime coalescence, of two men disclosing paradoxical masculinity, a fusion in which the orthodox, heterosexual meaning of masculinity is triumphantly violated, so that with one's partner one experiences the embodied irony and ecstasy of the homoerotic paradox. In homoerotic fucking, masculinity is not destroyed; it is at once violated and revered, brought to the paradoxical edge of its own dissolution.

There is significant irony in the title, *Take It Like a Man.* In

---

*Whether or not the masculinity here is orthodox would depend on the erotic view of the fucker.

140

the expression "take it like a man," "it" usually refers to punishment. But the word is a double entendre here, referring both to punishment and to being fucked. But no "man" would submit to such a complete violation of his orthodox masculinity—if he did, he would no longer be a "man." He might be, as Mailer's Meni said, "more of a woman." But that understanding of man-to-man fucking doesn't really comprehend homoerotic fucking, for the homoerotic ecstasy of being fucked is the incarnation not of transsexualism, but of gender paradox.

Such forte expressions of homoerotic ecstasy are not limited to the drama of gay pornography. Many times in gay bathhouses one hears through the thin walls rapturous men imploring, "Fuck me, fuck me, fuck that ass," and announcing, "I'm fucking your ass, I'm fucking you." These are verbal echoes of the incarnation of the homoerotic paradox. Genet's Riton and Erik represent this paradox at the vanishing point of the homoerotic horizon. But is this meaning intrinsic to all homoeroticism? Because this erotic meaning is implicit in the gender myth and that is the cultural foundation of homoeroticism, this paradox is at work in all homoerotic contexts. But not everyone likes to hear these erotic themes at such a volume. So, in the sexual lives of many men, the homoerotic paradox whispers, sotto voce, in their subconscious understanding of their sexual acts and erotic desires.

DESIRING MEN

Although getting fucked is the ultimate sacrifice of masculinity, the erotic desire for other men is itself a desecration of the meaning of being a man. The erotic confirmation of gender lies in the attraction that superiors have for their subordinates. The erotic desire men have for other men undermines their position of mythic superiority. A man who desires really masculine men, like athletes, botches his masculinity even further by not looking for signs of femininity in the object of his desires. While homoeroticism is a violation of masculinity, the very source of its attraction, that is, the desire for men, reveres masculinity. Quentin Crisp said of homosexual men, "If they succeed, they fail. A man who 'goes with' other men is not what they would call a real man."[13] This paradox is the nucleus of homoeroticism.

The triad of gay sensibility constitutes the ways in which homosexual men deal with the paradoxical meaning of their erotic desire. Sometimes the sensibility of *de-emphasis* goes to work, downplaying the significance of the paradox and claiming orthodox masculinity for gay men. There has been a tendency in some quarters of the gay rights movement to declare the homoerotic violation of masculinity false. Gay men, it is said, are just as masculine as straight men; one can be erotically attracted to men and even get fucked by them and somehow maintain one's masculine status in the gender myth. This is the sensibility of de-emphasis, preferring to ignore the paradoxical reading of the gender myth that is implicit in homoeroticism, and to identify, in an unwitting irony, with patriarchal heterosexual masculinity. It is rather like saying $2 + 3 = 4$ because it suits one; it completely ignores the culture that created the patriarchally based, homoerotic structure in the first place.

With the advent of gay liberation, there was an attempt to establish the legitimacy and viability of homosexuality both in the eyes of gay men and of the world at large. So there was a de-emphasizing inclination to assert the "normality" of homosexuality: the only difference between being homosexual and heterosexual is the choice of sexual and emotional partners. There was a battle waged by gay men—a battle that is still being fought—against the "effeminate homosexual stereotype." Over and over again it was asserted that gay men are just as masculine as straight men. Martin Levine said a new masculine image of the male homosexual emerged in the early 1970s.

The image of the post-Stonewall gay male is, as I foresaw, distinctly virile and light years away from the "effete martini sippers" of preliberation times. This emphasis on masculinity has proved as important to the elevation of consciousness for gay men in the movement as the feminist cause is for lesbians. Members of stigmatized minorities

142

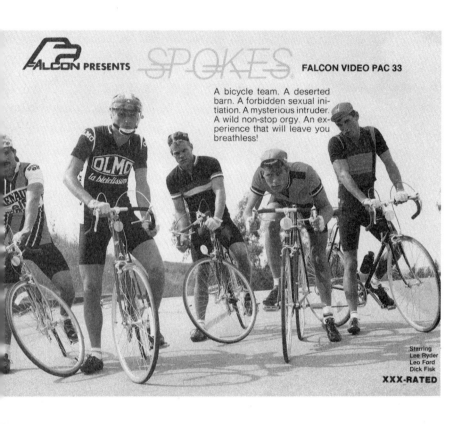

FIG. 1. The male athletic image has become a homoerotic icon for gay men. This picture from the well-known American gay video producer Falcon Videos advertised their video Spokes. The photo shows the intimate relationship between orthodox and paradoxical masculinities; the masculine, tough look of the cyclists invites its own erotic, paradoxical undermining.

COURTESY OF FALCON VIDEO

FIG. 2. The Other Side of Aspen II *is a homoerotic fantasy on the life*
of ski bums at the famous resort. The video plays on the erotic appeal
of healthy outdoor sports in the fresh, cold mountain air.
COURTESY OF FALCON VIDEO

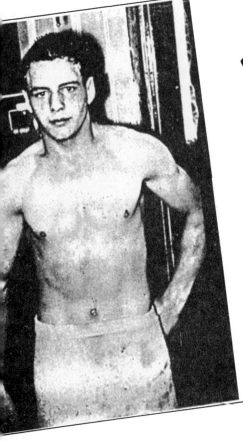

JR.
at
RINGSIDE

AFTER punching the bag for a while, **Sam Delany** (at left) tones himself up with a brisk shower.

B e l o w , little **Jimmy Dante** gets a few pointers on the manly art from **Walter West** (center) and **Bill Temple** (right). Photos by **HENDERSON.**

FIG. 3. *Pornographers, enthusiastic about the homoerotic appeal of athletes, sometimes show their ignorance of athletics. Showers do not tone muscles.*

FIG. 4. *The Greek god Apollo, because he is neither very young nor very old, maintains both the anal erotic promise characteristic of youth in the Ancient Greek tradition and the phallic potency associated with masculine maturity. His erotic diversity personifies the paradoxical masculinity of the contemporary homoerotic athletic icon. This illustration is of the Apollo from Piombino at the Louvre, Paris.*

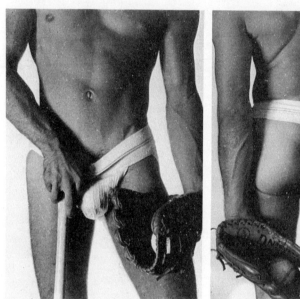
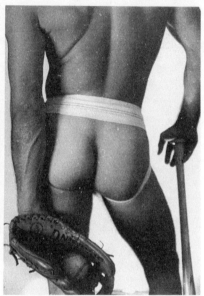

FIG. 5. *As suggested by the versatility of Apollo, there are two sides to the jock strap, symbolizing the homoerotic paradox; the pouch at the front as the shrine of masculinity, joined to the straps at the back, which frame its mythic violation. These pictures are from an advertisement for William Higgins's video* These Bases Are Loaded. *The Apollonian significance of the jock strap is enhanced by the athletic paraphernalia of bat, ball, and glove.*

FIG. 6. *"College Jocks" is a homoerotic telephone fantasy service which focuses on the homoerotic appeal of athletes. This advertisement employs a range of athletic signifiers as erotic enticements: jock straps, football gear, swimsuit, sweatshirt, and a stack of schoolbooks which are meant to confirm the Apollonian youth of the men in the advertisement. Notice that the company even offers to answer fan mail on behalf of one's favorite jock. The words "Play safe . . . play with us" remind the reader that telephone sex is a completely safe form of sexual practice in the age of AIDS.*

FIG. 7. *Duncan Grant's* Bathing 1911 *was painted for the dining room of the Borough Polytechnic; it is now at the Tate Gallery in London.*
COURTESY OF THE ESTATE OF DUNCAN GRANT

FIG. 9. Duncan Grant's biographer Douglas Blair Turnbaugh said that
Grant, "with a positive attitude that served him all his life, intuited
that sports was a respectable way to be with boys in a directly
physical (and sometimes naked) way." (Private: The Erotic Art of
Duncan Grant. London: Gay Men's Press, 1989.) This picture is entitled
Wrestlers.

COURTESY OF THE ESTATE OF DUNCAN GRANT

FIG. 10. Eadweard Muybridge's famous human locomotion studies, done in the late nineteenth century, are appreciated not only for their contribution to biomechanics and motion picture technology, but also for their homoerotic athletic appeal. The above are reproduced from Muybridge's Complete Human and Animal Locomotion, Vol. 1. New York: Dover.

FIG. 11. R. Tait McKenzie idealized the wholesome, youthful, hairless, budding masculinity of male athletes. The above statue is entitled Relay Runner and is dated 1910. It was given to the Montreal Museum of Fine Arts by David Scott Walker.

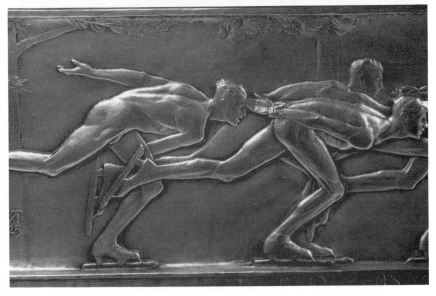

FIG. 12. *This metal galvano relief by R. Tait McKenzie is entitled*
Brothers of the Wind, *dated 1925. Although McKenzie's work is not*
usually cited for its homoerotic content, one cannot help but wonder
what would inspire him to portray handsome ice skaters without any
clothes, save their skates, out of doors in what must be the winter.
Notice the direction of the gaze of the man on the far left. This relief
belongs to the Canadian National Archives.
PHOTO BY JOHN DEAN

FIG. 13. *Gay male pornography, especially of the early 1960s, often appealed to the wholesomeness of athletes.*
PHOTO BY DAVE MARTIN

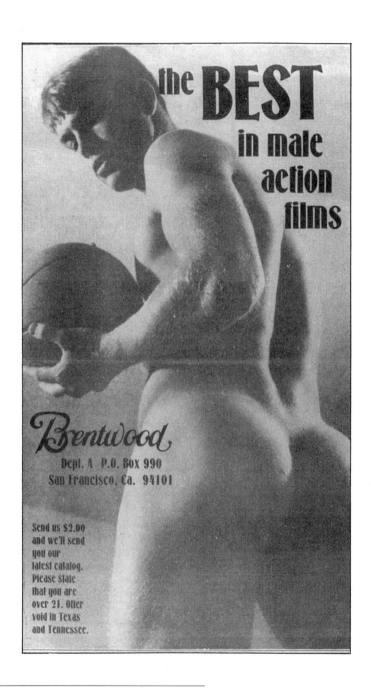

FIG. 14. *The combined appeal of youthful athleticism and masculine action was the subject of the pornography producer Brentwood in the 1970s and early 80s.*

FIG. 15. Physique photography has long been a covert homoerotic genre. One of the earliest professional muscle men was Eugene Sandow. PHOTO BY H. ROLAND WHITE, CIRCA 1900

FIG. 16. Sandow was the inspiration behind the early physique magazine The Strong Man.

FIG. 17. *The homosexual orientation of* The Strong Man *is discreetly attested to in the above. Note the two men holding hands in the top left corner.*

FIG. 18. Body-building competitions are covert, homoerotic burlesque shows. Exhibitionistic men line the stage, flexing their highly muscled bodies, playing to the voyeuristic pleasure of their audience.

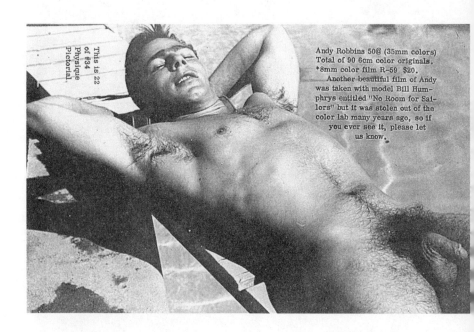

FIG. 19. Bob Mizer popularized the paradoxical, homoerotic "Take me,
do with me what you will, I can't resist you" pose in his well-known
Physique Pictorial.

COURTESY OF THE ATHLETIC MODEL GUILD, LOS ANGELES, CALIFORNIA

FIG. 20. *The professional wrestler "Ravishing" Rick Rude offered himself in the Mizer pose in the magazine* Superstar Wrestler.
COURTESY OF SUPERSTAR WRESTLER, *PHOTO BY JAMES PAPA*

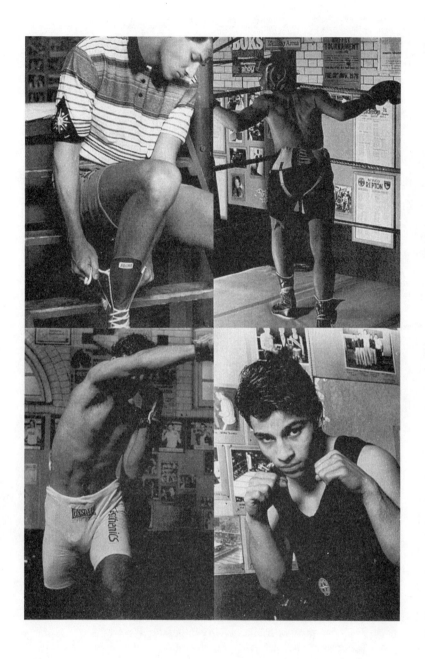

FIG. 21. *The homoerotic appeal of the athlete has become a theme in the fashion industry. The above advertisement appeared in the British fashion magazine* Arena. *The loose phallic prominence in the boxing shorts attests to the calculated homoeroticism of this advertisement.*
PHOTOS BY HELEN PUTMAN

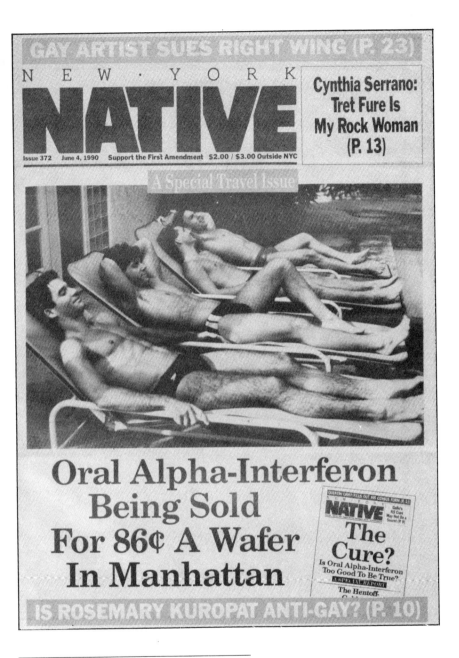

FIG. 22. *The image of muscular athletes has been used extensively by gay liberation publications to increase reader interest in their political messages. The* New York Native *frequently graces their covers with muscular young men.*
COURTESY OF THE NEW YORK NATIVE *AND FALCON VIDEO*

THEATER • CABARET • ART • PROVINCETOWN • PERSONALS

NIGHT AND DAY

June 4, 1990   All the Fun That's Fit to Print $1.00

1990
Guide to
Fire
Island
30 Years
of Gay
Roles in
Movies
Ruby
Rims:
Cabaret
School

FIG. 23. *This gay New York entertainment magazine uses the semiotic power of muscles and athletic gear to attract readers.*
COURTESY OF NIGHT AND DAY *AND FALCON VIDEO*

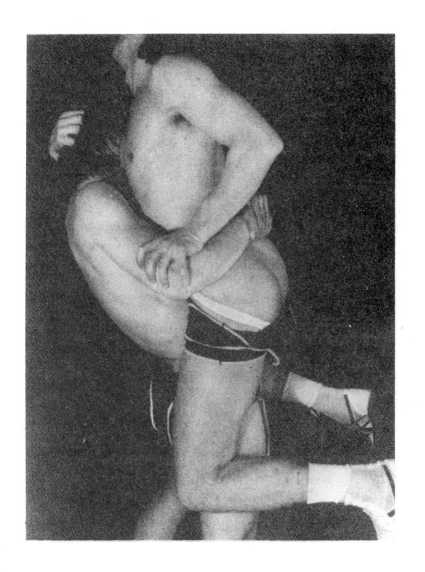

FIG. 24. Wrestling is a popular homoerotic activity. Video companies
such as BG Enterprise makes the often covert homoeroticism of
wrestling more overt.
COURTESY OF BG ENTERPRISES

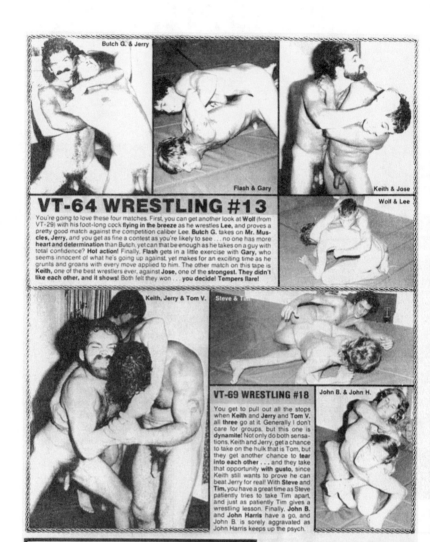

FIG. 25. Old Reliable specializes in films and videos of naked street toughs wrestling. Fledermaus, of Drummer magazine, says of the video: "The matches are good-natured horsing around, but the machismo of these guys will not let them cry uncle easily, and they keep going until totally exhausted. But not too exhausted for the next event in every Old Reliable tape, which is a J.O. (masturbation) session." (Drummer, 115)

FIG. 26. *The erotic thrill of brutal masculine contact is the theme of the boxing video* Gut Punchers *by Palm Drive Video. 1988.*
COURTESY OF JACK FRITSCHER, PH.D.

FIG. 27. *The Sydney Swans, an Australian Rules football club, decided to capitalize both on the homoerotic possibilities of the game's reputation as a rough guy's sport and on the attractiveness of their star full-forward Warwick Capper. Wanting to improve the "eye appeal" of their full-forward, they had special very tight-fitting shorts and vests made for Capper.*
PHOTOS BY ACTION GRAPHICS

FIG. 28. *Mainstream sports reporters like to allude to the possibility of homosexual liaisons among sports stars. The caption under this photo on page two of the June 27, 1988, issue of* Sports Illustrated *read: "KISS AND MAKE UP. After their spat—tsk, tsk—in game 4 of the NBA finals, Isiah Thomas (11) and best buddy Magic Johnson did their customary smooching before the fifth-game tip-off."*

PHOTO BY ANDREW BERNSTEIN

Flames
ut some
name.

ound, i.e.

nebody
evil And
d in the
agers to
oppo-
against
s to NHL
ve vice-
Maybe it
good/bad
ys when
d a vide-
revealing
e were no
spension.
umpy old
ins: Larry
ery happy
real these

p this sea-
k. Not one
Ciccarel-

be called
oalie Ron
trying to
Islanders'
ncing the
roximately
1 six-pack.
s an effec-
n that it dis-
om entering
ll seems to
nunity. The
hat an oppo-
him serious-

ade.

A great pair: Flyers goalie Ron Hextall, left, has shaken any suggestion of a sophomore jinx, while Wayne Gretzky, right, decided
this NHL half-season to finally take a bride.

at every night? And doesn't the NH

FIG. 29. *The Toronto* Star, *Feb. 6, 1988, made allusions to the hockey
star Wayne Gretzky's personal life with the following caption under
the above photo: "A great pair: Flyers goalie Ron Hextall, left, has
shaken any suggestion of a sophomore jinx, while Wayne Gretzky,
right, decided this NHL season to finally take a bride."*
PHOTO BY THE EDMONTON SUN

BOYS! What is it about soccer that brings out the eternal child in its players? They're certainly all great big strapping men and 100% heterosexual, we're told. Maybe it's those adorable costumes they wear, cute shorts, sexy knee sox that display their muscular calves to perfection, etc. Here we have two examples of what happens when these guys line up for team pictures, one from Britain (thanks to Tony Gillies), the other from the U.S. (thanks to Frank K.). The caption says that "Skipper Kevin Keegan can't bear to look, but Terry McDermott seems to have England's World Cup situation in hand . . "So *that's* what they mean by World's Cup! The caption writer for the American photo was left speechless by the open display of comradely affection demonstrated here, so I'll say it for him: Ain't they sweet?

oker
the
amp

ER Kevin Keegan can't
o look, but Terry McDer-
eems to have England's
Cup situation in hand—
o the amusement of team
Kenny Sansom (left) and
ariner. Ron Greenwood's
ers clearly in good heart
they appeared for this
ll yesterday. The squad
o Spain tomorrow and
e France in their opening
n Bilbao on June 16.
Picture: MONTE FRESCO

HOLD TIGHT!: The caption for this picture says that the lad sitting up has the other wrestler "under control." I'll say he has. And, as you know if you can read upside down, the controllee is from West Point! Actually, because of the poor quality of the newspaper reproduction, it looks like the cadet has really pulled his opponent's vital parts right out of his singlet and is giving them one hell of a pull? Harold M. of Tulsa sent us this exciting clipping.

BOTTOMS UP!: Tony Gillies of Lincoln, England, is always on the lookout for items of interest to I.T. readers and he came up with a lulu in this one! It seems that soccer star Robbie Savage, of the Bournemouth Cherries (I'm not kidding!), got into a lot of hot water, both figurative and literal, when he was shown on T.V. full-frontally nude in another moment of this after-the-game locker room shivaree. He and his teammates had just won the FA Cup after a fierce struggle with the Manchester United Team. Angry callers rang the station to protest but Robbie was unrepentant. He said, "I don't know what all the fuss is about. I'm allowed to have my bath, aren't I." To which his mother, Rose, added, "I didn't see him on the telly but someone told me about it. I don't think our Robbie's got anything to be ashamed of. He's always been a joker and a bit mad." Hurray for Robbie and Rose . . . and where's the clip of Robbie showing us that "nothing to be ashamed of"?

FIG. 30. In Touch, *a gay magazine, frequently editorializes on the homoerotic dimensions of sports with photo essays such as the above.*
COURTESY OF IN TOUCH

IN
PASSING

IT'S A
FOUL
WHEN
THE HANDS
ARE
USED
ON
THE BALLS!

FUNNY game football...   the close companionship,

those sudden squeezes...   bring tears to your eyes!

FIG. 31. Drummer *also likes to highlight the homoeroticism of sports.*
COURTESY OF DRUMMER

must not only counter stereotypes in their struggle for freedom but must overcome what I have discussed previously as the self-hatred that afflicts all oppressed groups.[14]

There are many problems with this, not the least of which is the impossible analogy of virile masculinity (that is, signs of gender difference and the oppression of women) and feminism (that is, a philosophy for the liberation of women). There is also the dual equations of effeminacy with self-hatred and masculinity with self-respect (which is what Levine is ultimately referring to by "the elevation of consciousness"). But masculinity and femininity are signifiers of the variable power differences between men and women. When men behave effeminately, they are not expressing self-hatred; their effeminacy is, rather, an assertion of the strength of their commitment to their paradoxical interpretation of gender. Levine's appraisal of gay masculinity has more to do with cashing in on the patriarchal prestige of orthodox masculinity than it does with appreciating the paradoxical masculinity of gay men. That interpretation of the masculine style of gay men de-emphasizes the way in which paradoxical masculinity *departs* from orthodoxy. This is an attempt to establish the legitimacy of homosexuality by thinking of it in orthodox terms. But because the legitimacy of orthodox masculinity lies in the subordination of women in patriarchal culture, it is the legitimacy of despotism. *The legitimacy of homosexuality lies not in its loyalty to orthodox masculinity, but in its violation.*

The sensibility of de-emphasis is an ironic trap in which unwitting homosexual men can find themselves. Shrinking back from the paradox, they believe they are masculine in the orthodox sense. Failing to appreciate the paradox of their homoerotic desire, they are the naive victims of that irony. The former professional football player David Kopay is a prominent example of the "masculine" man who "happens to be" homosexual. It is certainly true that he has performed many masculine gestures in his life, playing football being one of the more notable. Although for Kopay to come out of the closet was indeed laudable and no doubt encouraged many less famous Americans to do the same, his high profile as a "masculine gay man" exemplifies the inclination of some gay men to refuse to acknowledge the subversion of masculinity inherent in their erotic desire. Their urge to cling to an inappropriate world of patriarchal orthodox masculinity is a testament to their fear of estrangement and their own homophobia (fear of losing patriarchal power). This gay sensibility of de-emphasis is a willful deafness to the deep message about the meaning of gender that homoeroticism conveys to men who know its desirability. This is the irony of ignorance. While Kopay now lives as an openly homosexual man, like numbers of gay men he maintains the image of the "masculine man." The homoerotic desire for masculine men is a paradox. The sensibility of de-emphasis, rather than authentically appreciating that paradoxical eroticism ironically, tries to make it fit the orthodox mold.

The sensibility of *change* has also been at work in gay liberation's approach to the problem of the homoerotic appeal of masculinity. Here, the emphasis has been on highlighting the oppressiveness of patriarchal masculinity, illustrating the fundamental homophobia inherent in it. Gay men who are attracted to masculine men and who behave in masculine ways themselves are considered "self-oppressive" and are encouraged to liberate themselves from that oppression. This tendency aims to put an end to masculinity. But an irony lurks here also. To put an end to masculinity is to ring the death knell for homoeroticism. Although the demise of masculinity would no doubt elevate the humanitarian dimension of the erotic relations between people, it would obviously strike a fatal blow to the homoerotic attraction men have for other men. Over the last two decades, gay men have not shown much interest in destroying the masculine source of their erotic desire. In fact, masculinity has been much celebrated—it is one of the main features of gay culture. Just consider the names that are typical of gay bars: The Barn, the Anvil, Chaps, Buddies, the Dungeon, Crowbar, Dudes, the Ramrod, Garage, Komrads, and so on. But this masculinity is not the same as that that enforces and eroticizes hegemonic patriarchal heterosexuality. The masculinity enunciated in gay culture is paradoxical masculinity. The gay sensibility that appreciates this paradoxical masculinity and the homoerotic desire for it is *irony*.

Paradoxical masculinity takes the traditional signs of patriarhal masculinity and filters them through an ironic gay lens. signs such as muscles, which in heterosexual culture highlight masculine gender by pointing out the power men have over women and the power they have to resist other men, through gay irony emerge as *enticements* to homoerotic desire—a desire that is anathema to orthodox masculinity. Paradoxical masculinity invites both reverence for the traditional signs of masculinity and he violation of those signs. Take, for example, the advertisement or Spokes (Fig. 1). In this picture all the traditional signs of masculinity are present: muscles, athletic gear, ruggedness, and so on. But the ironic body language of these men suggests they are ready for more than a simple orthodox road race. The looks, the poses of these models (especially Lee Ryder, who is on the far right) invite the paradoxical violation of that masculinity.

The ironic process of destruction and reconstruction is at work in all masculine homoerotic happenings. The homoerotic attraction for athletes takes the orthodox masculinity of athletes and, in a process of ironic destruction, violates that masculinity, reconstructing it as paradoxical masculinity. This is almost invariably the text of gay athletic porn: a situation that in the beginning seems to be heterosexual and masculine, by virtue of its athletic setting, turns out to be homosexual. In *The Bigger the Better,* directed by Matt Sterling, a student goes to his high-school teacher's house to get some guidance with his weight-training program. His apparent interest in weight training turns out to be an erotic interest in his teacher. In Sterling's *Like a Horse,* there is a wrestling scene that is a kind of tag-team wrestling with three young, and somewhat accomplished, wrestlers. At least a third of the scene is devoted to aggressive, collegiate-style wrestling, one wrestler spelling off the other. There is a lot of grunting and groaning, which is natural in vigorous wrestling. But eventually they start tearing each other's clothes and trying to pull off each other's pants. What were athletic grunts evolve into moans of sexual excitement: "Unnh, unnnhhh, oh yeah." In the beginning of the video, the ruse of straight masculine wrestling is convincing. The aggressive grabbing and hurling to the mat, the straining and grunting, are perfect signs of masculinity. But this orthodoxy is undermined when legitimate wrestling holds give way to the unorthodox slapping of asses. The turning point, that is, the

45

peripatetic moment of ironic awareness when masculine wres tling is revealed as nothing but an appearance that must yield t erotic reality, occurs when one of the wrestlers in torn short pushes his ass into the face of the other and says "Suck that thing boy," and his opponent does as he is bidden. This wrestling scen is not a rape. The tearing of clothes and grabbing at bodies i mutual. When the ass is lifted from the face upon which it ha been pressed, the face follows it.

In this athletic homoeroticism, the masculine appearance i not lost altogether. Once the peripatetic ironic revelation has oc curred, masculinity remains as the paradoxical context for th unfolding of eros. One of the virtues of irony is that it is not simple negation of that which is false; it is, as Rodway said, " double exposure on one plate." Irony maintains the marbled coex istence of truth and falsehood. In *Like a Horse,* masculine aggres sion is not forgotten once homoeroticism has been ironicall revealed; it continues to play an important part in the hard-cor sexual scene that develops. The third wrestler, who has bee waiting to be "tagged," finally says, "Oh, fuck this, man," an strips down to his jock strap and athletic socks and joins the othe two. (To maintain the athletic context, jock straps are a feature prop in the sexual scene, and the boys never remove their athleti socks.) When he joins the other two, he gets down on his knees an proceeds to slap and brutally grab the bare ass of the fellow o top. The recipient of these attentions finds them painful and say "Ouch." This appeals to the recently arrived wrestler, who says "Oooh, I heard him say ouch," and he slaps him again and snap the jock strap so that it hits the wearer sharply. Orthodox mascu linity would not stand for these violations. A truly masculine ma would never cooperate in such a scene, at least not without coer cion. All three wrestlers are clearly willing participants; thei erotic interest in each other is an obvious betrayal of orthodo masculinity.

Gay athletic pornography invariably has as its theme the ap pearance of orthodox masculinity, which is, in fact, paradoxica that is, an ostensibly straight situation turns out to be gay. Thi fantasy reflects in many ways the ironic experience of comin out; until that revelation, one seems to be straight. It could be tha an important part of the attraction that some gay men have fo athletic homoeroticism lies in its resonance with their own experience of coming out.

Given the myth of gender, the most masculine men are obviously straight. The homoerotic desire for actual straight men is known as a "taste for trade."* It is a taste that is probably quite rare among gay men; no one I interviewed wanted to have sex with real straight men.

> It's a funny thing. You see, I'm into uniforms and all those kinds of things, and the thing that's so striking about it is if, for example, suppose you think about having sex with a Marine—if that's your fantasy. Well, if a *real* Marine appeared in the room, he'd be somebody that you'd have absolutely no interest in whatsoever. He'd be such a turnoff in terms of where he's coming from, what he believes, and all kinds of things. So this is the funny part of this thing: it's as if the real world of your fantasies actually materialized in front of you, it wouldn't be anything like what you want. . . . Fantasies abstract, they merely abstract certain kinds of masculine indices or characteristics but they don't abstract the person in the total context of his life.
>
> Imagine what it would be like to meet a straight man with whom you are going to have sex—one of these real, straight, masculine men, and he simply wanted to fuck you—that's what he does, the way in which some gay or bi men or kids are treated in prisons where they are simply taken to be fucked by heterosexual men—it's just like rape. I met one person once from Kingston Penitentiary who told me about this and he said it wasn't so bad for him because he was bisexual and he could deal with the indignity in a way. But that's not the way that gay sex is organized. I've never seen it organized that way. In fact, there's this guy, Jeff Stryker [a porn star], and people say

---

*Bruce Rodgers, in *Gay Talk: A Sometimes Outrageous Dictionary of Gay Slang,* says that "trade" refers to a "passive activist, nonreciprocal sex partner, usually straight."

he's not really gay because he doesn't get fucked. I think in [gay] sex there is a lot more reciprocity. If you think of that kind of [straight] masculinity and all those kinds of things and think how that's worked out in Mediterranean cultures, in Spanish culture, or where a person can fuck another man and not be gay as long as he's not on the receiving end of things. I don't think gay sex is really that way, although people very often want the people they have sex with to have these very masculine attributes, whether they are muscles or mustaches or leather boots or utility belts or whatever. I don't think that in the substance, gay sex is masculine—in the appearance it is.

This man has made explicit the distinction, as he experiences it in his personal life, between orthodox masculinity and paradoxical masculinity. Orthodox masculinity is the masculinity of oppression and as such is not attractive to him. On the other hand, paradoxical masculinity is that which is only a surface. And so, although straight men have potential attraction as fantasy material, in real life they are undesirable. Another said, "I found men in Italy very attractive, but because of the way they act they are not gay, so having sex with a family-oriented straight man is usually a disaster—nice to look at, but after a while I turn off." "Masculine" men who have a homoerotic appeal that one would like to follow up in sexual acts are for the most part men who only seem to be masculine in the orthodox sense. This ersatz masculinity lies at the heart of the homoerotic appeal of athletes.

The ironic homoerotic desire for seemingly masculine straight men is attested to in want ads. It is interesting that what is required is a straight *act,* that is, advertisers are not asking for real straight men, what is wanted is *ersatz* heterosexuality. That the masculinity is unstable, that is, under the pressure of homoerotic desire, that it gives way to paradoxical masculinity, is essential to the whole enterprise.

TIP TOP GUY Smart, successful GWM [gay white male], aggressive, late 30s, terrific body, gets turned on by in-shape young men who are straight-acting and masculine but like to submit to a hot man.

148

Bi-curious attr SWM [attractive straight white male] sks
[seeks] bi-curious SWM for mutual 1st encounter. No gays.[15]

The writer of the second advertisement obviously plans to stretch
the irony of his homoerotic desire as far as possible. It could be
argued that this is the plea of a deeply closeted man who is submerged in the gay sensibility of de-emphasis. But it is also possible that this is the work of a consummate homoerotic ironist
contriving a sophisticated scene in which he may be able to en-
snare a virgin about to experience his first ecstatic incarnation of
paradoxical masculinity, marking his ironic transformation
from orthodoxy to paradox.

Athletics, as I said at the beginning of this chapter, is a sign of
orthodox masculinity. The masculine leitmotif that becomes an
integral social aspect of sporting experience (see Chapter Two)
enhances the masculine aura of athletics. This sense of the compulsory heterosexuality of sport presents athletes as straight
and, with gay ironic sensibility, erotically desirable. Straight appearance is an essential ingredient in the erotic appeal of athletes. An erotic short story in *Jock* magazine entitled "Sportsex,"
by E. R. Ross, shows the excitement that develops with the
ironic realization that an athlete turns out to be gay. "I couldn't
believe it. One of the top jocks in the school [a quarterback with
sandy blond hair] was not only talking to me, he was coming on
to me."[16]

The ironic transformation whereby the ostensibly straight
athlete turns out to be gay is the major theme of the "classic" gay
pornographic video, *The Idol,* written and directed by Tom de
Simone. Unlike many American pornographic films, *The Idol* has
a fairly intricate plot, theme, and character development. It is the
story of Gary Evans, a college athletic hero who gradually discov-
ers his homoerotic potential. His first exposure to homoeroticism
occurs when he complains to his buddy that his girlfriend doesn't
"put out." His friend says, "Why don't you let one of the boys get
you off?"

"You're out of your head—you know I'm not into that scene."

"Nobody's asking you to switch; all you do is get your rocks off.

You should see what goes on in the locker room. Half of the guys aren't there to make the team; they're there to *make* the team— get it." And so Gary and his friend go to the showers and Gary watches as "one of the boys" does the buddy. The athletic context is maintained both by the fact that the showers are communal, typical of athletic facilities, and by background noises of athletes in the gym. When it's all over the buddy says: "Don't worry about it; it'll be a lot easier next time."

And indeed it is. The next time, he gets a rubdown from his coach, who trots out a lot of coaching "wisdom" about the need for athletes to relieve themselves sexually. While Gary is lying on his stomach, the coach repeatedly tells him to keep his head down, then he suddenly pulls Gary to the end of the massage table and proceeds to perform anilingus on him. He reassures Gary by saying that he knows what goes on in the showers between the boys, but he lets it go on because "it's tradition and good for us all."

Eventually Gary falls head-over-heels in love with another young man, a voyeur who happens to have been watching him throughout the film. The ultimate resolution to his ironic transformation from straight athlete to gay man occurs when he describes himself as "the best-kept secret on campus: Joe College becomes Homecoming Queen." The seeming masculine athlete is so only paradoxically. This irony reflects that fundamental irony of gay experience, which is that of seeming to be what one is not.

POWER PLAY

A popular homoerotic fantasy involves the older coach and younger athlete. Here, against the homoerotic backdrop of equal gender power, we have the enhanced eroticism of the power play that comes from disparate age and social position. This is the power a mature man can exercise over a younger—the power that an authority has over his subordinate, the expert over the neophyte. This erotic world shows that sex between men, while based on basic gender affinity, isn't always an entirely egalitarian enterprise.

In mainstream movies, the homoeroticism of the coach-and-athlete relationship may only be alluded to. *North Shore* is a movie about a young surfer who is taught everything there is to know about "riding the waves" by an older man (perhaps thirty-five years old); the boy's future is in his hands. The relationship between the two is intense; their mutual involvement is obvious at a candle-light dinner during which the older man serenades the younger with his guitar. This romantic homoeroticism is cut short by the presence of a wife and baby; the young surfer suddenly goes looking for his girlfriend. The relationship between the two men is quite clearly the important one; the women in the movie are peripheral and seem to have no other role than to exorcise the lurking homosexual potential of the men. The romantic relationship of coach and athlete is also a feature of Patricia Nell Warren's novel *The Front Runner.*

In the movie *Youngblood,* Rob Lowe plays an innocent rookie hockey player. There is a scene rich with Freudian homosexual "Oedipal" implications. The rookie is taught by his father how to fight. "Come on, grab me, grab me. Come on, kid, show me something," says the father, who then slaps his son. "Come on kid, come on," he entices as he slaps him again. We can't help but wonder if the rookie's reluctance reflects something more profound than his repressed desire to *fight* with his father. When he eventually does start to fight there is a sense of triumph, of barriers between them finally broken.

The homoerotic power play of coach and athlete is not confined to the subtext of mainstream movies or the text of gay pornography. In the actual world of sports, coaches and athletes can sexually explore the homoerotic possibilities of their relative powers. One of the men I interviewed was a champion hurdler at a prestigious private school for boys. The coach, who was the school's phys ed teacher, took a special interest in him.

The gym teacher was everybody's idol. He was tall and muscular, had a big voice he used with a great deal of authority.

151

He was very tough on the kids. He was also the coach of the basketball team and he'd be intolerant and tough—mean, mean, mean with the team. So the boys looked up to him very much. I was very effeminate in high school. He used to pick on me, saying I was a baby. I was fourteen and had already been through puberty, but he'd say that I was just a baby, that I didn't even have any pubic hair. So I'd say to him sometimes, and this wouldn't only be in private, "Listen, I can show it to you right here, if you like." I knew what he wanted.

He put on the pressure for me to prove to him that I was a man. So, eventually I went to his house, my knees were shaking. I really wanted it but I was dying of fear at the same time. I was very attracted to him—he was muscular and projected such a masculine image.

So here we were, he was watching the football game on TV. He was at one end of the sofa and I was at the other. He turned the conversation to sex almost immediately, wanting to know if I had sex regularly—I was only fourteen! He wanted to know what I liked to have done to me. Finally, I walked over to him and he pulled down my pants and his. Then he went and closed the curtains and we lay down on the carpet and had sex.

We had sex on and off for three years, in the showers at school, the locker room. Always alone, or hiding. I would take a shower—he would always come into the dressing room to watch the boys—I would intentionally be the last one in the showers; then he would come and take a shower. He would be across from me and we'd both start playing with ourselves. Then we'd start feeling each other up—when all the boys were gone we'd have sex. Sometimes in the showers and sometimes we'd go to the locker room. Because he was often involved with women, I couldn't go to his house, so we usually did it at school. When I think about it now, I can see that it was real fantasy material.

The coach had all the masculine appeal of a muscular athlete; the fact that he was hard on the boys intensified that masculine power. His young athlete was both erotically drawn to that power and ultimately troubled by it.

> But, it was only genital—no affection. He never gave me a caress or a kiss. He had a lot of power over me—he had me in his grip. If I had known, I could have blown the whistle on him—imagine the scandal, this was the school where all the cabinet ministers had gone, but I never did tell. It was pleasurable, in fact I wanted more, but it took awhile for me to put sex and affection back together again after that. I mean, I think it's fine for a horny teenager to have sex with his phys ed teacher; it was great. The experience was pleasant sexually, but I felt taken advantage of—I felt that he was using me. It was purely genital and that's not a good experience for teenagers. This is not the way I want to be with a man; I should have known. It hurt me in the end and it took a long while to recover. Feeling that he had so much power over me, it took all the courage I had, but I finally went to his office and told him that it had to end.

This eroticism of man/boy power was not staged, was not just a fantasy scene that could be transformed at will. They eroticized the actual power play of coach and athlete. Because this power play had no affective dimension, the relationship was, after three years, eventually undone. It could be that the coach was more attached to his orthodox status as a "masculine" man than he was to the full working-out of his paradoxical motivations. Because the coach liked that masculine, in fact, patriarchal, powerful position and the sex it afforded him, he had no interest in undermining the power and, no doubt, its erotic appeal by opening himself to an affectionate relationship with his young athlete. I am not suggesting that a caring and sexual relationship between a coach and athlete is not possible. But when the eroticism lies, as it does in this case, in the actual exercise of the power that one person has over another and in the erotic actualization of the pseudo-orthodoxy of the powerful partner, the human potential of a caring relationship is easily circumvented. If the coach had been more open to the ramifications of the paradox in his own life, he may well have fostered a man/boy relationship worthy of the praise of Socrates.

MUSCLES

As the Japanese novelist Yukio Mishima said, it is "a special property of muscles that they [feed] the imagination of others while remaining totally devoid of imagination themselves."[17] It is a truism in gay publishing that a muscled body on the cover of a publication sells more copies than any other image. In droves, gay men are going to gyms, pumping up their muscles, so much so that, at least in major urban centers, there are often more gay than straight men in many athletic facilities. Muscles have great power, a power that consists not only in their ability to move heavy objects but also as puissant symbols of masculinity. The preeminent symbol of masculinity is the phallus. But a muscular build is also an important star in the constellation of masculine signs. In a drawing by Ed Hartley in *Jock,* two masculine symbols are placed side by side: an erect cock next to a very muscular arm and shoulder. The ambiguous direction of the gaze of the arm's owner draws our focus to the relative importance of muscles and cocks as powerful symbols.[18] The poet James Kirkup compares cocks and muscles in a poem on body builders. The body builder, he says, "Inflates the pecs for all to see. / A growing cock will so expand."[19] Commenting on the relative personal significance of muscles and penises, several of the men I interviewed said they found muscles more interesting.

> I always wanted to see their biceps bulging—I wasn't as interested in their dicks—and even now, I can get away with just someone show[ing] me their biceps. •

And another said:

> Some of the best-looking people are swimmers. I like chests and buttocks, I find them more attractive than the penis, just to look at.

154

Keeping in mind the Foucauldian concept of power and its masculine embodiment in athletic bodies, the following comments on masculinity and muscles are illuminating. A man who lifts weights and wrestles, and who is quite muscular as an adult, hints at the significance that muscles had as a sign for him of heterosexual masculinity.

For me, because I didn't have [muscles] when I was a kid, I didn't perceive myself as being that kind of man. I didn't think I'd ever be that way, it was an unreachable goal, so it's part of the mystique about it, something to worship from afar. The greater the muscle, the less approachable the person would be. Actually, muscles never figured in sexual fantasies for me until really quite recently. In terms of adolescent fantasy, no, muscles weren't particularly important. Body hair was another masculine characteristic. I added the muscle later. You can just add these things as you please.

Finding masculinity attractive as sexual fantasy, that is, as a feature that is to be contrasted with reality, a runner told me how the *appearance* of masculinity is exciting to him:

There are some really attractive features to masculinity, the strength, the virility, the excitement—I mean, when you look at someone who looks masculine, that is, big, pumped-up, strong, someone with jeans and T-shirt and the muscled body and rippling stomach . . . he can be a total wimp, but the *image* of masculinity does excite. I think it's exciting because it feeds into some fantasies, maybe fantasies that we have about ourselves, but certainly fantasies that we have about lovers, friends, sex partners.

Many gay men find muscles beautiful:

Muscles interest me because they are beautiful, because they are part of this human art.
I've always been fairly muscular naturally. When I was competing in gymnastics I had fairly good tone and good

definition; it stayed for years after. I like a naturally toned body. I like my body and people with bodies similar to my own. My attraction to muscles is aesthetic and very much sexual.

There are many who would argue that the beauty of muscles lies in their adherence to high aesthetic, perhaps universal, principles of symmetry, balance, proportion, the play of tension, and so on. Although this is not the place to launch into a refutation of classical aesthetic theory, I would like to suggest an alternate explanation of the beauty of muscles. In Western culture, the characteristics of bodily beauty are dependent on gender. Consider the following physical attributes: substantial shoulders, wide, hard pectoral muscles, large biceps and thick forearms, a rippled abdomen, small muscular buttocks, strapping thighs, and bulky calves. Even if these coexist in some sort of harmonious proportion, they are seldom considered the defining features of a beautiful woman's body. Outstanding musculature, albeit in varying degrees, is usually considered beautiful on men. The nature of beauty lies in the experience of agreement. As David Hume said, "Beauty in things exists in the mind which contemplates them."[20] When we find that a phenomenon agrees with our notion of how it should be, we say it is beautiful and, conversely, when something is dissonant with our view of the world, we say it is ugly. Commenting on a boxing match, a person with a violent sensibility might say, "I saw a beautiful fight last night," whereas someone with less violent sensibilities may say of the same event, "Last night, I witnessed the ugliest spectacle." So it is not quite precise to say that the object of our attention is beautiful; beauty is constituted in *the experience of the agreement* between one's worldview and things one sees as positive in actual experience. Consequently, when we say that a man's muscles are beautiful, we are saying that they resonate with our concept of masculinity. From previous discussions we have established our culture's understanding of manliness. We also know that a gay ironic interpretation can undermine and recast that masculinity in a new, paradoxical mold.

Muscles, being a sign of masculinity, are beautiful to homosexual men because they reflect their interest in the paradoxical dynamics of masculinity in general. And so men who are intrigued by the more temperate expressions of masculinity are more inclined to prefer moderate musculature. One of the men I interviewed said:

> For instance, the young Iranian who I see frequently in the showers and sauna at my swimming pool has been working on his muscles. As he stood there the night before last, he was very attractive. Because his muscles are very natural. On the other hand, when it gets to be exaggerated, then it becomes rather ugly. The cords, when they stick out too far, and things are there for their own sake. Where I do find it very entertaining is in Tom of Finland, because he manages in his drawings to get the lines somehow and they stick out of his trousers or shirt in a very funny way, whereas the Arnold Schartzenburger [sic], that's the other kind that is funny, that I can't take seriously.

When I asked the former runner Jim Pullen if he liked muscles, without any hesitation he said: "Hmmm hmmm!" He said that he is attracted to muscles because they are aesthetically appealing and because he thinks men should be trim with muscles—he is attracted to such men. He doesn't like the hugely muscular bodies of body builders, finding the swimmer's body to be the most attractive. "Although, I can watch a body builder go down the street and think, 'Oh my goodness, isn't he big! Nice tits!' "

"Tits," known anatomically as pectoral muscles, along with various other muscular developments like biceps and abdominal muscles (the famous and much sought-after washboard stomach), have acquired high status as masculine signs. As signs of *athletic* masculinity, their prestige is probably greater than the phallus. And so, the homoerotic desire for these muscular machinations is the desire for masculine contact. To pass one's hands over the athlete's muscles is to come close to his masculine mythos. To run one's tongue over the hills and valleys of this athletic terrain is to offer homage to the myth—as a friend of mine once said, the greatest respect you can show for a thing is to put it in your mouth. And finally, for a man to experience orgasm while riveted to the mellifluous undulations of a muscular body is to make incarnate in his being his paradoxical penchant for that mezzo forte expression of athletic masculinity.

THE JOCK STRAP

In his book on homoerotic poetry, Gregory Woods says: "Three types of male physique, three distinct ideals, occur in Western art: the adolescent pliancy of Narcissus; Apollo's firm but graceful maturity; and the potency of Heracles, tacitly poised on the verge of deterioration." The attraction of the young Narcissus lies primarily in "the delightful promise of his backside" whereas "Heracles is unequivocally phallic. When he lays down his club, he is still heavily armed. His musculature seems designed for the pinning down of loved ones, while the phallus does its work." Maintaining both the anal and phallic natures of Narcissus and Heracles in one physique is Apollo. "He is best depicted in three dimensions: for we must be able to wander at will from penis to buttocks to penis, gazing at his statue as though in his bed, making love with each aspect of him in turn. . . . In the versatility of his manhood, Apollo is, perhaps, the ideal ideal."[21] (See Fig. 4.)

The athletic body, being typically neither very young nor very old, is best cast in the image of Apollo. And the jock strap, no doubt *the* garment of homoerotic athleticism, consisting as it does of an ample purse on one side and straps that highlight posterior potential on the other, epitomizes the twofold nature of Apollo. The jock strap, as the vestment of fluent anal and phallic aspirations, highlighting Apollonian versatility, draws us to the homoerotic paradox; by featuring the phallus it elevates masculinity, but its concomitant delineation of the buttocks draws us simultaneously to the violation of masculinity, thus stimulating the ironic homoerotic imagination. In his sexual versatility, enhanced by his youthful yet mature body, it is Apollo who fills the jock strap of homoerotic fantasy.

* * *

Masculine patriarchal culture is concentrated symbolically in the phallus. The Swedish psychiatrist Thorkil Vanggaard points out the distinction between "penis," an organ, and "phallus," a symbol, the purveyor of meaning. "By the symbolic term phallus, we express the idea that beyond the practical function of the genital in its fully erect shape as a means of procreation and pleasure, it is a pictorial representation of the essence of manliness, a representation of the synthesis of every imaginable aspect of proper manhood."[22] Contemporary euphemisms for the phallus also indicate that it is the symbol of masculinity. In pornographic literature and sometimes sexual experience, the phallus is referred to as "throbbing manhood," "man-pole," or "man-meat."

The myth of masculinity hangs on the penis. It is by the myth that a dangling tissue becomes a phallus. When a baby is born, it is with intense interest that doctors, nurses, mothers, and fathers look between the legs of the newborn. When they behold that tiny fleshy knob, with the happy performative proclamation "It's a boy!," they crown his little penis with the laurels of masculinity. For the rest of his life, that boy knows that the source of his masculine power, the thing that places him above his sister and all other women, is his penis, endowed at birth with the significance of the phallus, the potency of patriarchy.

Weaponry is among the chief artifacts of masculinity, indicating the masculine desire and capability for power over others by aggression, violence, and ultimately murder. The metaphorical association of the phallus with weapons is well established. Gregory Woods points out that Shakespeare referred to it as a dart, lance, pike, poleax, and sword. There are old Japanese drawings in which "wrestlers and muscle men fight, with no other weapons save their long, thick, huge-headed, and erect penises." The likening of the penis to guns occurs, among other places, in poetry: Gavin Dillard says his own penis discharges "like a rifle." Mutsuo Takahashi likens the combination of a man's genitalia to "a cannon with its two wheels." Harold Norse refers to his own "heavy artillery," while Frank O'Hara envisages a "missile with a smoking muzzle."[23]

The eroticization of the phallus is the incarnation of masculinity, intensified through its potent symbol, which is physically located, that is, actually made available for sexual exploration, at

159

the penis. The jock strap is the shelter and shrine for this apotheosis of masculine symbols. It enhances the already-powerful phallic myth with the mezzo forte mythic masculinity of athletes. And so, the jock strap as a symbol in its own right imparts phallic *and* related athletic myths. Visually represented, as it often is in both pornography and mainstream arts and entertainment, it is the key to this mythic world of athletic masculinity. Jock straps are icons of this masculinity.

The jock strap is perhaps the quintessential homoerotic ritual robe because, just as it enshrines the symbol of the myth of masculinity, so too the straps that originate in the top elastic circumscribe the buttocks and disappear at the anus, bringing us to that place where masculinity meets its mythic undoing. And so, as suggested by the versatility of Apollo, there are two sides to the jock strap that symbolize the homoerotic paradox: the pouch in the front as the shrine of masculinity joined to the straps in the back framing its mythic violation. (See Fig. 5.)

The jock strap, as the symbol of the fluent phallic and anal dimensions of homoerotic fucking, conveys the irony of this eroticism in its paradoxical conquest of masculinity. An 8mm film distributed by Coloraction Films is called *Jockstrap Romances.* Their brochure says:

> Paul invites Tom over for a workout. They strip to their jocks and begin their routines—which turn into a cock-and-ass workout. Tom delivers multiposition fuck. Paul then demonstrates some far-out gymnastics and sucks his own big rod. . . .

There is an interesting movement here from more peripheral signs of masculinity to central ones, while simultaneously there is the familiar process of a homoerotic ironic metamorphosis. Paul invites Tom for a workout, the ostensible butch reason for two guys to get together. They strip down to their jocks, presumably because jocks straps are *real* workout clothes—fantasy, of course, often involves stretching the facts. This constitutes an intensification of the masculinity: the workout gets tough and the guys strip down. The erotic appeal of the jock strap as the symbol of homoerotic paradox sets us on a course of gay ironic

160

destruction in which the straight appearance of two athletes having a workout gives way to the homoerotic reality of two gay men engaged in a homosexual encounter. Their workout becomes a "cock-and-ass workout," which is a movement from the peripheral orthodox masculinity of exercising muscles to the central paradoxical masculinity of homoerotic fucking. Emphasizing his athleticism and therefore masculinity, "Paul demonstrates some far-out gymnastics" in his performance of autofellatio. Autofellatio plays, perhaps, on the mythic self-sufficiency of masculinity. As Morse Peckham said, "Size is a pretty universal indicator of value and importance, or more generally, significance."[24] The fact that Paul's cock is large is the ultimate sign of masculinity. Its description as a "big rod" attests to its power, potency, and rigor.

There are some who take exception to the notion that the size of a man's penis should be considered a sign of masculinity. The logic is that that's not fair, because people can't help their physical disposition to large or small sexual organs. But the gender myth obviously has nothing to do with fairness. People can't help being born male or female, yet this is the physiological indication for the major division of power, prestige, and opportunity in our culture. Trying to claim masculinity for men with small cocks is an attempt to help some men to cash in on the symbolic power of mythic masculinity while still denying that power to half the population—and *that's* not fair.

Gay pornography dwelling on the size theme is extensive. The titles of magazines and videos often indicate the homoerotic preoccupation with this symbol of masculinity: *Inches, Like a Horse, Tall Timber, The Big Fantasy, Huge, Never Big Enough, They Grow 'Em Big,* and so on. In *The Bigger the Better,* Rick "Humongous" Donovan plays a student who fucks his teacher, played by Matt Ramsey. Jeff Stryker, also noted for his extreme genital endowment, frequently delivers a verbal commentary both on the enormity of his endowment and the sexual action taking place. A typical monologue Stryker delivers in a tough, low voice is: "Fuck him in his mouth," "Take all that big cock," "Choke on that big motherfucker," "Watch him suck that big dick," "Fuck him with that big dick—he likes that." "Stick that big cock all the way up his ass; pound it in him, pound it in him." While the language is, to say the least, coarse, and the sexual activity brutal, the recipients of Stryker's masculine ministrations are always very appreciative; this is not surprising since the scenes are such overwhelming incarnations of homoerotic paradox. After he has commented on his own masculine force, Stryker will draw attention to the joy of his partner by pointing out the rapture of the same: "You like that big cock going up your ass don't you? Huh?" "He likes that, don't he? See, he's got a big ole hard-on."

Although fucking is the most penetrating expression of homoerotic paradox, it is by no means the only one. As I have said before, the erotic attraction men have for other men is in itself an expression of paradoxical masculinity. Consequently, fellatio and any other sexual appreciations of masculinity may also constitute explorations of the homoerotic paradox. An interest in jock straps, while not necessarily dealing directly with fucking, is nevertheless an encounter with the homoerotic paradox. Jock straps that have actually been worn by athletes can become sacramental vehicles of masculinity. The sacramental role of jock straps in sexual encounters is one of gathering up the mythic world of athletic masculinity and making it physically present, available for eros and therefore the incarnation of athletic masculinity in the lived experience of the homoeroticist. It becomes, as Anglican theology says of the bread and wine in the Eucharist, "an outward and visible sign of an inward and spiritual grace."

In a contribution to a book of "true life" homoerotic tales entitled *Flesh,* a writer from California describes his fascination with jock straps:

> Ever since seeing jock straps in high school PE classes, I have been obsessed with them. Generally, the older jock straps that were made of cotton and rubber/elastic were more comfortable and absorbent, whereas the newer fabrics don't seem to hold the precious sweat aroma as well. . . . In high school, there were some studs who wore a jock more than is necessary; they were overly concerned about the care and protection of their cocks and balls. But there was one chap who had a pair of balls and a cock that had to be strapped in, as they were huge. His jock strap was filled to capacity. The jock fetishist loves this piece of men's

wear because it is the closest thing to the cock and balls, and thus all the sweat and other juices and aromas permeate the jock strap. A sweaty jock absorbs a hell of a lot of aromatic salts from an athlete. It also comes in contact with his asshole. Jock nuts love to breathe in this spicy scent. . . . There are guys who never wash their jocks, as they feel this is bad luck, and some of them get really well seasoned.[25]

The used jock strap, as the sacramental element of athletic masculinity, is highly desirable to men whose homoerotic inclinations inspire them to this dynamic of masculinity. There are at least two companies in the USA that cater to the homoerotic interest in jock straps. One, "College Jocks," offers a variety of athletically oriented homoerotic services: phone sex with "athletes," letters from one's favorite jock, and used jock straps, tennis shoes, socks, sweatpants, shorts, jockey briefs, posing trunks, and tank tops, all of which they claim are *straight* [emphasis theirs] from the locker room." In an advertisement the company explains: "My buddies and I started College Jocks when times were a bit hard. We put together College Jocks to tell the *untold stories* about the campus scenes, the prep boys, wrestlers, football players, swimmers, gymnasts, tough guys, and the so-called straight jocks; and, of course, *what really* goes on in the locker rooms!" An advertisement for College Jocks in *Jock* magazine is a cornucopia of gay jock signs. (See Fig. 6.) There is a telephone fantasy sex service called "Lone Star Jocks" that also sells used gym gear and T-shirts. *The Jock Book* ("explaining the stimulating world of jock straps and underwear") was advertised by the following:

Perhaps we have become jaded by all those hard cocks, sticking out at us from the pages of magazines. This volume is to answer all the requests for the young male, in his shorts, and the young athlete, in his "jock strap, with their [sic] firm, young malehood, full, stiff, and completely outlined in those sexy garments.

A pornographer called "A Very Different Studio" advertised its photos of "hot guys who have sex using, abusing, and playing with jocks, underwear, and gym gear."[26] Playing with used athletic gear is not just the stuff of pornographic fantasy. One man I interviewed said:

> I remember once [in the locker room], I was tying up my laces, and some behemoth stumbles in and rips his shirt off and grabs a towel and goes off to the showers, and I thought, I've got two minutes before he comes back, so I grabbed the shirt and just went [breathing in] so that I got this lungful of stale man-sweat. Which was rather jolly.

In Nova's (a pornographic filmmaker) description of the film *Gregg Donovan as the Jock,* a baseball player is helpless in the face of the overwhelming homoerotic power of a used jock strap. Lying in his bathtub he reminisces:

> Gregg had returned to a deserted locker room where he discovered a jock strap hanging on the locker door of one of his teammates. The jock strap had fascinated him for some reason. He'd picked it off the door and played with it for some reason. The fascinations with the jock grew as he studied it—and its erotic power grew also as the cock inside his own jock began to grow and throb and demand attention. Almost without being aware, he'd begun to beat off as he studied the jock. . . . The mysterious power that this cock-carrier had over him took total control and he'd picked up the strap and rubbed it all over his tense, muscled body. Finally . . . Gregg spewed forth a creamy load onto the powerful piece of cloth.

One man I interviewed told me:

> When I was a new boy at the senior school, the older boys would play rugby and they would get their clothes all sweaty and wet, they would pull them off and just drop them on the floor and I, along with all the other new boys, would pick them up after them and take them to the drying room. Then we had to put them in the boys' lockers. I used to love doing the jock straps. And I don't think that I was the only boy that did.

I remember once being in the athletic center at [the university] and there was a famous athlete at the locker next to me. He was a football player—he had taken his jock strap off and left it lying on the floor, while he was standing there naked, looking big and hunky. He had his back turned to me, I reached out with my toes and fondled his jock strap while he was talking to another guy. Here was this sweaty jock strap that I was fondling with my toes and he didn't know it! When you're fourteen you get interested in these jock straps, especially if they've just come from really interesting boys. I don't remember feeling funny about that or that other people thought it was a revolting thing to do with jock straps.

Because athletic symbolism enhances the masculinity of men, things that are normally associated with athleticism often come into play in homoerotic fantasy. Although the most prestigious of these symbols is the jock strap, there are many others that are featured in gay pornography and homosexual encounters: athletic socks, running shoes, football jerseys, athletic jackets, barbells, lockers, benches, shower rooms, sweatbands, bath towels, footballs, football shoulder pads, basketball singlets, Speedo bathing suits. . . .

IMAGE-MAKING

The homoerotic fascination with muscles, although obviously inspired by the paradox itself, has been reinforced by the arts, gay pornography, and the burgeoning fitness industry. This image has had an important influence on the development of a gay sensibility of athletics, contributing to a new and emerging gay fantasy of the "hot jock." The development of this image, and the many closeted ways it has played hide-and-seek with the viewer, deserve a fuller treatment than we have space for here. Nevertheless, it's hoped that the following, by no means exhaustive, account of this imagery will give the reader a sense of its ironic character.

The "respectability" of the visual arts and its well-established tradition of nude representation was an early vehicle for imaging the homoeroticism of young male athletes. Duncan Grant's famous painting *Bathing* (1911), celebrating the movement of muscular bodies through water, shows from behind a naked swimmer climbing into a boat, buttocks spread promisingly. (See Fig. 7.) Grant also took advantage of the erotically appealing practice of young men taking their shirts off to play basketball in *Basketball Game* (1960). (See Fig. 8.) The classic aesthetic homoeroticism of naked wrestlers is the subject of his painting by that name. (See Fig. 9.) In the 1870s, the joint respectability of science and photography gave the work of Eadweard Muybridge a legitimacy it probably would not have had otherwise. To study the biomechanics of movement, he photographed naked male athletes wrestling, throwing, running, and jumping. These pictures are admired not only for their contribution to the analysis of human movement, their artistic integrity, and their importance in the development of cinematography, but also for their only slightly concealed homoerotic potential. (See Fig. 10.)

R. Tait McKenzie was a physiologist and sculptor who idealized the youthful masculinity of athletes in his sculptures. In these homoerotic artistic treatments, the emphasis is not so much on "butch" masculinity as it is on the erotic appeal of the wholesome, youthful, hairless, budding masculinity of athletes. (See Figs. 11 and 12.)

The homoerotic appeal of wholesome masculine athletes is explicit in some gay pornography. A homosexual magazine, circa the mid-1960s, has "respectable" pictures of a clean-living young man. The text describes him as:

> An outstanding player on the tennis team at college, Perry Stevenson has also participated in football and swimming. He is 5′10″ tall and weighs 175 pounds and possesses a good body structure with ideal proportions. This young nineteen-year-old is quite talented in pen-and-ink drawing. He has illustrated many of the term papers he was required to turn in during school sessions. This has usually brought him an "A" grade. Upon completion of college he plans to take pro-

fessional training at art school to prepare him for the career of a professional artist. (See Fig. 13.)

The physical perfection of athletes is the theme of Brentwood's video *Eric.* In their brochure they say:

> The fact that he's a one-in-a-million discovery is excitingly clear as he moves his sleek muscular body around the basketball court. During practice he proudly displays his fantastic athletic ability. With trickles of sweat glistening over his classic All-American face, powerful chest, and down the ripples of his stomach, he's the perfect male for any sexual dream or fantasy.

There are many homoerotic scenes in mainstream, ostensibly straight, films about athletes. For instance, in *Youngblood,* the rookie hockey player played by Rob Lowe is often seen in that vastly significant homoerotic vestment, the jock strap. (See Fig. 14.) He even wears it at home. When he brings his girlfriend to his bedroom, there are jock straps strewn across his bed; embarrassed, he moves them out of the way. Is this not perhaps a symbolic gesture in which the homoerotic significance of the jock strap is moved aside in deference to the ensuring heterosexual episode? His initiation into the hockey team is the traditional one in which his teammates gather round and gaze upon his genitals while one, wearing a jock strap as a surgical mask, shaves the rookie's pubic hair; this is not an unheard-of homosexual practice. The director sets up steamy locker-room scenes that could easily be the context for gay porn movies—with boys in various states of undress, the jock strap, again, prominently featured. This homoerotic titillation is common in movies about athletes; half-naked athletes in jock straps, T-shirts, and towels abound in films like *All the Right Moves,* which features Tom Cruise. At one point in this football movie, a player on the field says to his opponent, "I'm coming after your ass, Riley." And Riley answers, "Do it man; make me happy." What is the director of *Youngblood* trying to suggest by using the same sexy red lighting in both the locker-room and bedroom scenes? Homoerotic paradox is suspended over this film like a cloud with a silver lining.

Over the last decade or so, a new athletic masculine look has emerged, the product of a burgeoning physical-fitness industry. Although muscles are the centerpiece of this form, it is not the brawn of brutes. These muscular fellows aren't rugged types—they will wear pretty, color-coordinated gym outfits, carefully placed sweat bands, and will be photographed with a tasteful patina of perspiration gracing their chests. This look might best be described as the "sissy athlete"—enticing muscles that wouldn't hurt a fly. It's an ironic gay style that reflects paradoxical gender. Scott Masden was the first to popularize this look in a well-known advertisement he made for an exercise machine called Soloflex. His success as a homoerotic icon no doubt encouraged him to publish a book of exercises, *Peak Condition*. It's as much a photo essay in soft-core gay porn as it is an exercise book. The photographer Bruce Weber was the major commercial/artistic force behind the photographic style that idolized pretty muscle boys. He did a series of photos on the 1984 USA Olympic team that were published in Andy Warhol's *Interview* magazine. Irony, here, is heaped upon irony; the photos are executed in Weber's trademark pretty-boy, sissy-athlete style (an ironic style in itself), but these are pictures of *real* athletes, and so those desirable muscles are not just fashionable erotic accoutrements, as his photographic style has always suggested, but are actually the creations of dedicated athleticism.

There are many books and magazines that exploit this quiet homoerotic genre, presenting soft-core homoerotic images under the guise of being guides to fitness. *Working Out,* by Charles Hix, features a different model for each muscle group. The effect of the photos is more erotic than illustrative. There is another volume with the title *Getting Hard;* whether it is meant for the gym, coffee table, or bedroom is an ambiguity the author clearly intended.

There is more than a soupçon of gay irony here. The homoerotic appeal of these books and magazines is barely concealed by their ostensible legitimacy as health and fitness texts. Before exercise became popular, gay men bought books on dance. Homosexual men who didn't want it to be too obvious that they had such erotic interests could, under the pretense of their devotion to the arts, buy *After Dark* magazine, which featured pictures of virtually naked dancers. Around their apartments, gay men could leave handsome volumes of photographs of famous dancers and troupes, attesting, not too convincingly, to their high aesthetic sensibilities. The erotic allure of the union of muscles and effeminacy that is traditionally associated with dance has been largely supplanted by the more masculine, but nevertheless paradoxical, allure of the "hot jock."

A homoerotic interest in men's bodies can also be disguised as an interest in physique, ostensibly a sexless pursuit of the "healthy" male body. The first popular body-building model was the nineteenth-century Russian strong-man Eugene Sandow. (See Figs. 15, 16, and 17.) Body-building magazines abound; for gay men who are charmed by the exaggerated masculine symbolism of the steroid-induced body, periodicals like *Muscle Mag* are of considerable interest. Although the muscles of body builders bespeak hypermasculinity, the sensibility of body building is not always a macho one. The preoccupation body builders have with men's bodies has often aroused suspicion as to where their sexual interests lie. An owner of a weight-lifting gym and manager of highly ranked professional body builders told me that disguised homosexuality is what body building is all about. Now that the well-known body builder Bob Paris has come out, other gay body builders may follow suit, and the closetedness of that covertly homoerotic world may begin to erode.

The connection between body building and homosexuality is suggested in the 1959 film *Boys in Prison.* The official synopsis is:

The plot is of a young body builder who is thrown into jail with a bunch of roughnecks. When he attempts to work out with his dumbbells and cables, they tease and ridicule him. The bully of the group tears his inspirational muscle-man pinup photo from the wall and destroys it. When the body builder tries to fight the bully, the other prisoners restrain him (for his own good). Then one day in the shower the final humiliation is visited upon the body builder. After being forced to wash the bully's feet, the body builder is given a kick in the rump that sends him sprawling. Fed up, he tackles the bully and gets some wrestling holds on him that put him out of commission. The other prisoners are quite impressed. Back in the dormitory, the body builder now gets the prized bunk, the other prisoners dutifully read the copies of *Physique Pictorial* that have been provided for them, and the film closes with them all going through their exercises.[27]

In this Athletic Model Guild film, body building is not only a metaphor for homosexuality but also a traditional excuse for sexy shots of men using their muscles. When the rest of the prisoners take up "body building," we certainly take a flight of homoerotic fancy.

Body building is purely cosmetic. Typical of the gay ironic fascination with appearance, the muscles are developed not for actual athletic activity, but for posing. Behind the facade of athletic competition, body building is homoerotic burlesque. (See Fig. 18.) Unlike straight burlesque shows, whose erotic mission is explicit, body building exploits gay irony by passing its eroticism off as "athletic." Videotapes of body-building competitions are readily available; their gay appeal is attested to by the fact that they are regular features on the video screens of gay bars. A special twist of gay irony is present in the annual New York City Police Department's body-building competition being shown on videotape in gay bars.

"Physique" was the major alibi for homoerotic images during the 1950s and 60s. Those being severely repressive times, homosexuality often deported itself in disguise. One of the most prolific producers of physique pornography since 1945 has been the Athletic Model Guild. The irony of this enterprise is evidenced just by the name. "Guilds" are usually organizations for artistic groups like musicians and actors. Churches, of course, have altar and flower guilds—all very respectable. "Athletes" are good, clean-living, healthy people. This admirable picture is tainted by the word "model." Life-models, after all, remove their clothes for art classes. Nevertheless, there is a campy air of respectability in the name. The irony is born out when we realize that this admittedly marginal respectability exists to mask the "seamy" fact that homosexual men use these photos of a guild of apparently clean-living athletes for masturbatory fantasies.[28]

A publication of the Athletic Model Guild was *Physique Pictorial,* which was featured in *Boys in Prison.* The force behind AMG is Bob Mizer, whose photographic style has had a considerable impact on the development of homoerotic photographic imagery. One modeling pose he has made famous is that of a reclining man with his hands behind his neck. *While standing,* this is a traditional body-building pose, effective because it highlights a number of muscle groups. But the same pose, *while reclining,* adds to the display of an already-desirable musculature the promise of homoerotic paradox. A muscular man lying down with his hands seemingly immobilized is vulnerable: "Take me, do with me what you will, I can't resist you." Figure 19 is typical of Mizer's work. This style has been imitated in less overtly homoerotic magazines. For example, *Superstar Wrestler* featured the professional wrestler "Ravishing" Rick Rude in that same reclining position. (See Fig. 20.)

The homoerotic appeal of athletes and sports settings are sometimes exploited for their potential to sell consumer goods. For example, *Arena,* a fashion magazine for men with a distinctly gay appeal, advertised Lonsdale sports equipment with four photographs taken at Newco Repton Boys Club in London. The phallic prominence in the models' boxing shorts attests to the calculated homoeroticism of this advertisement. Boxers would never expose themselves in such a way when working out. (See Fig. 21.)

The homoerotic image of the athlete, the "hot jock," has been reified by the arts, the gay press, the fashion and pornography industries, thus working its way into the erotic psyches of gay men. The arts, as forms that give their subjects an aura of "truth," lend a truthful status to the image of the homoerotic athlete. In their "artistic" treatment of the erotic image of the athlete, Yukio Mishima, Duncan Grant, and others lend that image the credibility of "artistic" insight. In the early gay liberation movement, the "objectification of the body" implicit in the hot-jock icon prohibited its inclusion in the movement's lexicon of acceptable, feminist-inspired erotic images. Images like the hot-jock were thought to obscure the humanity of those who have such bodies and to devalue those who didn't have hot muscular bodies. But because that feminist point of view tried to negate the aspirations of much of homoerotic desire, that is, idealized masculine bodies, such political correctness didn't last long, and athletic bodies can now be seen gracing the pages and covers of most gay magazines, thereby giving the hot jock the imprimatur of gay liberation (and conversely, giving gay liberation at least some of the allure of the hot jock). (See Figs. 22 and 23.) The fashion industry, with the help of its burgeoning subdivision, the physical fitness industry, has heightened the desirability of the hot jock by emphasizing the cosmetic athletic body as a requirement for personal attractiveness. The pornography industry has formalized the eroticism of the hot jock's muscular body, marketed it as a commodity, and through its availability, turned up the volume of its erotic potential in the day-to-day lives of homosexual men.

Sometimes pornography will attempt to invoke the myth of the hot jock simply by using locations, props, or scenarios that are vaguely athletic. At times, the only thing jock-like about jock pornography is the title. There is some athletic pornography that, because of the seemingly unathletic physiques of the models, requires a powerful, willful suspension of disbelief on the part of the viewer. A lot of pornography is just badly produced. Whether or not it is successful depends more on the mythic imagination of the fantasizer and his ability to endow the images with hot-jock eroticism than it does on the actual hot-jock sensibility of the pornographic production.

The mythic image of the hot jock, like its parent the myth of gender, shapes the way some of us see ourselves and others. That mythic fantasy-world imprints itself on the erotic relations between men who are inclined to this particular dynamic. This is where fantasy and life meet. When one has sex with a man and erotically admires, for example, the contours of his pectoral muscles, one may well be invoking the hot-jock myth with its paradoxically masculine, homoerotic implications. Because it is the nature of eros to transform mental life, to make incarnate in individual lives the culture in which we find ourselves, we endow our sexual partners with the cultural frameworks of myths. Of course, not everyone will eroticize the myths in the same way;

172

whereas one eroticist might experience the hot jock in a pectoral muscle, another may find the paradoxical pleasure of a construction worker, soldier, or policeman.

The hot-jock sensibility can be identified with the masculine leitmotif that I said in Chapter Two characterized team sports. It's a way of thinking that emphasizes the machismo of sports—playing football proves you're a "man." This sense of manliness, of course, implies heterosexuality, and so the "jock" is conceived as straight. Regarding the homoerotic desirability of these macho guys, a swimmer said: "They can be nice to look at and they can be fun. It can be sort of trippy. Self-consumed, red-necked, stuffy, aloof, not real emotional beings, denying that. Could be strong, physically domineering, big and brawny." The homoerotic fantasy of jocks is a desire for orthodox masculinity, a fantastic "taste for trade," which we have already seen as being, on the whole, undesirable in real life.

The erotic image of the orthodox jock is now being paradoxically transformed, making space for a distinctly gay image of the hot jock. Orthodox athletic masculinity is becoming erotically paradoxical; the power of orthodoxy is being overthrown. There is evidence of this change in gay pornography.* The hot jock of gay pornography is moving away from its direct reference to athletics. If we look at the evolution of *Jock* magazine, and the use of the word "jock" in other gay pornography where there is often nothing athletic in the imagery, it is clear that the intention is to preserve only a paradoxical masculine echo of athleticism. In the discourse of pornography, "jock" is undergoing an etymological development, maintaining its masculine associations and letting slip the athletic. The adjective "hot" is being incorporated into the meaning of "jock," so that its use is almost redundant. In the June 1988 issue of *Jock,* there is an obvious appropriation and confirmation of this new, not directly athletic, meaning of the word. In a four-part photo and textual essay, the editors of the magazine explicitly attempt to redefine "jock." Each section has a picture of a young man and a text that refines the new meaning of the word, climaxing with the ironic assertion that "jock" is a

---

*As I will discuss in Chapter Seven, there is also evidence of this change in gay culture at large.

dirty word. *Paradoxical* masculinity is the core of this new meaning. The orthodox significance of "the jock" is paradoxically undermined. The duality of active/ passive, dominant/subordinate, and masculine/feminine is made the heart of the concept of the (hot) jock. The new emphasis in the word "jock" is on the Apollonian masculinity we contemplated earlier in "The Jock Strap."

> JOCK. Say it. Be it. Take it. David is jock . . . tough and tight; a body with proportions able to please. He's hot and ready to meet your action. He knows how to please; he's sleek and sensual. . . .

Notice that the word has ceased to be a noun and is now an adjective. So one is no longer *a* jock but jock-like. Orthodoxy is being undermined. For the orthodox jock, pleasing another man sexually is anathema, but this paradoxical jock not only has a body he knows how to use homoerotically, he is also anxious to do so. This is traditionally more the position of the orthodox woman: there for the taking. He is described with traditionally feminine adjectives, "sleek and sensual"; so here is a slight feminization of the jock.

> JOCK. In tune with his body, he knows how to work it. Hard. Long. Rough. He wants to be stroked. Licked. Sucked. And he deserves it. Doug likes it deep. Slow and smooth. And you'll give him what he needs. Because you want it.

The fluency of Apollo is disclosed in the dual phallic and anal potential of jock: "you'll give him what he needs," which is, of course, to be fucked orally or anally. In the following section, we find that jock is not limited to being fucked; jock also does the fucking. And so the jock as "trade" is now seen as a reciprocal partner.

> JOCK. A new brand of sex. Wear it with pride. . . . Look for him next door. He's the one whose eyes excite you. Whose body fuels your sex. On your knees in an alley, after school in the park, be what he wants you to be. . . .

As a "new brand of sex" that is to be worn "with pride," "jock" suggests the homoerotic paradox and its acceptability in the light of the achievements of the sensibility of change and the gay liberation movement, which celebrates itself as gay pride, especially on Gay Pride Day. "On your knees in the alley" signifies the undermining of masculinity implicit in giving oneself over to another man. But it is with pride that you do so. "Be what he wants you to be" is the incarnation of the jock myth, the rendezvous of fantasy and life.

> JOCK. A four-letter word. The *dirtiest* four-letter word! One that you whisper under your heated breath when you see him, hot from a workout or wet from a shower. Go ahead. Say it out loud. Let him know how badly your body needs his action.

This is an ironic transformation of the word "jock." The orthodox understanding of "jock" is that of a masculine straight man. By embracing the homoerotic desirability of masculinity, this new sense of the word ironically destroys that masculinity and reconstructs it as paradoxical. "Jock" becomes "the dirtiest four-letter word" because it speaks of a desire for the violation of masculinity. The gay appreciation of "dirty words" is ironic also, because it sees through the orthodox appearance of filth and reconstructs it as respectability. The gay myth that this meaning of "jock" conveys already exists as the homoerotic paradox; whether the word "jock," percolating up through the pornography industry and common gay usage, will become the accepted name for this dynamic of the myth remains to be seen.*

What is common to all homoerotic experience is the paradoxical erotic transformation of the myth of masculinity. The image of the hot jock, although by no means the only erotic theme, is an archetype of one dynamic level in the myth. In sexual encounters, the hot-jock fantasy may be one element in a pastiche of erotic

---

Jock magazine is trying to redefine a word in its own image, a word that is, after all, the name of their product. The magazine is capitalizing on and therefore highlighting an important sense of the word that already exists; the homoerotic paradoxical desirability of jocks. Whereas traditionally jocks were always thought of as straight, this new sense of the word makes "jock" a gay phenomenon.

themes such as love, contempt, racism, competition, impropriety and so on. And, like many erotic themes, hot-jock imagery may well be the subconscious milieu of a largely unconsidered personal erotic world.

VI

Sex And Sport

"He shoots! He scores!"
—Foster Hewitt

SPORT AND THE HOMOEROTIC PARADOX

It's ironic that while sport is traditionally a sign of orthodox masculinity for men, emphasizing the conventional masculine values
of power, muscular strength, competition, and so on, it is also a
world that celebrates affinity among men, and therefore, paradoxical experience.

Women are excluded from most men's sports. Generally
speaking, men don't want women on their hockey teams, in
their rugby scrums, on their wrestling mats, in their locker
rooms. . . . The fact is that there are very few sports that integrate men and women. Given that orthodox men are interested
in women for the social and erotic production of mythic gender
difference, one would think that they would make an effort to
develop sports that include women. Instead, they have cultivated sporting styles, rules, and regulations that make it virtually impossible for women to participate. Rather than taking
advantage of the many similarities of male and female physical
capacities, sports have developed to emphasize the differences,
thereby reproducing in that athletic/social sphere the mythic
discourse of gender difference. The arguments about the physiological differences between men and women and their respective abilities to compete in various sports are legion. But since
there is a more fundamental cultural and erotic dynamic at

work here, one that precludes any mere physiological questions, one that may, in fact, construct the conceptual framework upon which scientific, physiological questions are asked in the first place, it's not necessary here to enter into the debate on the relative physical capacities of men and women.[1]

Given that all sports are the products of social relations (that is, their origins are obviously social, not physiological), why do we have sports that segregate rather than integrate men and women? Why are men so anxious to perpetuate that segregation? What are men getting out of their sports that might be lost if women were to become involved?

The orthodox world of sports is a covert world of homoeroticism. I am not saying that men who like sports are necessarily gay, nor am I saying that their intuitions of themselves need be in some way fundamentally paradoxical. But lurking *mythically* beneath the ostensible orthodoxy of masculine sport is the ironic subtext of the paradox. In Chapter Three, we discussed this theoretically as the "intimate relationship" between orthodox and paradox.* The irony of orthodox gender relations is that men become segregated from women; consequently, they develop a greater affinity for other men than they do for women. But is this the same gender affinity that we said characterizes homosexuality?

Inherent in the structure of the gender myth is a strange slippage between orthodoxy and paradoxy, a slippage that is in itself paradoxical. Gender is in its essence a myth of difference. But that myth has so subjugated women that they are often not perceived by men as worthy. The intentionally segregated organization of sport, and the remarkable enthusiasm of men to keep it segregated rather than redesigning it so that integration is possible, proves that women are not seen as the fellows of men. In the gender myth, women are tangential to the real world of men. We see this marginalization of women dramatized over and over again in segregated sports, both at the community level and in the prime-time television broadcasts of the NFL. So the paradox of orthodox masculinity is that the hierarchy of gender difference

---

*Cf. p. 75.

compels men to find satisfaction in one another. One of the ways they do so is in sports. It might seem that this is not erotic satisfaction in the usual sense; after all, it doesn't usually, or at least publicly, proceed to genital expression. Certainly, we don't see any of that in the television coverage of the NFL, or any other sporting event for that matter. But if one considers the wide range of experiences that one finds erotic, it becomes clear that for most of us, eroticism is not a strictly genital phenomenon.

Consider this popular, indeed legendary, scene that is played out time and again at high schools, universities, and community centers and is often featured on television, in newspapers, and magazines. A group of men get together in what are usually the rather close quarters of a locker room and take off their clothes. In various states of undress, they stand around talking to each other, preparing themselves for what is to follow. Ritual garments are donned. First of all, the jock strap. Then a coalition of pads and suspenders work together to dramatize and accentuate the masculine form. The men pull themselves into tight pants that closely adhere to the shapes of their buttocks. And not forgetting the twofold nature of Apollo, an elaborate set of laces frame the cupped and much-vaunted male genitals. The men then work themselves into a psychic frenzy of masculine unity and run out on the playing field ready to get the other team. One man bends over, while another, behind him, puts his hands between the inclined man's legs, grasps a ball that's shaped like a large testicle, and attempts to throw it to another man. Everybody wants the ball. Men along the line of scrimmage press themselves against each other enthusiastically. As a man out on the field runs with the ball, many others run after him, trying to grab him. Unless the ball goes out of bounds, each play climaxes with men lying on top of each other, the testicle-shaped ball forming the nucleus of this masculine clutch. The whistle blows and some variation of the same theme is played over and over. When time is up, the boys go back to the locker room, take their clothes off again, and shower together.

It could be said that this description has left out an important dimension of sport, a dimension that is usually cited as *the* essence of sport, namely competition, the masculine struggle for superiority. In the famous "gladiatorial" scene of his novel,

Women in Love, D. H. Lawrence probes the meaning of athletic masculine struggle.

So the two men entwined and wrestled with each other, working nearer and nearer. Both were white and clear, but Gerald flushed smart red where he was touched, and Birkin remained white and tense. He seemed to penetrate into Gerald's more solid, more diffuse bulk, to interfuse his body through the body of the other, as if to bring subtly into subjection, always seizing with some rapid necromantic foreknowledge every motion of the other flesh, converting and counteracting it, playing upon limbs and trunk of Gerald like some hard wind. It was as if Birkin's whole physical intelligence interpenetrated into Gerald's body, as if his fine, sublimated energy entered into the flesh of the fuller man, like some potency, casting a fine net, a prison, through the muscles into the very depths of Gerald's physical being.

So they wrestled swiftly, rapturously, intent and mindless at last, two essential white figures working into a tighter, closer oneness of struggle, with a strange, octopus-like knotting and flashing of limbs in the subdued light of the room. . . .

At length Gerald lay back inert on the carpet, his breast rising in great slow panting, whilst Birkin kneeled over him, almost unconscious. Birkin was much more exhausted. He caught little, short breaths, he could scarcely breathe any more. The earth seemed to tilt and sway, and a complete darkness was coming over his mind. He did not know what happened. He slid forward quite unconscious of Gerald, and Gerald did not notice. Then he was half conscious again, aware only of the strange tilting and sliding of the world. The world was sliding, everything was sliding off into the darkness. And he was sliding, endlessly, endlessly away.[2]

These are the familiar signs of the ecstatic experience of homoerotic paradox.* Gerald is "penetrated" and brought "subtly

---

*Cf. "The Meaning of Fucking," Chapter Five.

into subjection," imprisoned by the "sublimated energy"—the secret of the paradox—the "potency," of Birkin's muscles. Their wrestling is the "rapturously mindless" ecstasy of their abandonment to the "oneness"—which I called "coalescence"—of working out the "struggle" that is the emergence of the paradox. Orthodox masculinity is undermined as the "world," that is, the myth of orthodox masculinity, "slides off into the darkness." The mythic "slippage" from orthodox to paradox is now accomplished, so that Birkin, having experienced the paradox himself, "slides endlessly away." In the orthodox athletic experience of masculine struggle, we have the subtle homoerotic experience of paradox.

Thematically, a satisfying sports competition is much the same as a satisfying homosexual, that is, paradoxical, fuck. The paradoxical play of masculinity is essential to both. In both well-matched sports and homoerotic fucking, masculine power meets masculine power; men play with each other's masculinity, paradoxically probing those places where masculinity can be undermined, painstakingly bringing each other to the edge of masculine dissolution.* Crucial to fine athletic competition is the equality of the competitors. Likewise, fundamental equality in the gender myth is essential to a homoerotic encounter. Although they are often portrayed by the media as adversaries, competitive athletes are actually erotic accomplices. They are *accomplices* because the athletes must cooperate extensively with each other if the competitive struggle is going to take place at all. They are *erotic* accomplices because men's sport is a bodily, carnal experience in which the myth of masculine struggle is actualized. Just as in fucking there is an ecstatic meeting, a coalescence of equal bodies in the rapt oneness of the paradoxical project, so too in sports there is an exhilarating coalescence of equal bodies devoted to the carnal working out of manly struggle.

Ironically, men meeting men in sport, while pursuing an orthodox expression of their masculinity, also explore the paradoxical possibilities of their masculinity. Some are more aware of this than others. The paradox of homoerotic stimulation, the ecstasy of man-to-man struggle, disguised by the orthodox violence of sport, may be a deep secret whispered incomprehensibly in the

*Cf. p. 140 ff.

grunts, groans, and moans of athletes straining their bodies against each other. And for those who are themselves unathletic but nevertheless fascinated by the play of masculine power, the excitement of the homoerotic paradox may be hidden deeply, indeed unconsciously, in the enthusiastic voyeurism of the dedicated sports fan, guzzling beer, cheering on the men who actually get to rub against each other on the playing field, wishing they were doing it themselves. For these men, televised sports spectacles are a deeply disguised form of homoerotic pornography. As Gore Vidal said, " 'The only time when heteros may openly enjoy what they secretly dream of is when watching handsome young men playing contact games.' "[3] For the orthodox sportsman, the sensibility of de-emphasis is paramount; it keeps the secret power of the paradox under wraps, even for themselves. For these men, the "orthodoxy" of sport exonerates the paradoxical subtext of exclusive, masculine, athletic struggle and the cult of manly contact, jock straps, and naked male bodies. The hidden erotic paradox of orthodox sport is terrifying for some men. Homophobia in sport is the fear of the inherent slippage between orthodoxy and paradoxy realized in sporting scenes.

If the orthodox masculine world of athletics were to be known as a deeply hidden homoerotic world of paradox, the patriarchal power of athletics and of those men who pursue athletics for that power would be ironically undermined, making the entire edifice of orthodox athletic masculinity tremble at the very epicentre of patriarchal power itself. If deeply submerged in the orthodox pleasure of athletics, disguised by the "orthodoxy" of athletics, is the pleasure of the homoerotic paradox, then the masculine patriarchal significance of athletics will show itself as containing the seeds of its own paradoxical destruction. This is intolerable for men who truly desire the power that their orthodox relationship to patriarchy has so gratuitously afforded them. And so they homophobically deny that there is any homoerotic dimension in sport. The paradoxical erotic experience of sports can be concealed by the false consciousness of "orthodoxy." This alleviates the fear some men have of the concealed allure of the paradox, preserving for them their own orthodox patriarchal power. That de-emphasizing maneuver also sustains the patriarchal socio-cultural status quo.

For those who are more open to the paradox, however, whose intuitions of themselves in the gender myth motivate them to deliberately seek out the paradoxical eroticism of gender, the homoerotic dimensions of sport are full of promise. The more gay one is, that is, the more fully one has accepted the legitimacy of the paradoxical interpretation of gender, the more willing one is to draw out the homoerotic dimensions of sport. The intimate relationship between orthodoxy and paradoxy in contact sports is pursued by gay men both in the fantasies of pornography and the actual experience of sport. There are several gay pornography producers who are devoted to the homoeroticism of wrestling and boxing. These films make the implicit homoeroticism of main-stream sport spectacles explicit. (See Figs. 24, 25, and 26.)

One man told me that, as a boy, wrestling brought him to his first awareness of homoeroticism and has remained a source of erotic fascination for him.

It's more of a dawning, a realization over a long period. . . . When I was eleven, twelve, thirteen, and I was just becoming aware of my body, me and my best friend would spend the summer [at my grandmother's place at Cape Cod]. My uncle lived there, and he was maybe ten years older than us, and he was living at home, not working, he was a beach bum, but he was blond, muscular, and always wore this skimpy little blue bathing suit, and he loved to wrestle with the two of us, and we loved it, we thought it was great. We did it when we were eleven, twelve, and then we got to be thirteen, and the next year, we came down for the summer and said, "Where's Russell?" and my mother gave some excuse like he had gone to the city and wouldn't be there while we were there, and I found out later that he was homosexual, but we didn't know about it—we didn't know about anything. We just liked to wrestle with him.

As a legitimate activity for boys, wrestling allowed him the opportunity to explore, unwittingly, the homoerotic potential of masculine physical contact. He was fortunate enough to have a muscular uncle with whom he could encounter mature physical power. Another man remembered how his fascination with men's muscles evolved into a desire for wrestling contact. Unlike the fellow above, this yearning remained unrequited in his youth.

I can remember Adam's stepfather, Adam being my buddy, describing how he used to be on a high-school wrestling team and it wasn't so much because he really liked it but because he was so darn good at it, and I thought—! So that's the first time that it worked itself out into a little *Drummer* story as opposed to just the vague forearm fetishes.*

Boys and teenagers are intuitively aware of this kind of fun and wrestle with their friends. Some are content with the subtle, nongenital expression of the paradox; others use it as a mutual masculine ruse or prolegomenon to a more transparent homoerotic seduction. As Gregory Woods said, "Wrestling . . . is the heterosexually acceptable form of homosexual foreplay."[4] Often boys will wrestle with each other hoping for a more explicit homosexual action. Describing an ultimately frustrating teenage relationship with another boy who turned out to be more interested in orthodoxy, one man told me that he and his friend, "were very physical, we were always wrestling, doing everything but having sex, and I think I just got tired of waiting for something to happen."

Afraid of the homoerotic paradox, its power to undermine masculinity and the estrangement that may follow the pleasure of the paradox, some boys and men nevertheless manage to immerse themselves in the experience by disguising it as "orthodox" athletic combat. On the other hand, in *The City and the Pillar,* a novel by Gore Vidal, boys wrestle their way into sex: "Somehow the violence released Jim from certain emotions and he wrestled furiously with Bob, made free, for the time, by violence."[5] In this story, the wrestling eventually gives way to genital sex, leaving Bob feeling uncomfortable and Jim feeling that he has found himself.

Drummer is a gay pornographic magazine that specializes in hypermasculine images and fantasies that heighten the coalition of masculine aggression and homoeroticism.

184

A man I interviewed remembered the problems that competitive wrestling in high school caused him. He said he found wrestling:

> Very sexual. I'd often get hard, I'd often come. It was difficult to deal with: "How did you get that hard-on off me." That became a problem in high school so that I ended up, grade twelve . . . I stopped wrestling, I was too afraid that I was going to get hard and someone would notice. Actually, it rarely happens when you are really wrestling—it can't physiologically because the blood is going to the muscles and it's certainly not engorging your penis. So it has to be in a fooling-around sense, but still, it's happened to me, so you tend to become really cautious about coming out in grade ten in front of the gym class, it's not cool.

The homoerotic appeal of wrestling needn't always result in erections. As the wrestler above pointed out, when one wrestles intensely the muscles get precedence over the penis for the supply of blood. That physical economy, however, may have little to do with the erotic focus of the athletic activity. The lack of an erection does not signify a paucity of homoerotic attraction. As Neil Marks said, "There is a unique excitement in being aware of your physical attraction to a man and sublimating it into an athletic maneuver."[6] No doubt, there is also a *jouissance* in being *unaware* of your physical attraction to a man and sublimating it into an athletic maneuver. James Kirkup says that football is that game "Where players, colliding, shrink,/Yet with desired daring reach/Longingly at one another."[7] A gymnast I interviewed said, "I always enjoyed playing touch football; I remember in grades seven and eight we always played it during our lunch hour. It was great because it was a chance to jump on another guy." This is the concealed homoerotic appeal of contact sports.

Some of the masculine rituals that surround mainstream sport almost scream with homoerotic desire. Gary Shaw, a former University of Texas Longhorn football player, describes an after-dinner entertainment team members frequently enjoyed in the dorm.

Probably the varsity's most popular game was "record races." Here they would strip several of us naked and divide us into two groups. Then they would bring out our "toy"—an old forty-five-rpm record. They placed the toy between the cracks of our asses. We had to carry it from one end of the hall to the other without using our hands. We would then have to—again without using our hands—place it in our teammate's ass. If he happened to drop it, his partner had to pick it up with his mouth, and put it back in place. These races were considered the highlight of the evening.[8]

A straight-identified university football player told me of a strangely homoerotic team initiation rite. Rookies would be stripped naked and then required to extract from the foreskins of their uncircumcised teammates, without using their hands or feet, olives, which they were then expected to swallow.

There are men who feel no need for these pretenses and happily admit the homoeroticism of sport.

Wrestling and sex to me are the same thing; there's no difference. To get aroused, I need to wrestle, I need the physical contact, I need muscle, I need a response from someone else. If they just lie there and let you dominate them, that doesn't do a thing for me. It's the muscle, the meeting, the equal response, the body contact. That to me is synonymous with sex.

The homoerotic significance of masculine struggle can outweigh the importance of orgasm.

The orgasm is almost incidental to the fact of the wrestling; that you come is almost like blowing your nose at the end. After you've had your bout, he's off getting a drink of water, and you sit there and you jerk off. It's not the most important part.

One needn't be a participant in sports to enjoy its homoerotic potential. A multimillion-dollar spectator-sports industry exploits that homoerotic appeal. Certainly, there are men who watch sports on television or go to games because they enjoy watching the skills of fine athletes. But as I have said many times, the world of sports is not *just* a world of athleticism. As Denis de Rougement said: "Sportive struggles always and everywhere contain a strong dramatic and erotic element. In the medieval tournament these two elements had so much got the upper hand that its character of a contest of force was almost obliterated by its romantic purport."[9] One can't help but remark that many, if not the vast majority, of sports spectators are supremely unathletic themselves; the fat, beer-drinking baseball, football, or hockey fan is a legitimate cliché. Their lethargy leads one to suspect that *athletic* experience is not an important one to them. Those sports fans who are obsessed with the aura of athletes are known by professional athletes, quite pejoratively, as "jock sniffers."[10] Given what we know about the homoeroticism of jocks and jock straps, and also that hidden in the orthodoxy of sports is the homoerotic paradox, we can see that the interest male sports fans have in their athletic heroes probably involves the deeply submerged pleasures of homoerotic sniffing.

Although one may enjoy watching fine athletes accomplishing superb athletic feats in high-performance sports, the real appeal of sport lies in its exercise of masculinity. The orthodox appreciation of athletics as a masculine drama, involving the display of power, aggression, and violence, is well known to us all. The masculine combat of sport is thought to mirror the competitive, in fact war-like, relations between men. One need only consider the language typical of the sports pages to see the hostile nature of orthodox masculine relations as they are portrayed in sports: teams and athletes are routinely said to be walloped, bashed, thumped, crushed, slaughtered, and annihilated. The paradoxical appreciation of sports spectacles, on the other hand, views the games with ironic, homoerotic field glasses.

Typically, gay men are not inclined to be sports spectators. This is probably because the ostensible orthodoxy of that masculine world is incompatible with their personal reading of the gender myth. Most, however, are able to give that athletic masculinity a paradoxical interpretation and derive at least occasional pleasure from it.

I don't watch [sports] on television. I've been to one major-league baseball game and one major-league hockey game in my life, and the one I went to because my lover at the time got free tickets, and the other I went to because my brother got me a couple of tickets and wanted me to take his son. I like some things to watch, like gymnastics on television. The bodies are nice.

A number of the men I interviewed said that although they were keen to play some sports, they were not interested in watching except for the athletic bodies. A swimmer told me: "I'd much rather participate than watch." Another man said that he doesn't usually watch sports, although he has enjoyed

tennis, I watched Wimbledon on TV this year and quite enjoyed it. Unless somebody was going to a game, then I would go with them for company. I would never want to go to a baseball game. I enjoyed hitting the ball and playing when I was participating—if I ever went to watch baseball it was because of all those social sides of it and college loyalties, but I'd be awfully glad when it was all over, especially on cold nights. I suppose baseball is the sexiest game. Those uniforms, and all that bending over.

A gay phys ed student said:

I get bored very quickly watching any sport, unless there's somebody in it I know and I have a personal interest. I got a bit of a charge out of the pennant race a couple of years ago. I hadn't realized what an attractive bunch the Blue Jays were. I was surprised. I started watching ball games, and the next thing I knew there was a picture of Donald Sylveste in my desk I could pull out to look at. It was sexy watching Garcia slide.

A body builder I interviewed said he was very fond of watching sports for both orthodox and paradoxical reasons.

[My lover] closes the door and I watch the NFL, track and field, I look at all of them. Eighty percent of my television

188

watching is football, tennis, track and field, hockey, I don't watch boxing. The whole aspect of trying to beat up on another person in boxing doesn't appeal to me. But I do watch these other sports and my rationalization is that's how I channel my competitive urges, I admit I have them, I'm just not prepared to act them out.

[Is there anything sexual in watching sports?]

I'd like to say no, but I think I'd have to say yes. They played the 100m from Rome with Carl Lewis and Ben Johnson so many times. There's no question that I'm stimulated—although I don't get a hard-on—by seeing these beautiful masculine bodies doing what they do, and doing it very well. There is an element of sexuality there, maybe not consciously. I notice their cocks, but also the legs and the arms and how tight they are—all those things. When I watch tennis, yes, I'm watching the tennis, but whenever I get a shot of the front—I never noticed how cute the Australian, Pat Cash is, and then I think, I wonder what his basket is like, and it's all happening at the same time I'm noticing the score. . . . [The television cameras] give you crotch shots and bum shots. I'm sure they are subliminally seducing straights and overtly seducing gays. It does make me wonder sometimes who's behind those cameras.

A group of gay wrestling friends enjoy attending the wrestling matches at hockey arenas where they witness not only the exaggerated masculinity in the ring, but also the machismo of their fellow spectators. One of them described the experience:

We sat in the red seats, just in the crowd. That was *fascinating* because you really were in the belly of the beast. I can still remember the guy in front of us: this poor-white-trash, East-End type of guy with a loading-dock body, not a wealthy "fitness" body, with his chick and his mop of hair and his bad skin, and every time one of the wrestlers would do something great, he'd give a clenched fist—*"Awl right!"*—and there'd be all these muscles and bulges and ripples and so on that would just course through his body and our dicks, and it was just wonderful. And during intermission you get the sense there are lots of men there who aren't quite sure why they enjoy watching sweaty muscular men throwing each other around the ring. So the halls are oddly cruisy. There is a lot of aggression and masculinity and sex appeal involved in it. For eight-year-olds it's just cartoons, but I think that there are people between the sophisticated jerk-off queens like us and the eight-year-olds; between that range there would be people who would be there with sexual desires left unfulfilled.

It's obvious that some sports producers choose to play on the homoerotic appeal of athletes. A poster from The Sports Network (TSN), a Canadian TV channel that gives twenty-four-hour sports coverage, is a case in point. It shows a sweaty, muscular young man pulling off his singlet. Beneath the picture in bold uppercase letters are the words: "WE DELIVER THE MALE." This picture presents a muscular, wet torso seductively arched, the head back (perhaps in ecstasy), with arms above the head in a pseudo-Athletic Model Guild pose. That hallmark "take me, do with me what you will, I can't resist you" pose is subtly reinforced by the seeming bondage of the muscular model, tied up in his own sweaty singlet. This provocative juxtaposition of power and vulnerability bespeaks an invitation to the homoerotic paradox, a fantastic enticement to the violation of masculinity. The Sports Network must realize this significance; the poster, after all, is directed at potential advertisers, people with a sophisticated sense of the commerical appeal of the not-so-subliminal seductiveness of the homoerotic athletic body.

Some professional sports organizations, in an attempt to increase revenues, are capitalizing on the erotic appeal of their athletes. Australian Rules football is traditionally known as a rough guys' sport. The Sydney Swans decided to exploit that erotic potential, and hired a marketing company to refine their image. This resulted in the enhanced appeal of their star full-forward, Warwick Capper. (See Fig. 27.) The marketing company has designed special, very tight-fitting shorts and vest for Capper. Not willing to be too obvious about their intentions, they say they are improving the "eye appeal" rather than the "sex appeal" of the athletes. Acknowledging that they are attracting a gay following, the marketing manager said:

The crowds we attract are the most well-behaved and nicest people in the world. We never have any trouble. The most flamboyant people in the world come along and strut their stuff and have a great day. We're not catering to the "yob-bos." We'd rather have a smaller crowd of nice people that are really into the game than a whole mass of uncouth people. We'd rather have gay people coming to watch the match than all those yobbos from the western suburbs.[11]

A homoerotic text can be gleaned from the common discourse of mainstream sport. Photos of athletes feigning homoerotic interest in each other regularly grace the pages of newspapers and sports magazines. For example, *Sports Illustrated* pictured basketball players Isaiah Thomas and Magic Johnson kissing before a game. (See Fig. 28.) The *Toronto Daily Star* pictured Wayne Gretzky seemingly kissing the Philadelphia Flyers' goalie Ron Hextall. (See Fig. 29.) *In Touch* and *Drummer*, gay magazines, have run humorous photo essays, highlighting this hidden erotic dynamic. (See Figs. 30 and 31.) The vocabulary of sports can also betray hidden homoerotic significance. In collegiate wrestling, there is a hold by which one immobilizes an opponent by pressing one's pelvis into his backside; the move is called "the Saturday night." Dennis Potvin, in *Power on Ice,* speaks of "the orgasmic delight of seeing the black hunk of vulcanized rubber penetrate the deepest recesses of the net." And regarding the importance of "assists" in a hockey player's career, Frank Rose says, "It pays to help your buddy get off his shot."[12]

Male athletes will often sell their homoerotic appeal to companies for advertising. The late Canadian swimmer Victor Davis, who set a world record in the 200-meter breast stroke at the L.A. Olympics, lent his hard, shaved body to the Speedo swimsuit company as an image to help them sell bathing suits. Speedo then sold not only the bathing suits, but also the poster of Davis—a poster that made its way into the homes of numbers of gay men. As previously noted, the Sydney Swans want to "have gay people coming to the games" rather than "yobbos." Conversely, Speedo, hypocritically exploiting the homoerotic appeal of Victor Davis, prefers to distance itself from homosexuality. I asked them for permission to reproduce that poster in this book. When I spoke to the amiable general manager on the telephone, he said that he could foresee no difficulties in giving me permission; I should simply write to him explaining the context. The "context" turned everything around. I received a terse refusal. That the photographer and advertising directors who created the image the company now refuses to allow me to reproduce were unaware of its homoerotic appeal seems very unlikely to me. Advertisers put a great deal of thought into the nuances and implications of their work. So it would seem that the company prefers a covert assocation with homosexuality, making money from it without admitting it.

THE LOCKER ROOM

Looking

A gay phys ed student told me:

> It's an unusual situation in athletics, because in heterosexual society you don't have this contact. You can only suspect what may be underneath those clothes, but if you are gay, there are no surprises. My straight friends, they say it must be really tough, walking around the showers when you are gay. "I couldn't do it in a women's shower and try and be casual and talk with them."

A runner described the special experience of being gay in a locker room.

> When I was coming out and after I was out it was like, "Oh my God, all these gorgeous bodies." It was seeing all these terrific-looking men in one place. A "kid-in-a-candy-store" mentality—I want that one and that one!

192

But figuring out how one can get who one wants is not always that easy. He went on to say:

> When I was at college, just before I was out, I remember there was this one guy who I used to look at and I was worried that he would think I was staring at him. I only realize now that I was staring at him because he had such a huge basket. Well, the reason he had such a huge basket was that he had an erection! I *knew,* or I sort of knew, but at the time, I didn't think it had anything to do with me looking at him.

A swimmer recalled an experience he had in the showers with his team, all of whom knew he was gay. Only a few of the showers were working and those that were, were right next to each other. He remarked how nice it was that the swim team was becoming so intimate. They laughed nervously since the comment "came as it did from the queer in the corner."

> There I was and I was shampooing my hair, looking down, and Tom was talking to Frank and they were both about a foot away, and they both had about a foot each [the length of their penises]. Tom had this gorgeous bum. They were just chatting away in this terribly masculine sort of way, soaping up their dicks, and I was washing my hair and watching them; I know I had a grin on my face and I thought to myself, "Isn't this thoroughly pleasant." I had every right to be there—in fact, I was finished showering before them, I wasn't lingering and peering. I belonged there. It was like having chocolate sauce on your ice cream. It was a perfectly gratuitous, pleasant experience.

Finding it natural to look at men in the showers and locker room, a man told me: "I consider it perfectly normal. I am discreet about it. I do it and I feel fine about it."

Only one of the gay athletes I interviewed did not see erotic potential in the locker room.

> That's something the gay pornographic film industry has been trying to tap into for some time now, but I'm afraid

193

they're off the mark. There's nothing to me that's sexually attractive about a dirty locker room.

Several athletes told me that although they could see the erotic potential of the locker room, the fantasy about sex with teams and in locker rooms had little to do with real teams and locker rooms.

When you say that you play football, a lot of gay men who have never done that, they think about the locker-room scene from the porno thing. And nothing could be further from the actuality. Well, sorry to tell you, it's a lot more mundane than you think. You finish, you take a shower—if you win, everyone's patting each other's back and stuff—but essentially, you take a shower and everyone goes home. Not much happens. I can see where it would be a source of fantasy for people who [aren't athletes], but for people who are, you want to take your shower and go home, you're tired. For people who are fantasizing and are starting at that point, they still have all their energy, that's fine.

Myles Pearson, a former competitive swimmer, said:

In most locker rooms, that *I've* been in anyway, the only sex that's talked about is "Oh, I fucked this fox on a beach the other night, was it ever fantastic." I haven't heard gay men in locker rooms talk about things, or people talk about gay topics whether the person talking is gay or straight. It's something that if it's brought up, it's as a joke. So I would tend to think [the porn image] doesn't come from [actual locker rooms].

For some gay men, being in the presence of other muscular men is an inspiration to their own athletic activity.

I can remember pacing myself behind some particularly nice man on that running track and that making it possible for me to run an extra half-mile or so. I'm not going to pass this man for anything.

194

A gymnast told me that working out and the erotic potential of athletic facilities are mutually enhancing:

> Sometimes when I'd be lifting weights, I'd look out of the corner of my eye and see someone who has an amazing body and I would look at them and think, "Oh my god," and start pushing the weights harder and harder. It raises the motivation. It gives you a goal. Watching someone while working out hard is a lot like sex, minus the ejaculation.

In one's youth, locker rooms are often a source of erotic fantasy.

> When I was age-group swimming, there were people from ten to twenty, I much preferred looking at the older boys. I remember doing that at swim meets. Now that I think of it, I have had fantasies of locker rooms and stuff. I don't have that kind of fantasy now, but I did then. I can remember now during one of the big meets walking through and seeing all these swimmers getting changed and there were a few swimmers I would see at various different meets from different clubs who I thought were really quite something. I can remember having dreams where I could go into the locker room and sort of freeze time—everyone stopped except me—and I'd walk around and touch and feel whatever I wanted. But that's about all it was, touching and feeling. As I recall there weren't any erections in any of these fantasies, it was just naked bodies and I just wanted to touch and feel.

Athletic settings in general and the locker room in particular feed the homoerotic imagination and provide homoerotic contact for boys. I asked a masters* swimmer if there was a sexual aspect to athletics when he was in high school.

---

*Masters sports are geared to mature athletes. Although competition is important to some masters athletes, it is not generally the major focus, which is participation for its own sake. Competition is organized in age categories. The masters movement started with swimming in the early 1960s and has spread to other sports and developed into an international sporting movement that culminates in the World Masters Games, which are held quadrenially. They were held in Toronto in 1985 and in Denmark in 1989.

There certainly was. There were boys flirting with each other the way boys do when they are fifteen or sixteen years old. Some of it is just playful mockery insinuating that everyone else is a fag. Some of it is curiosity. There were a few who really wanted to touch other boys or show themselves off in the locker rooms. I remember being in the locker room one day—everyone was naked and there was this one fellow who was about fifteen years old playing around and generally making an ass of himself. He was pretending that he wanted to fuck this other guy by thrusting his hips forward into the other naked boy. It was interesting because this boy was the most butch of all the boys around. He liked grabbing other guys cocks. I think that he is probably straight; but he was awfully curious. He had a great body and he was an early bloomer! There was another fellow who would hug boys and liked to wrestle sometimes in the locker room but mostly out on the playing field. I remember being tackled by him a couple of times. I would have liked it more if there hadn't been so many people around. That rolling around had a nice sexual feel to it.

One man remembered that in his high-school gym class they took swimming lessons in the nude. Even when they did wear bathing suits, there were pleasant memories. "I remember one boy and he had this bathing suit, he was really cute, and when he got his bathing suit wet it would get all clear—it was just so devastating; it was quite wonderful. . . ." He would use locker-room sights as fantasy material when he masturbated. Although he was careful when he was in the locker room not to let on that he found it sexually interesting, he remembered getting caught once. A fellow accused him of staring at his "wiener." He told the boy that he wasn't staring at his "wiener"; he was simply staring into space. "He looked vaguely suspicious because I had, in fact, been staring at his wiener."

There are some men who get upset when the paradox is revealed by homoerotic voyeurism.

We all play voyeur, straights play voyeur all the time. I've seen just as much cruising from supposedly straight guys as

196

I've seen from gay guys. Gay guys just make it more obvious. Straight guys do just as much comparison and cruising as anybody does. I've noticed that a lot of guys will not shower anymore in the gym, they refuse to. If you ask them why— "too many faggots around here." They towel off and off they go, they shower at home. Anybody who's that homophobic, I automatically question their sexuality. What are they worried about, "You've got twenty-inch biceps, fella!" It tells me they are really uptight about their sexuality and have problems dealing with it. Anyone who is sure about themselves isn't going to be concerned when someone is looking at them. . . . It doesn't have to be in the locker room or the shower, there's just as much voyeurism going on in the gym, people hanging around the big guys, watching as close as they can get, but not too close. It just never stops.

That the locker room can be an erotic environment is undeniable. Men who prefer to ignore that erotic potential are sometimes upset about the appreciative glances that they receive from the more homoerotically inclined. I interviewed a heterosexual man who had been a college football player and national track and field coach. Although homoerotic voyeurism did not bother him personally, he suspected that he knew why it was disturbing to some.

I think with some athletes, when somebody thinks somebody else is gay: "Boy, I feel dirty, somebody's staring at me." And I think that comes from equating it with what they do to women, that is that it's dirty, the sneaky peaks at women, and therefore it's what they would be doing and what they would be thinking about women. I think we tend to relate things to what *we* do, and so what they're thinking about women they realize somebody's thinking about them.

Another heterosexual coach agreed that the straight interpretation of the homoerotic voyeur's gaze is that the look mirrors the erotic interest that heterosexual men have in women. He told me that he disapproved of homoerotic voyeurism because it reminded him of the way he would look at women. As a result of

197

having been cruised by men at a hotel, which turned out to be a primarily gay hotel in which he and his team had been unwittingly accommodated, he decided that he should no longer leer at women, but because the nature of homoerotic desire is fundamentally different from that of men's heteroerotic desire, the former being the eroticization of the paradoxical *violation* of mythic masculine power within a context of equality and the latter eroticizing the *affirmation* of that power within a context of inequality, it is incorrect to equate the meaning of a heterosexual man eyeing a woman with a homosexual man eyeing another man. The erotic intention of these two looks are, in fact, virtually opposite.

The combination of an intuitive understanding of the significance of homoeroticism as a violation of masculinity, along with the fragile status of their own mythic masculinity,* leads some men to homophobia. This fear is built into the masculine leitmotif of athletic culture, a culture that exists, after all, to celebrate and confer orthodox masculinity. The first of the previously quoted coaches said that growing up in sports, one grows up with homophobia.

> You get taught those reactions too. "I was going to beat the shit out of a fag the other day, he was looking at me"—you hear that from the time you are really young in locker rooms. What does it mean? But you've been *told* that. Long before, and I mean eight years old, when you're eight years old on the hockey rink you hear that from the older guys, being twelve. . . . There's a real aversion to homosexuality around sport, and I really believe it's because people aren't sure of themselves. That's the bottom-line reason; certainly all the enculturation too, but it's an *aversion*—a "get-away-from-me," infection type of aversion, perhaps I might get it. It will *breed* like athlete's foot.

---

*Masculinity is fragile because of the "intimate relationship," the all-too-easy slippage, between orthodoxy and paradoxy. Because it is fragile, some men feel compelled to reinforce their orthodox masculinity by playing football, or at least watching it (which we can now see is rather ironic), beating up women, fighting among themselves, and "beating the shit out of fags." Homophobia is the fear of the allure of the homoerotic paradox and its concomitant destruction of the orthodox myth of gender and the knowledge about oneself that that would bring.

But there are many men who appreciate the attention of the homoerotic voyeur. Weight rooms are notorious as places where men and boys like to admire each other's bodies. They will spend a great deal of time admiring themselves—the notion that mirrors in weight rooms are aids to good weight-lifting technique is a macho conceit meant to disguise the narcissistic and homoerotic intrigue that surfaces as muscles flex and get bigger. Many of the men I interviewed said that there are seemingly straight men who appear to appreciate their adulations. And, of course, for gay men, being the recipients of the homoerotic voyeur's attention has its pleasures too.

One meets a whole range of people [in the locker room]. There are some who seem to be there a lot of the time. Some of them don't ever do anything, they just hang around and look. They are often quite good-looking. I think they just enjoy exchanging knowing glances and having people look at them—it is very flattering to have people admiring your body. A lot of that happens.

Hard-Ons

The erotic potential of the locker room can lead to an obvious physical sexual response: an erection. Such a prominent testament to one's desires can be embarrassing to men and boys who are trying to keep those desires a secret. Said a man who generally shied away from sports:

I didn't like going to the "Y" because you had to take your clothes off. [I was] scared to death of the locker room—it's partly frivolous but partly true—because you betray yourself, or might [that is, get an erection]. And all that towel flipping and so on might be just a little too attractive.

John Argue, a former varsity swimmer, told me, "By the time I was in university, I was getting a little more sexually frustrated, I would be acutely embarrassed about the possibility of getting an erection in the showers." He was in the uncomfortable situation of not yet having accepted his erotic attraction to men, yet while in the showers his body was giving him the all-too-obvious signal that he *was*. So, for him, there was a negative feeling associated with being in the showers; it forced him to confront something he would rather just repress. Nevertheless,

> I would be looking at them and enjoying their physiques and fantasizing about touching them. But I would have to fight with myself because the more I would fantasize about them, the more likely was a budding erection, which I really didn't want to get. When I got home, now that would be a different story. Sometimes I would go to the gymnasium washroom and jerk off in the toilet, hoping no one would hear me. If all those guys knew how many of them had been jerked off to! I think some of them would have been complimented.

The fear of getting an erection can lead some boys to avoid showers after gym class; others avoid sports altogether because of that anxiety. Most learn to control their sexual response. Even so, a former gymnast told me that he still finds it difficult to restrain himself.

> I have to get dressed and leave right away. If I've seen a guy in the gym and he starts getting undressed beside me, I'll have a strong sexual desire for him and I'll get an erection and there's nothing I can do about it. I have to get out right away because I've had the experience of being in the steamroom and if someone comes in and starts staring at me in the genital area, I'll get an erection; any admiration in that area just hits me the wrong way. I have a strong sex drive and so when I see someone I want, I have a terrible urge to go over and grab him. You know you can't, but you still have the urge. It shouldn't be embarrassing because it happens; everyone gets erections, although some people can control it better than others; I'm just one of those people who can't. At least I let the guy know where he stands right away. If they want to laugh, fine, then I'll laugh too.

Not everyone is embarrassed about getting erections, in fact, it is often the prelude to more involved activities or at least a sign that the owner of the erection is keen. Some men are amazingly adept at controlling the exact amplitude of tumescence in their penises—they will signify their desire with varying states of erection—it goes up and down like a Geiger counter. A man said that in the university locker room:

> I had a guy flashing a hard-on at me, he was holding a towel over it so that he could expose it whenever he wished. I was in a real hurry that day. He was straddling the bench and lifted his towel for me to see his little pink erection. I remember the only thing I could think of was that I was in a hurry. I saw another guy with a hard-on; he was masturbating, looking at the people in the shower. He wasn't jerking off vigorously, just long slow strokes. He knew people were watching, I certainly was and he knew that; and I wondered what was going to happen next! There is another guy who gets hard-ons in the showers and he just looks so embarrassed; I see him trying to put on little Speedo things but his cock just shoots out from underneath.

The locker room sometimes becomes the place of sexual activities.

> There is a surprising amount of cruising and sexual activity going on in the university locker room and showers. I've certainly had sex there. It's generally initiated in the sauna, it's just a look and then you go to the small shower room next door. I was in there one time masturbating this guy when someone pushed open the door and caught us in the act. He looked and said, "Oh, I'm sorry."

A swimmer told me that although he has been involved in sexual situations in the locker room, he finds the idea of it more comfortable than the actual activity.

> I was in the shower and watching this guy who was obviously interested, he became visibly excited. The more I

stared at him, the more excited he became. I found it kind of a thrill, there we were in the middle of [the athletic center], and this guy is sporting an erection right in the open. So, we left the showers and went down to the end of the lockers and did a few things—we touched and stroked each other. He was a big guy, a bit goofy, it seemed like the only thing that interested him was sex and that was fine with me. When we weren't touching or stroking it was kind of exciting to think that we could be caught, but when we were actually touching each other it was too frightening and stressful. So I guess the thought of it was better than the actual act.

Another man told me a story about a brush with a sexual encounter in the locker room.

I used to swim twice a day, early in the morning and in the afternoon—I was training for the World Masters Games. One morning I'd finished my workout and I was at the end of the row of lockers combing my hair. This muscley guy came swaggering along and I thought, "Oh God, here's some straight guy that thinks he's hot shit." And then just when he was about to pass me he winked at me and said, "You look hot in those Jockeys." I remember he had a really deep macho voice. And then he reached out and grabbed my crotch. I didn't know what to do so I said, "Thanks." So he went down into my row of lockers, stood on the bench so he could see over the top of the lockers, and then dropped his towel and started swinging his cock around. Then he sat down, straddling the bench, by this time he had a huge hard-on, and he started slapping it against the bench and then his stomach. It made this kind of thwacking noise. I was still pretending to be combing my hair, but I got a hard-on too, and I couldn't stay like that because there were these two guys speaking Hebrew in the next row. So I went into my row of lockers—the guy was really hot and I wanted him so bad but I thought it was just an impossible situation. So I was still gonna pretend that I wasn't into it—which was pretty silly because I had this boner. As I tried to walk past him, he grabbed my hips, yanked my shorts away from my crotch, and started sucking my cock. Anyone could have come along, and there were these guys talking Hebrew right next door. So I whispered something like "This is impossible!" and he said, "Hey guy, just get into it." I think he thought I was straight! So I said, "No, no, no, it's just that there are too many people here." He tried to suck my cock again so I pulled his head away by the hair. I think I might've said something like, "I really want to, but I can't here." So he got up and said, "Yeah. Maybe next time, guy." And he swaggered off. I jerked off to that one for months.

Responding

A university physical education instructor told me:

All these men with their clothes off. I really find the whole thing about walking around, straight or gay, in a room of twenty-five other people without anything on, is unnerving. And you find people walking around with towels around their waists, and then you have the studs strutting around without a towel, and these are the straight ones, and you wonder, "Are they flaunting it?" because they know there are only males in the locker room, they aren't flaunting for the women. They are strutting around in front of other men, are they gay? They are trying to do their peacock-attracting number to other men. That blows me away.

Who is interested in whom in locker rooms? Life in the locker room illustrates the fluidity of homosexuality and the role of gay sensibilities. If we think of sexual orientation as the essence of one's being, as an identity, then the interest that "straight" men might have in men's bodies is problematic.* But because homo-

---

*It's often said that it's "normal," i.e., heterosexual, for men to look at other men's genitals and bodies; it's only a matter of comparing these masculine signs. While it may be a matter of comparison, there is also good reason to believe that the interest runs deeper. My own experience and that of a number of the men I interviewed suggests that the glances and the overt genital sexual response, i.e.,

eroticism plays with desire in that slippery mythic world of orthodox and paradox, it may be that when confronted with naked
men, homoerotic potential presents itself to all men. Some men,
because of their attachment to orthodox power, either refuse to
see or are blind to the paradox and its erotic promise; they exercise the sensibility of de-emphasis to the utmost. These are the
men who seem the most straight in the showers. On the other
hand, there are men who are keenly aware of every nuance and
erotic possibility of the paradoxical understanding of gender;
they seem the most gay. And there are those in the showers who
arouse great curiosity among gay men because they show some
awareness of the paradox and perhaps even a glimmer of interest
in its erotic potential. They may seem to be straight, but their
slightly lingering gaze and sometimes semierections suggest a
sensitivity to the paradox of which they themselves may not be
truly aware.

One gay man said:

It can be quite fun to watch. The straight guys like to show
off but then they get nervous when you watch too much.
They like being looked at and they like looking. It's like a
pot boiling of suppressed things, especially for straight
men. There's a whole vocabulary of behaviors that are not
clearly defined that are incredibly interesting in the locker
room—exhibitionists who roam the locker room, whether
gay or straight, they like the attention. Gay people playing
with themselves, looking out for sex, straight people turned
on by being with other men. There's a feeling of being with
other guys, naked. I find it very sexual. A lot of guys like it.
You see more than one man, and not all gay, with half-erect
penises, taking their time, lounging around. Being naked
with the boys, being part of the team.

Life in the locker room, and in sports in general, because of
their exonerating orthodox jock associations, creates a safe place

---

erections, of some "straight" men while in the locker room indicates some degree
of homoerotic imagination. The suggestion that this phenomenon is just a "comparison" is probably more of an alibi born of homophobia meant to disguise the
awareness of homoerotic desire.

for the paradoxical imagination to feed itself. Here, there is a concentration of desirable masculinity in which men can immerse themselves and pretend that it's all orthodox masculinity. The degree of paradox and orthodox in the interpretations of these men is often a secret that only they know. It may be a secret kept even from them, deep in the subconscious. Athletic settings facilitate the potential of homoerotic paradox. Given that potential, various sensibilities go to work.

The sensibility of de-emphasis is at work for many men and for a variety of reasons. Men who take great pride in their orthodox masculinity, who feel they would be compromised by an erotic interest in men, de-emphasize the presence of the paradox in the locker room, ignore its potential, and claim not to be aware of it. Seeing the interest that other men may have in the paradox when confronted with naked men, they are disgusted.

Although heterosexual men generally do not get to shower and change with naked women as homosexual men have the privilege of showering and changing with other naked men, there are heterosexual arrangements that are similar. Consider life on the beach and around swimming pools where men and women wear as little as possible. Generally speaking, these arrangements for the stimulation of heteroerotic desire are not considered disgusting. But ethically, such arrangements should be a concern because they raise the spectre of the erotic consummation of orthodoxy in the gender myth, the erotic celebration of the power of men over women. The difference between hetero- and homosexual voyeurism is substantial. The power difference of the gender myth always puts women at risk in their relations with men; rape is an ever-present fear for women. Men, on the other hand, are virtually never raped by women, and very seldom by gay men (they are, however, often raped by straight men in prisons and other all-male environments). When a gay man looks at another man in the showers or locker room, it is never from the position of power that straight men have when they look at women at the beach or on the street. In fact, the erotic world that is invoked in homosexual voyeurism is one of equality in the gender myth and the paradoxical *violation* of masculine power rather than the orthodox, heterosexual *confirmation* of power difference that is fundamental to heterosexual desire. The homoerotic aura of the locker room is disgusting to some, because it brings to the fore the potential for paradox, the violation of orthodox masculinity. Those who want to cling to their orthodox masculine power usually prefer to de-emphasize the homoeroticism of their athletic environments.

There are gay men who are happy to explore homoeroticism in other situations, but prefer to de-emphasize its potential in athletic settings. This is often the case with high-performance athletes. The athleticism of high-performance life can outweigh homoerotic possibilities—one's life is devoted to athletics. Immersed in the heterosexual athletic environment, the homosexual high-performance athlete will often ignore the homoeroticism of the locker room. John Goodwin's experience (he was the rower we met earlier) highlights the complex interactions between the fluidity of homosexuality and the sensibility of de-emphasis when a homosexual high-performance athlete is confronted with the homoerotic possibilities of the locker room.

> At that time, sports were a bit secluding—I trained hard from 1972 to '77. I don't remember anybody cruising me—I remember people looking at me and talking to me. I go there now and it's like night and day—I don't think there are any straight people there! Then, we were all on teams— we lived together, showered together, did everything together so that you learn to ignore everybody else and you purposely allow everybody their privacy in a very public place. I still do that—consciously not look at people so that I walk past people I know without seeing them. It's a way of behaving in changing rooms. . . . I think I purposely kept my perceptions or involvement in the sexual thing very quiet. Getting into the boat, you're always close to everybody there. It was a very closely knit group that I just don't remember as being sexual.

He said he became so accustomed to ignoring the erotic implications of being with the other men on the team that it seemed to disappear as a dimension. The assumption of orthodoxy among the crew members made physical contact easy among them.

The guys I rowed with, I don't know whether any were gay or not, but they thought nothing about going up to someone they didn't even know and telling them how wonderful they looked and how great their legs were, and feeling their arms. It was very physical and complimentary, admiring, but nothing sexual. The people I rowed with I wasn't attracted to—there were other oarsmen, yes, but everyone was quite comfortable about talking about someone else's body. I didn't pay attention to what was going on, but now, in the last four years, I notice more of that going on—perhaps it always was and I didn't notice. If somebody admired the way I was doing bench presses and wanted to hold the bar for me I would have thought it perfectly normal, but today if somebody said that I'd interpret it as cruising. I can't remember anything ever happening to me with the team, when I was alone I was cruised a few times at the university but I only recognize that fact now.

For John Goodwin, understanding the homoerotic implications of his high-performance athletic life came only in retrospect. But as a young athlete, a combined lack of familiarity with the conventions of homosexual liaisons and his wish to avoid them, a wish based on his negative image of homosexuality, kept him from following through on desirable sexual possibilities.*

There were some really gorgeous guys that I remember talking to and having these nothing conversations with but thinking all along how good-looking this guy was, and trying to interpret what he *really* meant. I know now if I was in that situation—somebody chatting with me and I thought he was very sexy—I'm sure I wouldn't have any difficulty in clearing the air. . . . Why didn't I do that? I don't know.

He said that although he felt very sexual at the time, the combination of a demanding training schedule and the seeming dearth of homosexual men made a sexual life impossible.

---

*Cf. pp. 101 ff.

When you're in that kind of shape you're very sexual, you're like a high-performance vehicle, everything is finely tuned, but having sex with men, no, it just wasn't possible. I would have had to have gone to [the city] to have sex because I didn't know a soul [where I was]. Besides, in the whole rowing season we might have had one day off—and we didn't even want that, because if you take a day off, it throws you off, and it takes a week to get back to normal. Some of the guys had steady girlfriends and they would have sex. When women's rowing was brought in, a lot of men went out with those girls because they were always at the course at the same time.

Because heterosexuality is acceptable in sports, the advent of women in rowing introduced easy heterosexual relations in a busy athletic environment. John Goodwin remained "secluded." Now that he is out of his competitive career, he sees the erotic potential of the locker room. But he finds voyeurism unfulfilling.

I don't like it that much. It doesn't work with me. There's something missing. If somebody's looking at me and smiling, it's not enough, too vague, not that I think everyone should be having sex in the showers. I don't like the voyeurism, I think there are people there who only want to look, and that I don't understand. I could see only wanting to look a couple of times, but to keep going and only ever looking is a bit bizarre. I've never done it but I've wondered, what would happen if I made a pass at this person who's been looking at me, supposing I went over to him in the sauna and touched him—what would he do, scream?

He told me about meeting a boy in the sauna at the university athletic center; he had walked up to him and put his hand down John's bathing suit. After a few seconds John told him that he shouldn't do that. The boy said, "Well, I guess I should go take a cold shower then." John said he was flattered by the attention but found it frustrating to be in a situation where he couldn't follow through on what was started. It turned out that the boy was one of the lifeguards, and every time John would see him in the pool

after the episode, the boy would turn away; he found this discon-
certing.

Because one can disguise homoerotic desire in the orthodox masculine facade of the "straight" locker room—masculinity, as we
have seen, has great homoerotic potential when it *seems* to be
heterosexual—the locker room invites homoeroticism. The irony
here is obvious. As one man I interviewed said: "The exciting part
is that you think most of the people in there are straight and
you're all walking around nude, and it's thought of as being very
straight and masculine, and the excitement is to take it out of that
context."

A heterosexual man asked a gay phys ed student what was
different about being gay in physical education. The gay student
asked the nongay man to imagine what it would be like to change
and shower every day, several times a day, with the most physically fit women on campus. How would it feel to walk down his
row of lockers and find sixty or seventy of those women pulling
off their clothes? Imagine sitting on the bench between the lockers and engaging in conversation for twenty minutes at a time
surrounded by naked women in various postures. Then try to
imagine what it would be like for none of those women to know
that he was a man and erotically interested in them.

Tony Curtis and Jack Lemmon starred in the movie *Some Like
It Hot,* in which they portray unemployed musicians who pass as
women in order to get jobs in an "all-girl band." Frequently, they
find themselves in close quarters in dressing rooms with the
"girls," who quite naturally are removing their clothes. Being gay
in a men's locker room is a lot like being Curtis and Lemmon in
Some Like It Hot. In the movie, the women are innocently unaware of the presence of men in their midst. In fact, at one point
a male stagehand almost comes into the dressing room; everyone,
including the disguised men, is quite upset that a man might
come into the room and find them undressed. Curtis and Lemmon
passed as women; gay men pass as straight men. As in most
uniquely gay experiences, both eros and irony are at work in
locker-room voyeurism.

The showers can be the place in which double irony unfolds.

It has happened that there has been more than one gay man in the shower room in the presence of other, probably straight men. The first irony becomes apparent to the gay men in the private realization that they are not alone in their ironic voyeuristic pursuits. However, rather than making this interior irony exterior and acknowledging each other as ironists, they suspend their recognition of each other as ironists, to build a second irony upon the first. Pretending not to recognize each other as gay voyeurs in a shower room surrounded by ostensibly straight men, they treat each other as though they were straight, thereby finding ironic voyeuristic pleasure in each other.

These gay men are manipulating appearance and reality. The appearance is that they are straight and simply taking showers. The reality is that they are gay and deriving voyeuristic pleasure. In the case of the first irony, ironic interpretation has been suspended, which allows for the experience of a second, richer, irony. They choose not to reject the original appearance, that is, that each other is straight. By choosing not to reject the original appearance, they have not opted to accept the appearance either, preferring to hold it in a kind of ironic limbo. Aware of the potential to reject and demolish the original appearance, leaving it intact, they proceed to the second irony. This will be an elegant voyeuristic pursuit of the homoerotic paradox. The second irony involves finding paradoxical pleasure in each other as "straight" men. The erotic voyeuristic appeal lies in the pretense that everyone involved in the encounter is straight. Eventually, they develop erections, which gives away their "straight" ruse, but offers them the alternative pleasure of knowing they are fellow erotic ironists.

They were gay, pretended to be straight, got "off" on the pretense, and through ironic destruction and reconstruction (signaled by the appearance of their erections), came to know the truth, which is that they are gay. The experience is satisfying because, as Wayne Booth says of irony, it's like moving to a better part of town: in this case, from seeming to be straight to being gay. In the creation and interpretation of irony, there is a special sense that one has accomplished something, and that the choice to reject appearance has led one to a better understanding. This voyeuristic encounter is a dramatization of a profound fact of gay life that involves the play of paradox and the manipulation of appearance and reality. It is the experience of things as they actually are, marbled through with the equal presence of things as they are not. Since irony brings with it a sense of superiority, a sense of looking at the world from a higher place, each gay ironic experience is a sublime reaffirmation of a gay world view. Such is the erotic and ironic joy of locker-room voyeurism.

While being in the locker room brings many pleasant erotic and ironic possibilities, it is important to be responsive to the sensibilities of others. Tactful honesty in the locker room is the best policy. A masters swimmer said:

> There are different kinds of voyeurs in the showers. My friend and I are different kinds of voyeurs. I don't like the kind that I am that much, which is to say, the discreet voyeur—although maybe I'm not as discreet as I think I am. But I do try to go for discretion, which my friend really doesn't go for unless he thinks he's about to get punched in the nose. I'm trying to train myself to either be brazen or not do it at all. The idea of covertness is so old-style homosexual, taking what you can get in little bits; it's not an attractive pose. The modern homosexual doesn't want to be seen to be doing that. On the other hand, it can go in the other direction, in which you are the other kind of homosexual— the kind who hangs around showers and leers.

Another fellow commented on the importance of tact when gay men are in the locker room.

> Locker-room voyeurism is a great opportunity to see a lot of men without their clothes on. I'm not always that subtle about it. It depends on who it is I'm looking at, whether he seems to like being watched, whether he seems to be gay, in which case I don't have to worry about it so much. Sometimes I'm quite blatant with people who I think are interested in my watching them. People should be allowed to look at other people. It's quite natural to be curious about

what another person looks like. I'm sure that all the straight men look at each other. It is perfectly reasonable to expect that if you are anywhere where there are other people around, they are going to look at you whether you have your clothes on or not. If you're interested in sex, it's important to be sensitive to the person that you're trying to approach. I don't enjoy being stared at if I'm not interested; it makes me feel uncomfortable. I think that one should be aware of whether the person one's looking at appreciates the attention one's giving them.

The sensibility of change can also shape one's gay experience of the locker room. Given that there can be hostility from homophobically orthodox men when they find gay men in their midst, it is important for gay men to have a strategy, the most effective of which is to claim the high ground of legitimacy, which comes with being out of the closet.

When I decided to go into phys ed, I had to decide how to present myself; was I going to let the boys with whom I change, shower, play basketball, and wrestle know I was gay? I made it clear to everyone that I was gay and I think because of that I had absolutely no problems. I never heard homophobic comments and got along amiably with my classmates. When I asked one of my coaches what he thought of such a personal policy for gay athletes, he said:

It sounds like the best course of action because I think you set yourself up for ridicule if you put the other person in the power position, in other words, "There's something wrong with me"—and then they jump on that because they smell fear. When we're talking about people who are not sure of themselves [which is how he described many straight male athletes earlier in the interview], and you come out strongly one way, what they tend to do is not say anything, at least not openly to you. They probably did behind your back, but they are not willing to confront; whereas had you showed some signs of being weak, you would have got many more comments because then people would have felt they could get away with it.

Another gay man agreed that it's best for the men in the locker room to know who is gay.

> I think that when straight men know that there are gay guys around them, they feel more comfortable. That's my experience in the locker rooms. They understand what the person is about so there is not the same fear of the unknown. I have never felt bad in the athletic center. Confidence makes all the difference. Truman Capote was very effeminate but also very self-assured, and he went down to research *In Cold Blood* in a very rough part of America and he didn't have any problem. People can sense that you can be intimidated, and if you give that impression, then they will intimidate you. They never bother me.

VII

Fraternities: Gay Culture, Athletic Culture

"The institution of the dear love of comrades."
—Walt Whitman

GAY CULTURE

Throughout this book we have looked at the experience of being strange in a familiar world. As a homosexual adolescent, one comes to realize that one's erotic desires are different from one's peers, so shockingly different, in fact, that one should keep them hidden. The difference between oneself and one's orthodox friends is a difference of interpretations of culture—interpretations that have an enormous impact on the rest of one's life. For those boys who pursue an *orthodox* course, life will unfold as an almost endless opening-up of personal patriarchal erotic and social opportunities that, for the most part, are considered the authentic destiny of men.* The more ethically sophisticated of them will question those opportunities and attempt to change at least some aspects of their orthodox reading of the myths. Whether many of their examinations will reveal the deep patriarchal

---

*These privileges are, of course, also limited by ethnicity, class, ability/disability, and so on.

meaning of their erotic desire for women is doubtful—the consequences of such thinking may well be too disturbing. Most men, however, don't care about the implications of their orthodoxy, and those who do will adapt their orthodox understanding only enough to continue to have access to women who demand change.[1] Those men and boys, on the other hand, who have embarked on a *paradoxical* course find themselves ignoble and estranged in a culture that is also, ironically, their home.

It is the paradoxical intuition of the gender myth that leads to the estrangement of some men and boys. But this estrangement has its resolution. In coming out as gay, two of the most joyful discoveries are that one is not the mythical homosexual monster-in-the-flesh, and that one is not alone; there are others who share, albeit with varying depths of insight, the paradoxical interpretation of our culture and the experience of estrangement. The sociologist Max Weber said that culture is a web of meaning. Paradoxical gender and eroticism, together with the sense of estrangement, constitute such a web. Orthodox gender, its eroticism and sense of belonging, obviously create a web of meaning, a culture that is realized in a multitude of social institutions—such as athletics—and is portrayed in works of art, religion, and the standard histories of our civilization. Orthodox people are integrated in this web and live their lives on the basis of those meanings. Living on the paradoxical edge of orthodox culture is not easy. The threat of the homosexual monster, as it looms in institutions like religion, medicine, and law, as it menaces in the orthodox masculine world of athletics, and as it lurks in the psyche of homosexual men, is just one of many discouragements. But for those who are so inclined and who have the courage to see the world in a different light, paradoxical culture awaits.

The relationship one has with paradoxical culture is filtered through the triad of gay sensibility. When *de-emphasizing* paradoxical culture, one moves toward orthodox culture. Seeing life in the context of *irony* and *change* allows the paradox to illuminate life. The word "gay" represents a positive attitude to the paradox and its implications, and so paradoxical culture is best understood as gay culture. Because we live in many contexts, in some of which gender and its eroticisms are of no, or at least negligible, significance, we should keep in mind the fluidity of these cultures.

216

Shared Sensibilities

The gender paradox is the heartbeat of gay culture. Grounded in the integrity of the paradoxical reading of the myth of gender, gay culture is the principled world in which gay men can meet each other and understand themselves: socially, intellectually, linguistically, artistically, ethically, emotionally, politically, spiritually, erotically, athletically. It is a world that both creates and is created by gay people—people who are in a constant "discourse" with the complex and extensive world of language, ideas, history, gender, class, and other cultural environments. It's essential to remember that gay culture is but one element in a vast synergetic cultural existence. Depending on a host of personal and social factors, some men will emphasize the role of gay culture in their lives more than others will, and pass in and out of its influence at different times and periods in their lives. The discovery of gay culture opens up a world of understanding in which the paradox has pride of place and which, therefore, allows an authentic cultural understanding of oneself and others in the myth of gender.

Gay culture is not purely individual; although subject to a multitude of interpretations and emphases, it is a world that many have in common. It is also a world that is different from that of many others; an important part of coming out is grasping the fact that one's sensibilities are shared by some and are much at odds with others'. As gay men become more aware of the paradox and resolved as to its role in their lives, they come to see that orthodox culture has been organized around patriarchal heterosexuality, giving credence to this orthodoxy through the creation of traditions, ideologies, and institutions and claims to "respectability," "naturalness," "God's plan," and so on. They come to see that the culture in which they have grown up is constructed to serve interests at odds with those emanating out of paradoxical intuitions. Gay culture is one that is *not* orthodox.

It is that distance from orthodoxy that some homosexual men find uncomfortable; despite their knowledge of paradox they prefer to live in orthodox culture, which is, after all, the place from which they came. By de-emphasizing the paradox and their association with gay culture, these men are able to feel at home. The

217

sensibility of de-emphasis is a matter of turning away and ignoring the insights of the paradox. One of the lessons of the paradox and estrangement is the personal experience of the oppressiveness of orthodoxy. Choosing to ignore that lesson, some homosexual men identify with orthodoxy, embracing some of its worst attributes, emphasizing orthodox masculinity and becoming dreadful misogynists. They may join orthodox institutions like the Roman Catholic Church, or Christian biblical fundamentalist sects that are dedicated to preserving the sexist status quo. Or they may work for right-wing political parties, thereby hypocritically taking advantage of their invisibility as homosexual men, keeping orthodoxy in power. Or they may associate themselves with the athletic theater of masculinity, injuring both themselves and others by boxing, playing football, or joining fights in hockey.

For those interested in pursuing a more authentic culture, that is, one that is in harmony with their deeply paradoxical reading of the cardinal myths of Western culture, gay culture is home. In gay culture one finds a "respectability," a "legitimacy" that is denied in orthodox culture.

One way to view gay culture is to see it, in its various forms, as resistance to social regulation. Foucault has argued that the development of sexual categories and the restriction of sex to the family constitute a relatively new form of social regulation, one that emerged out of the developing needs of capitalism, which, as Weber pointed out, required a high degree of social discipline among workers so that they would produce at a maximal level. But we needn't embrace Foucault's seductive history of sexuality to recognize that homosexuality has been socially regulated. The edicts, prescriptions, and legislation of religion, medicine, and law demonstrate the importance that those institutions place on the regulation of sexuality. In a more nuanced, but nevertheless effective, way, through its emphasis on the orthodox masculine leitmotif, athletics has played an important role in maintaining orthodoxy.

One of the interesting effects of this regulation of homosexuality is that it isolated people. Homosexual men saw their plight as individual and so their response to their oppression was individual. Because homosexual men understood their oppression on an individual basis, it was easy for orthodoxy to maintain control

218

through isolation. It has been common for the police to raid gay gathering places in an attempt to destroy the possibility of community. The first major collective gay response to that kind of police attack was the riots at the Stonewall Inn in New York City in 1969. This occasion is generally seen to mark the birth of the modern gay liberation movement.

Gay culture, as a response to homosexual oppression, existed long before gay liberation. It was expressed, however, on a smaller scale. Before the emergence of the overt institutional artifacts of gay liberation, such as independent gay presses, gay-owned gay bars, and gay sporting clubs, gay culture was geographically more transient and frequently more covert. Not having control over their gathering places, gay men were at the mercy of nongay, sometimes hostile, bar owners and the police. Publications that dealt with homosexuality sympathetically were few and far between.

Until the 1970s, there were no gay sports clubs. Gay culture was hidden from the general public. Private parties were the major social venue. Gay culture circulated through extensive "underground" social networks. Some gay athletes knew each other and would socialize quietly and out of view of their nongay teammates. Until gay liberation, many homosexual men remained locked in their closets. This was especially the case for athletes, and among professional and high-performance athletes, it still is. A major contribution to the development of the triad of gay sensibility has been this covert aspect of gay life.

Although the lives of many gay men were successfully circumscribed by the horrors of the homosexual monster myth, many others refused to bend to its power. As was mentioned earlier, one of the effects of the social regulation of homosexuality was that it isolated people; the response to social control, therefore, tended to be individual. Gay men, in order to survive, become keenly aware of how to behave in different circumstances. This is at the heart of passing and the fluidity of the gay world. Gay men would make their paradoxical orientation known at selected times and in selected ways, depending on the situation. There were some gay men who chose not to pass. Their response to society's attempt to control homosexuality was to be blatantly homosexual.

Quentin Crisp, the "naked civil servant," embodied flagrant

homosexuality. "Blind with mascara and dumb with lipstick, I paraded the streets of Pimlico."

> I assumed that all deviates were openly despised and rejected. Their grief and their fear drew my melancholy nature strongly. At first I only wanted to wallow in their misery, but, as time went by, I longed to reach its very essence. Finally, I desired to represent it. By this process I managed to shift homosexuality from being a burden to being a cause. The weight lifted and some of the guilt evaporated. . . . I went about the routine of daily living looking undeniably like a homosexual person. . . .[2]

One of the foremost techniques for social control over homosexuality was denial and silence. Homosexuality was known as "the love that dare not speak its name." Some people found this hypocrisy intolerable; they refused to deny their paradoxical orientation. "My function in life . . . was to render what was already clear blindingly conspicious," said Crisp.[3] One of the ways to strike back at the silent social denial of homosexuality was to behave in a way that forced people to take note. In the minds of many people, including many homosexual men, effeminacy and male homosexuality are indistinguishable. "I was over thirty," says Crisp, "before, for the first time, I heard somebody say that he did not think of himself as masculine or feminine but merely attracted to other persons with male sexual organs."[4]

Fem

Flagrant effeminate behavior by men is commonly taken as a sign of homosexuality. Frequently, when gay men want to call attention to the gayness of a situation they will use effeminate signs, such as a lisp, swish, limp wrist, reference to "ladies' " clothes or jewelry—"darling, where are my pearls?"—or the use of feminine names, pronouns, and habits in reference to gay men: "Oh, Eunice! Who does her hair?" It used to be common that when a young man came out, he would be given a feminine pseudonym, a metaphorical new dress for the debutantes' ball.

220

Effeminacy is a sign of homosexuality because it emphasizes the gender paradox. Kate Millet describes the effect of drag:

> As she minces along the street in the Village, the storm of outrage an insouciant queen in drag may call down is due to the fact that she is both masculine and feminine at once—or male, but feminine. She has made gender identity more frighteningly easy to lose, she has questioned its reality at a time when it has attained the status of a moral absolute and a social imperative. She has defied it and actually suggested its negation. She has dared obloquy, and in doing so has challenged more than the taboo on homosexuality, she has uncovered what the source of this contempt implies—the fact that sex role is rank.[5]

Feminine signs, whether they are used by women or men, signify deference to power and subordination. When people use those signs they indicate their sense of place in the myth of gender. A woman behaving in an effeminate way expresses her sense of her subordinate place in the gender myth. Interestingly, while very few people find limp-wristed women offensive, many find limp-wristed men offensive. This is because an effeminate woman is doing what is expected, namely, expressing her lack of mythic power. An effeminate man, however, expresses his abdication of power. For a man to behave effeminately is an expression of the paradox. With each flap of his wrist he slides deeper into the underclass and, in so doing, betrays the birthright of men to mythic power. Such gestures are violations of masculinity, insults to the meaning of manhood. This is why they are met with such contempt by so many, including many gay men who long for the power of patriarchy. Fear of effeminacy in men is the fear of breaking, overtly, with orthodoxy in the myth of gender, which is, after all, the usual way of seeing oneself and others.

Effeminacy in men is a revelation of paradoxical intuition. Whereas getting fucked is, for a man, the ultimate erotic experience of paradox in our society, the effeminacy of drag is the ultimate nonerotic experience of paradox. Men who feel the paradox most powerfully may allow themselves to give it its most obvious nonerotic expression by doing drag. Because drag is such a powerful, blatant, and radical undermining of masculinity, many gay men feel uncomfortable with it. Consequently, most gay men adopt modified effeminate expressions.

And this brings us to one of the bare nerves of contemporary gay culture: "the effeminate homosexual stereotype." This is a difficult issue for some men. Perhaps the most uncomfortable part of knowing the paradox is also knowing the estrangement that goes with it. Homosexual effeminacy intensifies estrangement by making the paradox, which is in some ways easier to keep secret, public. A phys ed student, illustrating his fear of being seen as different, told me:

> The only thing I still don't like about [being gay] is the public attitude toward it. And I think a lot of gays bring it on themselves, the so-called obvious gays give the rest of us a bad name, if you want to put it that way. It's how I look at it and it's not fair. If I were straight I would look at a stereotype and say, yes, that's gay because they are the ones that are visible, that walk around not being masculine, really being feminine, as far as I'm concerned. . . . The stereotypes are exactly what I see in the bars. I don't want to be associated with it.

His fear of association with effeminacy is homophobic. One of the painful experiences of homosexual youth is of being different, being on the outside of orthodox culture. Many gay men prefer not to see themselves as outsiders. A gay runner told me:

> My images of gay people were the stereotypes, the gay person who is very effeminate and very obvious. I remember sometimes riding on the bus and watching men who lisped when they talked or were very flamboyant and I thought, "That's not me. That's not the image I have of myself. . . ." So I rejected the images that I saw, [that] offended and threatened [me]. Effeminate men threatened me, not to the point where I would be abusive to them, but where I would ignore them. There was part of me too that was angry at them because this is where people are getting the image of what we are like and we're not.

Many gay men find it easier to come out of the closet by thinking that they are just as masculine as their straight buddies. That portrait of homosexual masculinity, as we have seen, is not true to its subject.

Because of the stigma against homosexuality and the fact that people read the orthodox/paradoxical interpretations of the myth at different degrees at different points in their lives, in daily life gay men often temper their effeminate self-expression both to make life easier and more congruous with the personal ebb and flow of paradoxical understanding. The impulse to behave effeminately depends on a number of factors. One's temperament probably plays a major role. Social settings, of course, can make an enormous difference. If one is working in a conservative law firm, it is unlikely that while there, one will "flap" too much. Living in a homophobic society, many gay men are reluctant to make their homosexuality conspicuous by behaving effeminately. The extent to which one feels the need to hide homosexuality determines one's behavior.

Behaving effeminately is understood as a "flaunting" of homosexuality. Said a wrestler, "[Effeminacy is] the negative image in terms of something *not* to be—if you've got to be gay, then don't be like *that*. I've got that from people at work. They can deal with me as I am, but if I ever let my wrist go limp or make a blatant 'queenlike' comment, they hate it—it's going too far; 'don't flaunt it!' "

I have known many hundreds of gay men in my life, and virtually all of them express themselves, at least some of the time, in traditionally effeminate gay ways. Sometimes they do it deliberately to call attention to the gayness of a situation. But often it is a seemingly subconscious nuance that informs their speech and gestures. In fact, some gay men are surprised when their effeminate manners are remarked upon. There is a gay way of speaking, what might be called a "gay accent."[6] It tends to pursue a melodious development of the phrase, which emphasizes the lighter qualities of the male voice, dwelling on some vowels while perhaps drawing out the sibilant qualities of the letter "S." It may exaggerate a style of speech, be it a precious English accent, the drawl of the Southern belle (Truman Capote and Tennessee Williams were famous for that one), or the special qualities of famous leading ladies: Tallulah Bankhead—"Daahling"; Joan Rivers—"Can we talk?"; or Gloria Swanson—"All right, Mr. De Mille. I'm ready for my close-up."

Gay effeminacy is not a confusion about gender or a form of transsexualism. Having a paradoxical interpretation of oneself in the gender myth doesn't mean that one feels less of a man or more like a woman. "I certainly don't feel un-male. I like my cock. . . . I sure don't feel like a fake female. That's not a cunt by any stretch of the imagination," said one of my interviewees. All the gay men I spoke to were uncomfortable, to some degree, with the orthodox division of masculinity and femininity and its relation to themselves. Said former runner Jim Pullen, "I'm just what I am. I have noticed throughout my life that that's somewhat less than completely masculine. I know that the way I do things, the way I move and the way I talk, is different from heterosexual men my age. I don't consider myself masculine or feminine."

A swimmer said:

> I don't think I'm ever really very masculine. I'm not sure how I walk, if I have a certain gay look when I'm walking. But I think my voice sounds very gay, and by watching my face, the way I move my eyes, the way I use my hands when I'm talking; so I think I look very gay. I've never really tried to look any different. Before I came out I wasn't really aware of it and when I was aware of it I didn't really care anymore. I don't know, when I'm swimming—do I have a certain stroke that denotes it! Or in a gym, I wonder what I look like in a gym. I wonder if they can say, "Huh, that's a faggot over there." They probably can.

Many of the men I interviewed contrasted their appearance of masculinity with their true sense of themselves. "If someone sees me when I'm perfectly still, because I have heavy masculine physical features, they will think I'm masculine. The minute I begin to move and talk, it's game over. I don't think of myself as masculine but I don't think of myself as fey either, so I don't know what I am. I think my body is very masculine. I like my body in the ways that I like other men's bodies. I don't think of myself as masculine genderwise."

Above all, gay effeminacy is an ironic expression of the insights of the gender paradox. Because irony is the authentic understanding that emerges out of the gender and homoerotic
paradoxes, estrangement, and the experience of passing, irony
is basic to gay culture. This is why effeminacy has been a feature of "homosexual" culture for centuries. Except during the
seventies and eighties, homosexuality was associated with effeminacy among gay men.* Standard entertainment in homosexual bars and clubs has been drag shows. The effeminate
homosexual was the hallmark of gay culture. Mary McIntosh
points out that in eighteenth-century England, effeminacy and
transvestism seemed virtually synonymous with homosexuality.
The terms for homosexual men used during that period emphasized effeminacy—Molly, Nancy-boy, and Madge-cull, for example. "Edward Ward's *History of the London Clubs*, first
published in 1709, describes a club called 'The Mollie's Club'
which met 'in a certain tavern in the City' for 'parties and regular gatherings.' 'The members adopt[ed] all the small vanities
natural to the feminine sex to such an extent that they try to
speak, walk, chatter, shriek and scold as women do, aping them
as well in other respects.' "[7]

The history of homosexuality is the history of gender paradox;
that's why throughout that history the words for homosexual men
have referred to effeminacy: fags, nancies, sissies, and so on. Our
contemporary use of the word "faggot" as a derogatory term for
homosexual men comes from the contemptuous term for women
as worthless.** In reference to homosexual men, this usage was

---

*In the seventies and eighties, masculinity became a preoccupation of gay cul-
ture. An interpretation of that masculinity will be discussed in the "Butch" section. (p. 230 ff).
**There is a false belief that "faggot" refers to the medieval practice of burning
heretics at the stake; buggers, being considered heretics, were burned like a bunch
of sticks, a faggot. Warren Johansson argues that "faggot" is an Americanism of
the twentieth century. Any relation to burning heretics at the stake, he says, is
erroneous folk etymology. (See Johansson, "The Etymology of the Word 'Faggot,' "
pp. 16–18.) Although the *Oxford English Dictionary* fails to include any reference
to sexuality in its definition of the word "faggot" (the OED did ban certain words),
it does include "a term of abuse or contempt applied to a woman." Eric Partridge,
in his *Dictionary of Slang and Unconventional English*, concurred, giving as the
first definition of "faggot": "a 'baggage'; a pejorative word applied to a woman."
The *Dictionary of American Slang* says that since 1940, "fag" has meant "a homosexual; an effeminate man." They suggest that the etymology ensues from "fag"

unknown in England at the turn of the century. It appears in America for the first time in an American dictionary of slang in 1914: "Amongst female impersonators on the stage and men of dual sex instincts, 'drag' denotes female attire donned by a male. Example: 'All the faggots (sissies) will be dressed in drag at the ball tonight.' "[8]

There are many gay expressions that illustrate the work of irony in the effeminate dynamics of gay culture. The word "Mary" calls up a world of ironic significance for gay men. "Get you, Mary!" With this, artifice is in the spotlight. Under ironic scrutiny, an appearance is held up as such, destroyed, and replaced by a deeper understanding of the truth.[9] Gay irony has a nose for artifice born of the special understanding that gender paradox gives some men of the so-called naturalness of orthodox gender and sexuality. The intuition of the paradox leads attentive gay men to an appreciation of the *artifice* of gender. Gay men, being aware of the fluidity of gender from the experience of passing, know its superficiality. When a gay man "butches it up" and takes his masculinity as orthodox, as do some athletes, the gay observer's response is "Who is *she* trying to kid!" Such masculinity, given the gender paradox, is a conceit. By using the feminine pronoun in reference to a man, the gay ironist calls into question the orthodox manhood of the man. (The feminine pronoun "she" has become more popular than "Mary" as of late. They mean the same.) Gay men will use the feminine in a nonaccusing way also. Having the shared experience of the paradox, passing and so on, we are all "Mary." Gay men will call each other "girlfriends"; two men who are just friends and not lovers are called "sisters."

Edmund White said that this use of the feminine is sexist. "Since one man generally calls another 'she' in an (at least mildy) insulting context, the inference is that the underlying attitude must be sexist: to be a woman is to be inferior."[10] To be a woman in our culture *is* to be inferior—that is what the myth of gender is all about, but, for the most part, the gay use of the feminine is not insulting; in fact, it articulates the subtle criticism of being

---

as a cigarette, since cigarettes, when they were introduced at the end of World War I, were considered effeminate by cigar and pipe smokers. The association between "fag" and negative effeminacy is, therefore, clear.

placed in the gender order, a criticism that is deeply rooted in the paradox. Primarily, it is an invocation of the paradoxical view and an intensification of ironic apprehension. It may be true that gay men who would not refer to *themselves* as "girls" are being both sexist and insulting when they place *others* under that parasol; but that is a dangerous position to put oneself in, Mary. When a man refers to a man as "she," he is saying that "she" is a member of "the club," which is to say that he has a place in the irony of gay culture. As Wayne Booth would say, irony is instrumental in "the building of amiable communities."

Effeminacy in gay culture is an ironic expression of gender paradox. The orthodox masculine disapproval of effeminacy in men is a fearful reaction to the undermining effects that gender paradox has on mythic masculinity. People will say that effeminate men make them sick. I believe them. I was once on a carnival ride, a kind of ferris wheel, that turned me upside down and spinned me around, causing me to lose my focus on the world as I knew it; I found that nauseating too. Resistance to gay effeminacy is an attempt to de-emphasis the significance of the paradox, and for those who know the paradox personally, it is a willful ignorance of the meaning of their own profound intuitions.

Camp

One of the manifestations of gay ironic sensibility that has become a distinct cultural form is *camp*. Camp abstracts the ironic experience of the gender paradox and applies that form to phenomena that are not necessarily related to gender and eroticism. Because it resonates with the basic intuitions of paradoxical life, camp has been an important part of gay culture. Although gay men do not have sole title to the estate of camp, they are, in all likelihood, its chief tenants. Susan Sontag, in her famous essay on camp, said, "Not all homosexuals have Camp taste. But homosexuals, by and large, constitute the vanguard—and the most articulate audience—of Camp."[11]

The sensitivity gay men have to camp is born out of their experience. Camp is a form of disguise that intentionally gives away its identity. Philip Core, who has written an encyclopedia of camp, said: "There are only two things essential to camp: a secret within the personality which one ironically wishes to conceal and exploit, and a peculiar way of seeing things, affected by spiritual isolation. . . ."[12] Camp sensibility arises out of the history of homosexuality as a hidden world aching to uncover itself; it is born of the painful experience of estrangement that finds its antidote in irony. The title of Core's book is *Camp: The Lie That Tells the Truth.* Drag can be seen in this light: dressing like a woman when one is not is a fabrication that reveals the paradox. It is the element of camp that distinguishes drag from female impersonation. A female impersonator is nothing more than a man in women's clothing, a simple deception, a mere imitation of feminine style; a drag queen, on the other hand, is a sophisticated interpreter of gender paradox, expressing herself through the juxtaposition of masculine and feminine accoutrements and bodies. It's for this reason that the most expressive drag is radical drag—muscular, hairy men in slinky, sequined gowns and bouffants.

Camp, above all, is style. One of the great camp aristocrats of homosexual history, Oscar Wilde, epigrammed: "In matters of great importance, the vital element is not sincerity, but style." This appreciation of forms is integral to camp. For gay men, this stylistic acumen grows out of their experiences of the paradox, the deep intuition of gender as a form, and of passing, the conscious appropriation of forms for the sake of survival. It renders the notion of "naturalness" shaky. Forever astute in these matters, Wilde said: "To be natural is such a very difficult pose to keep up."[13] Camp is like a postmodern sensibility: form is content. "Camp sees everything in quotation marks," said Sontag.[14] Camp style is characterized by exaggeration and extravagance—witness typical examples of radical drag. (See Fig. 41.) Art nouveau, art deco, and much of postmodernist design are camp styles. Camp is a loving appreciation of failed seriousness; it converts the serious into the frivolous. "The whole point of camp is to dethrone the serious. . . . Camp involves a new, more complex relation to 'the serious.' . . . One can be serious about the frivolous, frivolous about the serious."[15] The camp sensibility expresses a true disdain for the earnestness that is born of a shallow grasp of life and conventions. "One must have a heart of stone to read the death of Little Nell without laughing," said Wilde about Dickens's sentimental novel *The Old Curiosity Shop*.[16] By using the camp sensibility, gay men can communicate their shared worldview. The use of camp sensibility depends on the company. A volleyball player told me:

> I'm definitely a lot more campy with a certain group of friends that I play volleyball with—mind you, if I play volleyball with another group of friends, I probably wouldn't be half as campy. I think it has to do with how well I know you.

The camp implications of gay men getting muscles were illustrated by a remark on exercise I heard this fellow make to one of his friends. "If you use a rowing machine, you'll get a stomach you could wash your nylons on!"

The camp sensibility percolates through gay culture and is manifest, among other places, in gay community sports clubs. Probably the oldest gay sports organization in North America is the Judy Garland Memorial Bowling League. Its devotion to camp is perhaps more significant than its interest in bowling. (See Fig. 42.) Judy Garland was a singer and movie star of particular significance to gay culture. *The Wizard of Oz* is camp heaven. Gay men identified with Judy because she was cast into a world over which she had no control, in which she was expected to be what she was not. In real life, she was eventually destroyed by drugs, drink, and loneliness, a fate that many homosexual men saw— perhaps see—for themselves. Judy's pathos is not something with which all gay men identify. It is true that there are many "sad homosexuals"; a history of oppression is not easily eradicated. To many gay men, the sad era that Judy represented is finished but not forgotten. Indeed, the riots at the Stonewall Inn followed immediately Judy's death; having lost their heroine, that police raid was the last straw for gay men. The following is a report of one man who was there:

> I had been to Judy's funeral that afternoon, and I went home to cry a little, and listen to some records. I was going to go out that night, meet some friends, hit the bars. We

couldn't get into the funeral, but we stood in the street, and I had had enough of crowds, but decided, oh what the hell, might as well go out. Ron, a guy I knew, called and said that a lot of us were going down to the Stonewall, because a friend of ours was going to be Judy in drag. I thought that was a little tasteless, but I went and we stood around and talked about how awful it was. And then all of a sudden the cops burst in and the first thing you know, I'm screaming and kicking. Some cop starts pulling me toward a wagon, and I shout: "Take your hands off me."[17]

And so with this shift in attitude, the modern gay liberation movement was born. But "lest we forget" our past, the Judy Garland Memorial Bowling League is a kind of camp memory to "our war dead."

The names of the teams in that league and its "sister" camp league, the Toronto Historical Bowling Society, are a cornucopia of camp sensibility: Wilde Oscars, Betty Boop's Bowlerettes, Bugtussle Beauties, Flo's Floozies, Judy's Vice, Betty Ford Clinic, The MunchPins, Carmen's Mirandas, Beauty School Dropouts, Three Jacks and a Pair of Queens, Vaseline Alley, Altered Straights, Twisted Sisters, and MGM Grand. The players, the large majority of whom are men, often take pseudonyms as a joke. One year, many picked names that would make them wives of famous Canadian athletes: Mrs. Victor Davis, Mrs. Wendel Clarke, Mrs. David Steen, Mrs. Alex Bauman. One of the bowlers, Jim Pullen, told me: "I became Mrs. Victor Davis, so anytime I was bowling badly under my name, I would change my name to Mrs. Victor Davis and see if she could do any better." At the annual bowling league picnic, which they call the Garland Games, there are events like girdle hurdles, purse put, drag relays, and the high-heel kick.

Butch

Effeminacy was a major characteristic of gay culture until the 1960s or early 1970s. After a short period in which gay liberationists aped the pseudo-androgynous style of the sixties' New Left

230

hippies and love children—who turned out to be notoriously and hypocritically homophobic—a new style emerged; here the emphasis was on manliness. This seemed to reach its peak with the popularity of a disco music group, The Village People. One of their best-known songs had the lyrics "Macho macho man. I wanna be a macho man." Gay bars ceased to be the milieux for "pink poofters"; the style became distinctly masculine. Blue jeans, construction boots, leather jackets, and lumberjack shirts were de rigueur.

The rapid change in the appearance of gay men at this time was curious. Many civilized homosexual men took on some of the worst features of crude American heterosexuality, trying to be "natural, casual, and manly." At that time, *all* of style underwent a change; under the influence of the counterculture, "formality" was discredited. It was, in many ways, the heyday of the American way, the pinnacle of an American sensibility: "Gee, shucks, I'm just plain old me." In the seventies, even *haute couture* had "natural" pretensions: earth tones, handmade belts, beards, heavy, crude jewelry. People reupholstered their fine furniture in burlap-like fabric, paid extra money for used-looking blue jeans, and bought blow-dryers to style their new "natural-looking" long hair. Gay men were not immune to this trend.

For gay men, being natural and manly was just another affectation, a new form. Camp was at work in the extravagant manner in which gay men took up the down-home style. It was rather like Marie Antionette and her friends, who often enacted the *bergerie* in the garden at Versailles, pretending to be simple folk tending the farm. Bogusly dressed as construction workers and telephone linemen, gay lawyers and hair dressers stood around in smoky grottos that had been tarted up to look like barns, drinking beer out of cans and eating unshelled peanuts from open barrels. It wasn't unusual to find elegant gay men at posh dinner parties wearing lumberjack shirts and construction boots, rapturously discussing Dame Joan Sutherland's performance in the Metropolitan Opera's latest production.

This gay affectation of masculine style was much more than a commitment to the dernier cri. It was a response to perhaps the most appealing call of the gay liberation movement: sex. Gay liberation made homo-sex both respectable and immensely avail-

231

able. Everywhere in gay culture there were enticements to having sex: bars, baths, and pornography proliferated. There were even learned books published on the sociology of "getting sex," explaining the advanced state of gay sexual-delivery systems.[18] Being basic to homoerotic desire, masculinity became the plaza of a flourishing culture committed to homo*sexual* expression. With this surge of homosexual commerce in the 1970s, there was a shower of masculine homoerotic images. And so as sex moved to the center stage of paradoxical culture, gay men were faced with a puzzle. The erotic and nonerotic expressions of the gender paradox lead one in two seemingly different directions, masculinity and effeminacy. Put simply: butch is hot and drag is not.* Looking masculine is a definite boon to homosexual life. Butch drag, consequently, became the modus operandi for many (ironic) gay men. By dressing up as camp real men, gay men were able to satisfy both their erotic desire for paradoxical masculinity and their talent for ironic self-expression. Ersatz masculinity became the pith and soul of gay masculinity as it emerged in gay culture in the 1970s. The "hot jock," which I described in Chapter Five, is a contemporary distillation of that ironic, homoerotic masculinity.

In the gay liberation literature of the time, much was written about the change from effeminate to masculine style.[19] In much of this literature there was considerable disapproval of the development. I think that many of the earnest writers of this period failed to see, or at least appreciate, the ironic eroticism that was then at work in gay culture. The style or manner of gay men became macho—but it was *only* a style. A famous leather bar in Amsterdam was known as Leather and Lace. The name highlighted the irony of the men who frequented the bar. Beneath the butch leather exterior were men who, (perhaps) metaphorically, wore lace panties. The gay macho anthem by The Village People had a very important sense of irony. The lyrics are not "I *am* a macho man," rather "I *wanna be* a macho man." The Village People were not real macho men; they affected the style of macho

---

*There are men who find drag queens erotically desirable, although the testimony of some drag queens is that they are significantly in the minority.

men, and thus manifested the camp irony of paradoxical culture.

AIDS has dimmed, somewhat, the sexual flame of gay culture. Fear of infection has forced many gay men to de-emphasize the sexual expression of paradox. But this doesn't mean that the paradox is any less present. A variety of safe-sex practices make it possible to continue to engage in healthy homosexual activities; condoms have become a staple sexual precaution. But there are gay men who don't like using condoms because they are wary of their tensile strength, find them cumbersome, too inhibiting of physical stimulation, or have not yet been able to eroticize them, to overcome or translate their association with the orthodox world; some of these men refrain, therefore, from sexual activity. The ecstasy of fucking has been diminished; for some, this is a considerable loss of paradoxical expression. The long-term psychic costs of this repression of desire have yet to be seen.

Gay culture, however, is not limited to fucking with or without a condom. The implications of the paradoxical interpretation of the cardinal myths of Western civilization are enormous. (Tracing those implications in the works of notable homosexual artists, intellects, writers, and athletes would be illuminating, and I hope some will make it a project. What role, for instance, did the paradox play in Alan Turing's brilliant decoding of the messages encrypted by the Germans' "enigma machine" during World War II, in Cole Porter's music, or in Bill Tilden's revolution of tennis technique?) As I have already suggested, gay culture has important nonerotic dimensions. When gay men say that coming out allows them to be themselves, they are not only saying that they are comfortable having sex with men; just as importantly, they are saying that coming out has allowed them to make sense of their lives within the nonerotic contexts of the gender myth.

Gay Culture in Gay Sports

Gay culture is manifest in a variety of social organizations. The offspring of the gay liberation movement, gay sports groups have grown to be a dominant force in that fraternity, institutionalizing in sports the shared sensibilities of gay culture. The International

233

Gay Bowling Organization has affiliated leagues in more than sixty-five cities and membership in excess of twenty-five thousand. The North American Gay Volleyball Association has 135 competitive teams playing at the AA, A, BB, B, and C levels, and in cities like Toronto and New York the number of recreational versus competitive teams is at least two to one. The North American Gay Amateur Athletic Alliance, which oversees gay softball, has member leagues in twenty-four cities. In many cities there are a variety of gay sports organizations. In Toronto, for instance, there are clubs offering soccer, softball, running, tennis, swimming, wrestling, volleyball, cycling, bowling, curling, and an outing club that offers a range of activities such as bicycle tours, cross-country skiing, hiking, camping, canoeing, horseback riding, parachuting, and white-water rafting. Most gay community newspapers list the activities of the clubs in their respective cities; gay hot-lines usually have information on local sports clubs; there is also a publication, *The Gay Yellow Pages,* that is published yearly in several volumes according to North American geographic areas, listing information on bars, baths, hotels, and gay organizations including sporting groups. Gay sports groups, although concentrated in the largest cities, are active in smaller centers as well.

Gay sports are seen by most of their participants as primarily a social enterprise where they can be themselves in a place other than a smoke-filled bar.

> I write a sports column for *Xtra!* [a gay community bi-weekly magazine], and I've interviewed everybody from curlers to guys on the volleyball team, tennis players, etc., the whole spectrum, and from all of them, inevitably, you get the same comment, "Well it's a really healthy environment; you get to meet somebody out of the bars."

In the age of AIDS, health promotion has become an integral part of gay culture. Gay sports club offer a healthful alternative to the alcohol-dominated world of bars.

A former college basketball player and now avid gay sports participant described how he saw the relationship of bars and sports in the gay world.

The most common form of the subculture is the bars, but there are a lot of gay people who don't go to bars or who used to go to bars but don't drink or smoke anymore. I don't go to bars socially very often, but being involved in gay sports—and since the biggest money-maker in the gay community is the bars, and they support the teams—you are sort of required to go to the bars and spend money there because they are buying your uniforms and paying for the team to go to Houston or wherever. So even those who don't like the meat-rack kind of atmosphere in the bars still end up going. That's why I think gay sports is so important, because it's a healthy alternative to the bars, away from smoking and drinking.

For many men, with the discovery of gay culture comes a sense of finding a home. This is a resolution to estrangement: finding a culture in tune with one's deep interpretation of the cardinal myths. A competitive swimmer told me how he feels about gay society.

It's a whole society within itself and I like to think that it's compassionate, not superficial. I'm really surprised at the size of the gay community. There are so many facets—the swim group, all sorts of support groups. I'm glad that they are there, especially now with the whole AIDS thing. I haven't been overly involved, my swim club is the first real involvement in it. [How did it feel the first time you went to the swim club?] Strange, I wondered whether it was some-one's excuse for a raging video. Is this going to be some sort of scene? Once I was there and in the water, it was fine. I *was* curious—also, it was the idea that drove me to go there. It seemed novel; it made sense. Yes, I felt I was part of something, you're with people you have something in com-mon with. It felt good all around.

Myles Pearson, also a swimmer, said:

All the gay sports, gay fathers and lesbian mothers—there are so many organizations that are so helpful to people coming out, people in the community. I think it's wonderful. It ties it together in a stronger community. I guess it gives me a sense of security. There are people there who care. I'm not here alone. It's a comforting feeling. Like the Italian community or the Portuguese community, they have their organizations. I sort of feel that although we are considered an invisible minority because you don't look . . . well, I guess some of us do, but yeah, I feel a sense of security, and of pride, too.

Along with being gay goes much thought about its significance and estrangement. Gay sports is a milieu where the paradoxical view is given space; its meaning can be probed, casually, informally, in the context of ordinary life, such as athletics. In gay sports, being gay is infused into an everyday activity rather than isolated as it is in gay politics, coming-out groups, or other forms of gay activism. John Goodwin, the rower, described the difference he sees between mainstream and gay athletics:

Just the essential part of running, there isn't any difference, it's more of an unspoken thing. If you choose to do a lot of running and you want to get into racing, it's going to be a struggle if you're working at the time, to find time to train, and you're doing that *and* you're gay, you kind of incorporate the two. It's a social thing as part of your sports and a lot of the conversations that I have with people when I'm running kind of bounces back and forth between running and your sexuality. So that in one breath you're talking about the issues of being a gay person and also being a person who's interested in running, but in a straight running group, that would never happen. You would talk a lot about running, but you certainly wouldn't talk about being straight with them.

Straight runners talk about things, but they aren't necessarily struggles, not struggles that are common. If they are having trouble with their family life, I don't see it's being a group struggle, it's a private thing. The gay thing is—you can talk about everything from counseling to organizing benefits, dances, to being members of other groups that are connected, and on and on. Finding new members, getting a higher profile, and setting an example.

Goodwin's involvement in gay sports has made him think somewhat differently about his involvement in sports in general. "It's a rebound from my original involvement in sport." He remembered the estrangement he felt as "the only gay athlete" and now hopes that the increased visibility of gay sports groups will change that perception with other young gay athletes. He sees himself as helping to create a positive image for young gay people.

It's not only a lot of fun but I'm also with a very large group of gays and lesbians and that's new for me. I didn't really think gay groups were that good an idea but now I've changed my mind, I think it is very supportive. So, for example, this gay running group that I'm in will probably get some profile so that some kid in high school who is on a track team will hear about it—Front Runners, this gay running group—which at least gives him some indication that there are gay people around who can organize and do this running that parallels what his experience is on the track team. It wasn't around when I started out so I think that my goal is, I suppose, to enjoy all those things but to also ensure that it's never mistaken for anything but a gay group and there are reasons for it being a gay group.

As I said earlier, in the mainstream world of sports it is assumed that everyone is heterosexual; so for gay men there is not usually a sense of a shared sensibility. Many young gay men and boys avoid team sports because they feel estranged in those orthodox groups. Gay teams offer them the opportunity to enjoy the camaraderie of teams, which was impossible in orthodox settings. Being a member of a gay club, one becomes aware of commonality. John Goodwin said:

When you're competing in sports in a straight environment, you're never walking around thinking, "Oh, here we go, we're a straight group and we are going into the restaurant to eat dinner." But when you're with a cycling group of ten fags and we stop at the Swiss Chalet and everyone's talking about the busboy, you think differently. I'm thinking, "Quiet, stop staring at him," and everybody else is asking these probing questions about the busboy or about the boy at the next table, and you can do nothing about it, you realize that you're in a straight restaurant and in that environment, you are a little nucleus sitting in there. So I think that's a lot of fun.

Another man emphasized that he can feel more at home in a gay sports setting than in more orthodox environments. He, too, said that a shared sense, a sense of community, was part of the experience of gay sports.

I actually played volleyball at work for a while and really enjoyed that also. The nice thing about playing gay sports is, again, that it's really nice to interact with gay people in other than a bar environment. And it's also really nice to do sports and do activities where it's very comfortable, you can talk about whatever you want. You don't have to be on guard. You can joke around, you can play. That's a good feeling. It's also the sense of community that comes from it. The sense of being part of and of also fitting in. It's not that I didn't fit in at the work one, I did, but it's more fun. It is probably more relaxed in gay sports. It's nice to be able to hug each other too.

Normand Boucher, a volleyball player, said that the way that gay culture is integrated into gay sport makes it a more attractive venue.

Probably I would play in a straight league if I wasn't in a gay league now, but I might not get so much pleasure out of it. I've made so many friends in the gay league and it's nice to play with people that I have something in common with. Part of the fun is the three-day trips to Chicago, etc., the drag cheerleaders and all of that and the parties.

238

The gender and homoerotic paradoxes become institutionalized in gay sports clubs. At volleyball tournaments there are drag cheerleaders. The Sisters of Perpetual Indulgence, an ironic order of gay male nuns, will often make appearances at athletic events like the Gay Games. The Judy Garland Memorial Bowling League places camp at the center of their affairs. The homo*erotic* paradox also plays a role in gay athletic institutions, sometimes overtly, as in various wrestling networks that help connect gay men who like to openly mix wrestling and sex, and at other times more covertly: gay sports groups simply make it possible to meet athletic men.

In New York City there is an extensive gay body-building center called the Chelsea Gym, which has over three thousand active members. It has reciprocal arrangements with other gyms across the U.S., including Boston, Washington, Atlanta, Houston, Denver, and Los Angeles.

Gay sports clubs create an easy milieu for socializing. Myles Pearson said:

> The gay club seems a lot more fun [than straight clubs he has been in], it's a lot more social. Maybe gay people like to party more. Straight people just seem too straight. They have a straight sensibility—they have to get home and cook for their husband or do this or that. They seem afraid to socialize. But gay people don't. They are usually quite anxious to do so.

In large cities, gay social life has in many ways revolved around bars and steambaths. But these can be rather impersonal settings where a premium is placed on physical beauty. They are also socially demanding: one needs to be at least somewhat aggressive just to initiate a conversation. The gay sports leagues create a more intimate and familiar setting not unlike that which straight people have with community groups and families. Orthodox lives tend to be centered around children and their schools, extracurricular activities, taking the kids to this and that, visiting with grandparents; there is an established social superstructure that supports their way of life. Gay people, generally, don't have that superstructure; they have been estranged from those elements of mainstream culture. Jim Pullen described the social function of the Judy Garland Memorial Bowling League.

> The bowling league is a place for people to hang their hats. They can feel that there are friends out there. There is something to do once a week that doesn't involve work or bars, but it does allow you to see the same people on an ongoing basis. You have a team, there are five people who are counting on you to show up—so you are committed to a little group. You get to meet a lot of people on the other teams that you are playing with. It gives you something in your life that's a constant, gives you a place where you are wanted whether you are gorgeous or homely, tall or fat—those other people really want you to be there. Even if it's that superficial a level, it's good to know that people are counting on you.
>
> Gay sports is especially good for people who do not have the social graces that others might, people who find it difficult to meet other people and talk to them. Bars are stressful places in which it is very difficult to talk to people. When you're bowling, you have to talk to the others and you start giggling about how badly you're doing—suddenly, you get to know seventy-five people by name. It creates a social world. The gay peer-counseling center sends people who are having trouble coming out or who feel very uncomfortable in the bars to the bowling league.
>
> You can see the groupings of friends who started [in the bowling league]. They may no longer be playing sports but now they do bridge and have dinner parties. We must have had thousands go through our league over the last fifteen years or so.

Another man said that he became involved in gay sports because he found the alcohol-centered life of the bars progressively less attractive. He also found that the human dynamics of gay sports were more appealing than his experience in bars. In gay sports he is more comfortable being himself.

> I was very tired of bars and there was only so much social outlet you could have drinking. "Being myself" in my situa-

tion means getting away from being dealt with as an object, which seems to happen so much in society, period, straight and gay. But I did not like or ever try to treat people as objects—which, in a bar, "that is attractive," and it's like, "that *physically* is attractive, I want to possess that body for ten minutes to do with it what I want." I don't like that kind of reaction. I have difficulty with that. When you're involved in sports, what counts is how you are reacting with people, putting forward your best effort on the field. It didn't matter if you made eighty-five errors, if you're putting forth your best effort, that's hot.

From softball I went into bowling and they were trying to organize a bowling league for people going to San Francisco for Gay Games One. All of a sudden you were meeting a lot more people who had something in common with you, and again, there wasn't the objectification that I was used to in the bars, so I spent much more of my time doing these things.

Through gay sports groups, gay men develop networks of friends. These networks may extend well beyond the limits of one's own city. Jim Pullen said that traveling to softball and bowling tournaments over the years has given him friends in most major cities across North America. The gay wrestling network also establishes contacts in far-flung places, making it possible for a man to call another man in an unfamiliar city, get together to wrestle and socialize.

Often, one social sports structure gives birth to another. The Judy Garland Memorial Bowling League threw annual lavish camp banquets with drag shows, strippers, and many members in exotic costumes. To raise money for the Lesbian and Gay Community Appeal (a gay version of the United Appeal), some of the bowlers produced an extravaganza called DQ (Drag Queen), based on the show they had created for their banquets. Eventually it developed into a structure of its own, producing fundraising shows annually. In Toronto, the softball league grew out of the Judy Garland Memorial Bowling League, as did the volleyball league.

Gay sports offer gay men an opportunity to enjoy athletics and camaraderie without the masculine leitmotif, a feature that has often kept gay men and boys out of athletics. A former competitive swimmer told me:

> You're more likely to find the machos among the straights and you're going to have some difficulty with them; they tend to be afraid [homophobic]. There's a closer bond, another dimension to all you have in common when swimming with gay athletes. With straights, there's a missing element, you're excluded from the camaraderie, or you might exclude yourself. I'm more comfortable with gays but I don't have great difficulty with straights. In the gay club, I'm completely free to be myself, within reason. I can't do my Esther Williams, although, actually, it might go over very big. It's very liberating, you're among your brothers and sisters. I enjoy it. There's so much commonality.

A volleyball player told me that in the North American Gay Volleyball Association, machismo is more the exception than the rule.

> It's a very competitive sport, especially the North American Gay Volleyball Association, but those wonderful, superb athletes are the most outrageous screamers you've ever seen and they'll do it right there on the court. And to me that's like, one for us. So masculinity and sports . . . I've never seen so many hot-looking men per square inch in my entire life. They are beautiful, gorgeous men. In the NAGVA—these are the competitive teams chosen from each league. They are in really good shape and they're wonderful to watch, but as far as masculinity and sport is considered . . . The ones with the stupid phoney butch images don't last long. They just don't, it's a team sport. You're the exception, not the rule. The only exceptional team—no, they were very genuine guys, but they just happened to be Middle America butch, that's all. These are farm boys from Kansas, but that's what they were really like. They seemed quite butch and I thought, "Oh shit, don't tell me, act bored,"

and no, this was them. The edge was taken off, it wasn't harsh butch, almost like innocent butch.

Gay outing clubs make it possible to go camping, canoeing, parachuting, and so on without pretending to be butch.

I went winter-camping as part of my phys ed course. Although the men I was camping with were certainly very pleasant, they were all straight and I found that the greatest strain was not that it was forty below zero, or that I had to ski all day with a fifty-pound pack on my back and I'd never been on skis in my life before, or that my shoes didn't fit properly, or any of those usual physical hardships. The strain was that we were all supposed to be taking it like men. Now, I like challenges, I find hard portages satisfying; I like running hard, long distances and that sort of thing, but I don't like it so I can prove that I'm a man—because I don't care about that sort of thing. I'd rather make light of the difficulties by saying something like "My God, these ski boots are so tight they're going to ruin my pedicure!" But you know, they just wouldn't have found that very funny. And I would want to stop and quietly look at the scenery, but they were so into being adventurers they thought it was a waste of time. When I go camping or skiing or whatever with gay people it's entirely different. We like the hard work too but we see it in a different light, a more ironic one perhaps.

Gay men who are truly out of the closet are generally not interested in proving orthodox masculinity through the masculine leitmotif of sports. Among the many organized gay sports, with the exception of water polo and wrestling, there are no contact sports.* (In these sports, serious injuries are rare, whereas in hockey and football they are commonplace; in fact, injury is part

---

*There are gay touch football clubs. But touch football, which is meant to avoid injury, is nothing like real American football, where the point is to prove you can take it.

of the orthodox masculine appeal of these games.) It is true that sports such as tackle football are expensive, in that they need a lot of equipment; but I doubt that that is the major reason for their being ignored in the pantheon of gay sports. The brutal orthodox masculinity involved not only symbolically but also physically in football is at odds with the paradoxical reading of the myth of gender. Once one has accepted the paradox as the authentic understanding of oneself in the myth of gender, there is little reason to subject oneself to such warlike barbarism. A man who is very active in the organizing of gay sports said of violent contact sports: "Sports like that, you'd have to spend too much time trying to pass [as straight]—you know, who cares, fuck it! I'm going to play sports and relax, and not to play more of that."

There are some gay men, however, who even in the context of gay sports pursue an orthodox masculine style. One of the founders of a gay softball league, Jim Pullen, said:

> I think we have a great deal more fun; we are not so serious about team sports as are straight men who have gone through the hockey and football syndrome and are used to the big team thing where it is really important to win. Most of our people come into softball not with a team sport background, but as individuals with little background in sports. There are some gay athletes who have been through the team sport syndrome who become terribly competitive in the gay league, who really want to win and are really bad-humored when there is a call against them or when someone on the team doesn't do well. They have every bit of difficulty dealing with it as a straight athlete in the same situation. There's the throwing of the gloves and the swearing at the umpire, calling each other assholes—they get into a whole masculine aggressive stance, and it's every bit as prevalent on our competitive teams. [This league is divided into recreational and competitive teams.] There are whole teams that can't stand other teams. I was taken aback in softball, how much gay people can mirror their straight counterparts. That you can get yourself that worked up about a sport—you are there on your own free time, the umpire is a volunteer who isn't getting paid for this—that

you can get that nasty to somebody because they called you out when you thought you were safe, I personally have trouble with it. Even at the recreational level, there are gay men who get so worked up. I would say that 25 percent of gay men are as aggressive in sports as straight men, the other 75 percent are less so.

This masculine aggression may be a symptom of the sensibility of de-emphasis: "I'm gay and just as masculine as a straight guy." As we have seen, this is an inauthentic turning-away from the meaning of paradoxical intuitions. These men will sometimes band together in recreational leagues and try to get rid of less-competitive players. "We're not going to win with *you* on second base, so go somewhere else!" In Toronto, the softball league divided into competitive and recreational leagues. Most players are interested in recreational softball. There are twelve recreational teams and four competitive teams. After the split, Jim Pullen said, "I don't know who's gotten rid of who."
There is sometimes tension between gay competitive and recreational leagues.

The gay volleyball started at a grass-roots level where it's not all that important how good you are. When we started, it was half women and guys who had never played before, it was just an evening out to yell and scream and hit the ball around. Then they gradually got organized and gradually got better, which is what happened to the softball, when they had the big catharsis where they split into two. Of course, the recreational was three times as large as the competitive section. The gay American leagues haven't been able to find that water level; the competitive players have driven the recreational players out so that in huge cities like Los Angeles and San Francisco, there are only three teams. If you aren't flawless, a really good athlete and an excellent ball player, they don't want you on the team. So there's really no room for a beginner or someone who is not so talented; until recently, they didn't have recreational leagues. Now they are starting to spring up. But in Toronto we have the largest league in all of North America, which is odd because softball is not a major sport up here, we never played it in school. It just came through Toronto's gay community. They're just beginning to get this sort of thing in the USA.

In bowling, there is no conflict between competition and recreation because the system of handicaps evens out the good and less-than-good players. "From the worst to the best, everyone is on an equal footing. It's rather more how you play on a given day against yourself. This is why bowling is so popular—you don't have to be good at it to do well. You can be the worst bowler in the league and still be a star on a given night."

Volleyball, at least in Vancouver and Toronto where they operate similarly, has addressed this problem by developing a symbiotic relationship between the competitive and recreational aspects. Of the Toronto league:

Our gay volleyball league was so successful last year and we only have so much gym space that this year they didn't even advertise when the first night would be, and they just said the first 144 people who sign up are going to be it. And they had 126 people sign up the first night. So we are very successful because it's a recreational league and they pick the best players from that to be on the competitive team. The competitive team also does its part by helping coach and instruct and by being team captains and referees. And, in turn, the recreation league pays the entry fee for the competitive teams to go to various gay volleyball tournaments.

Gay culture is in some ways an amorphous creature. Although the paradox gives people a common basic intuition about the nature of gender and its eroticism, according to the triad of gay sensibility, people respond to that intuition in different ways. One man I spoke to came out of the closet in the context of the gay liberation movement (the sensibility of change); in fact, he was president of a university gay organization *before* he had had sex for the first time. He has gradually moved away from a social circle dominated by gay liberationists' commitment to the sensibility of change and has found such a variety of responses to paradoxical intuitions that he finds it difficult to believe there is gay culture.

I don't think there's a gay culture. There may have been till five years ago, when the community was small enough so that there was a commonly held group of assumptions. Five or ten years ago you could have said that it meant a range of things from specifics like reform of the Police Commission and Human Rights Code, stopping queerbashing on the streets, to a broader sense that being gay also meant aligning yourself with other communities in struggle or in crisis. That you could assume that a gay man would also be progressive and nonsexist and nonracist and all that kind of stuff and now you can't. You find lots of conservative, misogynistic racists around who have taken advantage of all kinds of things in the gay community. And so earlier, the culture would have produced a certain kind of larger view that was identified with gay and also more than that, but I don't think now you get that. You get people whose gayness influences how they behave, but I don't think it can be pulled together and called gay culture. Now, that doesn't mean you can't have things like Fruit Cocktail [an annual gay community revue in Toronto], that it isn't important for artists to identify themselves as gay, or for novels to deal with gay themes and so on, but I don't think it's quite so rigidly frontiered.

If we think of gay culture as a common political commitment, as he is suggesting above, then there is obviously no culture common to all gay people. But if gay culture is thought of more fundamentally as the common intuition of gender paradox and its attendant estrangement, which is then filtered through the triad of gay sensibility, then it is possible to speak of gay culture that is common. To draw a parallel: there are aspects of "American culture," patriotism for example, which are seen differently by different American people. American patriotic culture exists as a web of meaning, but it is the subject of substantially different interpretations. Likewise, paradox and estrangement are cultural phenomena that give rise to various responses among those who are aware of them.

Whereas politically oriented gay organizations tend to be concerned with being "politically correct," such as being overtly *gay* organizations and expressing solidarity with other minorities and "progressive" causes, gay sports groups are sometimes more conservative. There are gay sports organizations that have made explicit decisions not to use the word "gay" in the name of their organizations, preferring to maintain a somewhat covert facade. There are groups that will state in their constitutions that they are purely social groups and "are not political," and they purposely distance themselves from other gay organizations. Here there is a mingling of the progressive and conservative sensibilities of change and de-emphasis: although they want to create positive gay social environments (change), they prefer to ignore, at least officially, the political implications of their organization (de-emphasis).

One of the principles of "movement" politics is solidarity with other oppressed people. Most gay organizations will make a point of declaring their nondiscriminatory policies. The North American Gay Amateur Athletic Alliance (NAGAAA) calls itself a "nonprofit organization dedicated to promoting amateur softball for all persons with a special emphasis on gay participation." (Although they have implemented "sexual orientation statutes" for participation in some tournaments—at the Gay World Series there is a requirement that there be an 80/20 percent ratio of gays to straights—one can't help but wonder what test might be given if someone's declared "sexual orientation" is challenged.)

Many of the men I interviewed found their experience of being gay leads them to sympathy with women and other oppressed groups. Normand Boucher said:

> I cannot believe that straight stereotype that gay men don't like women. Gay people and women seem to get along so well, naturally. I feel very close to what women are fighting for, politically and socially. I feel very close to most minorities, just because being a minority gives you an experience of having to fight for whatever you have.

248

Listening to the implications of the paradox, some gay men understand their plight in the broader context of oppression. This, of course, contributes to their understanding of gay culture. Eilert Frerichs, a Protestant clergyman who was once married, said that it was his patriarchal sensibility that was the problem in his marriage, not homosexuality. Until he came out as a gay man, he did not personally understand the oppression of women.

> I was quite patriarchal myself until I came out. I was unbe-
> liveably threatened. My innermost security, the sense of
> who I was, and I think that's the reason why Heather and
> I separated. I don't think it was the gay thing at all. She
> forced me to confront patriarchy, not even terribly subtly.
> All of a sudden mail arrived for her addressed to her in her
> maiden name and I wondered, "What the hell's going on
> here, aren't you my wife? Why don't you use my name any-
> more?" Our marriage deteriorated from then. I experienced
> a strong sense of competition from her. She was a highly
> accomplished person in her own right, and now we talk
> about that quite a lot and we can confront *now* that history
> in a way that I couldn't then, not at all. The reason is that
> only since coming out—not since becoming a homosexual,
> but since becoming a gay man—have I begun to identify
> myself with the oppression of gay people, have experienced
> it in some sense, and identified with that whole history, and
> it no longer is an intellectual exercise for me. Now I know
> I'm an oppressed man myself, goddamn it all. I can under-
> stand, I *know,* what it is like and what it is all about.

Some gay men devote much attention to the way that their being gay influences their perspective in general.

> I've thought about that a lot, especially in my view of the
> role of women in society. I consider myself a nonsexist per-
> son; although I've been conditioned similarly to all males in
> society, I still feel I'm fairly nonsexist. I like to believe that
> I would be this way even if I were not gay, but I really feel
> that my experience of being gay has influenced definitely

my sensitivity to certain issues. When you are a member of a group that has been marginalized and ostracized from the mainstream, for me it's heightened my awareness of prejudice and ostracism and things that go along with that. I have a hard time when I see gay men that are blatantly sexist or racist. I think, "How can you be that way—you've experienced discrimination based on your sexual orientation," and to me, how can a person not make that link with the commonality of other people who are ostracized or discriminated against? It's beyond my comprehension. I think, definitely, being gay has made me more aware and more sensitive to other people's pain in different life situations.

Solidarity with gay men, women, and ethnic minorities, although certainly not a universal sentiment among gay men, is one of the texts of gay culture. In the early days of the gay liberation movement, solidarity was a political concept born of a variety of leftist sociopolitical analyses and tied to revolutionary theories. Many people now benefit from the revolutionary politics of the early gay liberation movement, but that rigorous political analysis is not, for the most part, the basis for the solidarity that gay people may have with each other.

Gay Culture and the Gay Games

The spirit of the gay movement changed through the eighties; the meaning of being "gay" modulated. Under the influence of the New Left, gay liberation began by rejecting the medical conception of homosexuality as a pathological condition; it preferred to see homosexuality as a political issue. This analysis of oppression, it was thought, would sow the seeds of liberation. Some gay activists made distinctions: "gay men and lesbians" grappled with the dialectic of oppression and liberation; "homosexuals," on the other hand, didn't. Both the medical and political treatments of homosexuality were "objective." By studying the pathology of homosexuality, the illness could be cured; by understanding the objective conditions of oppression, liberation could follow.

250

Gay liberation in the 1980s became more self-consciously subjective; the focus was on a special experience of being gay—gay pride. Most people have given up "rapping" about the politics of their oppression. That is not to say that gay men are not oppressed or that the politics don't exist, but there is a new, more personally meaningful, less-defined, and also less-rigorous gay way of looking at the world. This new worldview is focused through the prism of the personal experience of gay pride. Less a formal political agenda, gay pride is more an attitude, a disposition gay men and lesbians have toward themselves and each other. Gay pride has become the contemporary axis of gay culture, which comes to life in events like the international Gay Games.

The ideological impact of gay athletics is important and not without precedent in other political arenas. Athletics have been used by nations as an expression of ideology and as a means for galvanizing the population and building its support for the government's political agendas.[20] Consider the hoopla around the achievements of national teams at the Olympics or the effective way in which the prohibition against South African athletes participating in international sporting competitions has expressed international distaste for apartheid. Gay liberationists have seized upon athletics as an ideological instrument of gay politics, the fruit of the gay sensibility of change.

The major gay event throughout North America, drawing literally hundreds of thousands of lesbians and gay men to major gay centers such as New York and San Francisco each year, is Lesbian and Gay Pride Day. Said a gymnast: "Part of gay culture is Gay Pride Day, that's our day. Just as there's Christmas for everybody else, we have Gay Pride Day. We can say 'Look, I'm gay, this is my day, get off my case, I'm going to do what I want.' That to me is culture for homosexuals and you know we need more days!" An important expression of that pride can be found in gay athletics. In New York City, a major event in the gay pride festivities is the Gay Pride Run. But the most prestigious international gay athletic event is the Gay Games, which were first held in 1982 in San Francisco.

The Gay Games were founded by a former USA Olympic decathlete, Tom Waddell, in 1982, and organized in 1986 by a community-based alliance, San Francisco Arts and Athletics Inc., and supported by hundreds of volunteers and benefactors. The 1982 Games involved 1,300 male and female athletes in sixteen sports. In 1986, the Gay Games attracted 3,482 athletes with a ratio of men to women of 3:2 in a total of seventeen sports. (This is to be contrasted with the 1988 Olympics in Seoul where the male/female ratio was 2.5:1.) Among the events were basketball, soccer, bowling, cycling, diving, triathalon, softball, physique, track and field, marathon, power-lifting, volleyball, swimming, tennis, and wrestling. In conjunction with the Games was an artistic festival, called "The Procession of the Arts," which featured over twenty events including dance, theater, and plastic-art exhibits. Although athletes came from many parts of the world, the majority were from North America. Gay Games III in Vancouver, called Celebration '90, had over 7,200 athletes registered (which totals over 120 more than participated at the 1984 Los Angeles Olympics) in thirty-two sports. There was also an extensive cultural festival of films, plays, art exhibits, readings, book launches, and music concerts.

The organizers of the Gay Games I and II had considerable legal difficulty with the United States Olympic Committee. Originally, the Games were to be called the Gay Olympic Games. In the USA, the USOC has a legal monopoly on the use of the word "Olympic." Although they have not protested in the past to the "Diaper Olympics," "Dog Olympics," "Police Olympics," and "Rat Olympics," the USOC took legal action against the Gay Olympic Games, forcing the organizers to rename the games simply, Gay Games. After winning their legal battle against the Gay Games, the USOC tried to recuperate their legal costs by, quite viciously, putting a lien on the house of Tom Waddell, a former U.S. Olympian. In retrospect, Waddell said, "We were using it [Olympics] initially to describe our games, but let's look at the Olympics. The Olympics are racist, the Olympics are exclusive, they're nationalistic, they pit one group of people against another, and [are] only for the best athletes. That doesn't describe our Games."[21]

In her opening address at the 1986 Gay Games, highlighting the ideological focus of gay pride, Rita Mae Brown said, "These games are not just a celebration of skill, they're a celebration of who we are and what we can become. It's a celebration of the best in us."[22] The Gay Games constituted for many athletes an exciting experience of self-affirmation. Everyone I interviewed who had participated in the Games was enthusiastic.

> It felt marvelous. I really felt like I was making history, and you know I'm not some silly, starry-eyed faggot who's . . . It really was marvelous, fantastic. This from a hard-assed, capitalistic, corporate son-of-a-bitch, but it's true, it was wonderful. An experience of a lifetime, I wish that some- how I could impart that to other gay athletes. So that they would all want to be there, they don't know what they are missing.
>
> The sheer size, the numbers, the sense of festivity the entire time, the pride that you are representing your city, camaraderie . . . a lot of people who played volleyball had played against us before [at other tournaments] and we knew them as friends, so it was really quite marvelous. This was something I feel every gay man should really try to achieve. There are age categories, and it doesn't matter how old you are, you can start training now for something. I think the participation aspect is great.

Another man tried to describe his experience of the Gay Games.

> I still haven't been able to put that into words. The very first Gay Games were definitely emotional. I haven't been able to exactly measure how—I certainly know that I have not experienced the emotional shock that I had the very first time, with walking into the opening ceremonies and all of these people, spectators, in the stands. I know the experi- ence made me grow as an individual. It was personally gratifying. I think a lot of it had to do with gay pride. A lot of it had to do with the fact that no longer were people hiding part of themselves.

A former college basketball player described his experience of Gay Games II:

> The opening and closing ceremonies were in an old football stadium in San Francisco, it wasn't full capacity, but there

were about twenty-five thousand there. It was modeled after the regular Olympics, and so when you have all these people marching in behind their national flags, state flags, and city flags, it was just amazing. You walk in and there have already been two thousand marching ahead of you and they are all on the football field, all lined up. These people are standing and giving you an ovation that has gone on for half an hour before you, and still clapping, everyone's crying, and it's very emotional. It was the high point of my life. I've played basketball in Madison Square Gardens with ten thousand people watching, and that still wasn't the feeling like this was. It was gay pride—here's the cream of the crop, the ones who are willing to put their identities and reputations on the line and say, "Here I am and I'm a gay person."

The emphasis of the Gay Games was on participation. There was one thing in swimming that really showed how well things went, and they even reported this in the straight papers. There was this forty-five-year-old housewife entered in one of the swimming events. It was only two laps of the pool but she got up there and hadn't swum since high school, and people had already swum and finished and she was still finishing her first lap, and she finished, like, ten minutes later than everyone else. But while she was doing it everyone was getting up and cheering for her and giving her a standing ovation, and she was so embarrassed and saying, "Why are they cheering for me, I came in last," but the feeling was, we're cheering for you because you're doing the best you can. The whole idea of personal best. And that was what epitomized the whole feeling of the event. And afterward the media interviewed her and said, "Why are you here?" and she said, "Well, my son's gay and I'm here to support him." There were a lot of little events like that.

At the athletic events the ambience was not unlike mainstream masters sports. Gerry Oxford, who swam at the Games, said that around the pool, the primary feeling was that it was an athletic event; only secondarily did it feel like a gay event. "However, the athletes did kiss each other when they got to the end of the pool and touch each other's bums. So in this respect it was unlike mainstream sports.... Well, you know, you spend four days in the hot sun wandering around the pool in a swimsuit, there's going to be a lot of bum touching." At the physique contest, the MC said, "You seldom go to an event like this where the audience looks just as good as the contestants." Gerry said of the physique audience, "Tits for days. I mean, muscle queens abounded and they were just going to see what others were doing."

Gerry reported that "sex was there in a really up-front, really all-inclusive kind of way." He said that there was not a sense of athletes on display with the spectators being the consumers of their sexiness. There was a sense that everyone there was a sexual being, that sex is part of everyone's life, that everyone desires and everyone is desired. "It really didn't have the feel of sex as a consumer item—it was something that everyone experienced."

Commenting on the similarities and differences between Gay Games II and the World Masters Games, which were held in 1985, in which he also competed, Gerry thought they weren't the same. "I went to the Gay Games alone and didn't know very many people, so there wasn't the sense of being there with a group like there was at the World Masters. That was the difference for me. It's funny, the World Masters struck me as being more comradely but that's because I went with comrades, half of whom were gay." He said that at the Gay Games, there was a sense that things were really happening in teams. "If you weren't there with a team, you felt sort of out of it. There wasn't a lot of interaction between teams." He found there wasn't a lot of intermingling. "It was hard if you weren't with a big group to get to know people."

Tom Waddell, in his "Welcome Letter" of the official handbook of Gay Games II, said, "The message of these games goes beyond validating our culture. The Gay Games were conceived as a new idea in sport based on inclusion rather than exclusion. Since anyone from anywhere is welcome to participate in this event, we transcend the traditional problems of ageism, sexism, and racism, and just as importantly, nationalism. There are no competing world ideologies in these games." Waddell's claim that inclusiveness in sport is the creation of the Gay Games is overstated. The masters movement had been promoting these concepts for many years. Exclusivity is confined to qualifying times for some competitions—at the first World Masters Games, there were no qualifying times, nor are there at many local, regional, or state meets. But that inclusiveness is the central philosophy of the Gay Games is vitally important, regardless of whether they are the originators of the concept. In this policy of inclusiveness is a powerful response to estrangement, especially that which gay men feel in sports. By creating a festival of athletics and arts dedicated to inclusiveness, the Gay Games are working to change the myths surrounding athletics in our culture. Just as the Olympic Games of Ancient Greece celebrated Hellenic culture through athletic competitions, artistic festivities, and religious rites, so too the Gay Games are a celebration of contemporary gay culture as it is conceived in gay pride.

In the Gay Games, two of the hallmark myths of mainstream sports are undermined. Obviously, the compulsory heterosexuality that characterizes mainstream sports is rejected in the Gay Games. And the masculine leitmotif of athletics is downplayed in that environment. The Gay Games are a place where gay men and lesbians can be comfortable; they can be themselves, they don't have to pass as straight.

Currently, one of the most important issues for gay men is AIDS. Not only is AIDS a deadly syndrome, which in North America has claimed the lives of tens of thousands of young gay men, it is also being used as the springboard for homophobia. With the threat of AIDS, religion, medicine, and the law may reclaim power over the lives of gay men. Some Christian fundamentalists claim that AIDS is God's punishment for promiscuous homosexuality. (This must mean that it is also God's punishment for being black and from the Third World, since it is "heterosexual" black Africans who are the major sufferers of the disease.) The authority of medicine is reasserted through the association of homosexuality and pathology. The power of the law is being brandished with threats of mandatory quarantining of those whose blood tests indicate exposure to the HIV virus; there are estimates that over 40 percent of the homosexual population of America has been exposed to the virus. Ideologically, gay athletics are an attempt to counteract this encroachment of religion, medicine, and the law.

256

Rita Mae Brown also said in her opening address to the Gay Games:

> These Games are very important to us, not just because they bring us all together, but because here we show the world who we really are. We're intelligent people, we're attractive people, we're caring people, we're *healthy* people, and we're proud of who we are.[23]

Athletics is mythically understood as a sign of health.[24] The Gay Games, as a gathering of thousands of physically fit lesbians and gay men, demystifies the pathological homosexual monster. For the participants, AIDS was an important dimension of the Games. When they registered, the package of information they were given included condoms, lubricant, and AIDS information. There were some athletes competing who were diagnosed as having AIDS—one died two days after winning a silver medal. Another of those athletes was Tom Waddell. Four weeks before the Games he was diagnosed with pneumocystis carinii pneumonia; nevertheless, he competed in track and field and hurled the javelin 104 feet, winning a gold medal. He died in July 1987. The vision of vitality these men gave—not only gay men, but also people with AIDS—is striking.

The Ghetto

When gay men come out, they find themselves trying to appraise their relationship to orthodox culture. Some take a great leap and dismiss that culture altogether, immersing themselves in an entirely gay world. Often they will move to a large city, find the gay ghetto, get a job in a gay bar, work for a gay newspaper, play on a gay baseball team, and generally do everything they can to leave behind the orthodox culture from which they came. They will talk disparagingly about the suburbs, their families, and heterosexuality in general. Others prefer to take a more measured approach to their estranged situation. They don't dismiss the orthodox world entirely; they try to see how their paradoxical orientation is related to the orthodox world that was their home. They strive to maintain some connection with their families; they

257

will continue working or studying in predominantly "straight" environments. They will also develop a gay network of friends, become involved in gay causes, and perhaps play on a gay volleyball team. They understand themselves through the mingled sensibilities of the orthodox and paradoxical worlds. Still others restrict their estranging paradoxical experience to the occasional homosexual affair; some are more successful than others at de-emphasizing their estrangement in this way. They will get married, have a family, and see themselves as members of the orthodox world. Their interaction with the gay world is fleeting and has little bearing on the way they see themselves, their families, or their place in the world. There are many men who will live their lives in all these ways during different periods of their lives or, depending on the situation, from day to day.

In all of these cases there is an interplay between orthodoxy and paradoxy. Gay men who throw themselves completely into the gay ghetto are doing so because they find little hospitable meaning in the orthodox, straight world and find comfort in the shared worldviews of other gay ghetto men. They are immersing themselves in paradox while cutting themselves off from orthodoxy. Those who are trying to find a balance between the gay and straight worlds by purposely living in both don't feel uncomfortable with all aspects of orthodox culture and want to derive the benefits of both it and gay culture. And those whose sojourns in the paradoxical world are only occasional and restricted to sexual events see little or no meaning in gay culture, and understand themselves primarily in the light of orthodoxy.

A number of the men I spoke to said they found that in gay society there were expectations of them that they found discomforting. All the serious athletes I interviewed said that they have had negative responses from some gay men they tell they are athletes. Outside of being hot, being an athlete is often seen as an attempt at being too butch. Consequently, gay athletes can feel that they fit neither in gay culture nor in mainstream culture; as gay men they shouldn't be athletes and as athletes they shouldn't be gay. A runner told me:

A lot of people joke about my interest in sports. When I rush for the sports page they go, "What are you doing?" I've had

258

many people, gay people, basically say, "You're interested in sports?!" I know a lot of gay people who participate in sports, but I don't know a lot gay people who are actually sports fans in terms of watching. There aren't that many who will want to go to Blue Jays games. We're a minority among a minority, and do get ribbed about it. It's almost like getting ribbed about living in the suburbs. Again, it's not fitting into some defined category. But I've always been good at breaking those categories, and enjoy being the rebel, being outside the mainstream, even if it's mainstream gay.

A phys ed instructor said that he avoided gay society because of its confining social life.

I had very few gay friends. I think it was my choice, I had access to friends that were gay, but I did not want to hang out with them because they did all the gay things, the stereotype gay things, and I wasn't into doing that. The Sunday brunches and the going out to dinners, but it was all gay, gay, gay, gay, gay. They would be freaked out if you did something athletic or some sport thing, and that bothered me a bit. And they'd think you were just trying to be straight or trying to be butch.

When you talk to someone in a bar and they ask you what you do and you say you're in phys ed, and they say, "Well, you don't look like you're in phys ed," because I'm not a big football-player type. Stereotypes people have of the dumb jock, the whole thing, but being in a gay bar, my only response was, "You think I shouldn't be in phys ed because I don't look like a football player or because someone who's in phys ed shouldn't be in a gay bar," and that's what's happening. They think both. "Why are you in phys ed, you're not allowed to be gay, you're supposed to be straight." So you can't possibly be gay because gays are in hairdressing or they do flower shops. They are saying, you shouldn't be here because you aren't in one of the typical gay professions, you are in something that's not considered gay, unless you're a woman, and then you're okay. And the gay community ends up being a ghetto of pure stereotype gays, and the rest of us do not want to break into that—we just don't want it.

Gay men, like many other people, have become aware of the healthful benefits of exercise. Especially in light of the onslaught of AIDS, more men are taking greater interest in physical health. A runner said:

I don't know if being gay has anything to do with it. I think it's just wanting to enjoy a healthy life, a good lifestyle, with proper exercise and diet and stuff like that. The awareness of AIDS and just maintaining a healthy lifestyle is very important to me physically, mentally, emotionally, trying to lead a balanced life—rest, nutrition, things we learned way back in—when did I learn it?

The growth of the fitness movement in North America and the new interest gay men have in developing muscular bodies has made athletics somewhat more respectable among gay men. John Goodwin said that he has noticed a change in attitudes toward athletes.

In college I was teased for being a jock and it had bad connotations that don't exist today—it meant being a moron who pumped iron. I was always racing off to the sports complex and getting back late, and was teased so much for this sports thing. Then when I got on the team, I was teased about going to art college. There's a new syndrome, almost like a born-again Christian thing, I have people telling me how to run, giving me tips as to how much my mileage should be. These people who just quit drinking and smoking three weeks ago going on about this. So now I'm happy, I can talk about sports and I don't feel as uncomfortable, as everybody seems predisposed to embrace any physical activity. The gay world used not to be supportive, but now it is. It's a lot of fun to see people of thirty-five become fanatical, because it's exciting, it can happen at any age. The environment has changed.

BEING GAY IN MAINSTREAM ATHLETIC CULTURE

Integrity and Coming Out of Hiding

As the gay environment has changed, making it more comfortable for gay athletes to be athletes with their gay friends, so too has the environment changed in much of mainstream sports. Although it is not yet usual for gay men to be known as such in athletic settings, such openness is now possible for some. A canoeing and kayaking coach I know made it known to his club that he was gay. No one seemed bothered by that revelation and his coaching has continued uneventfully. His athletes are comfortable with him coaching, in the locker room, and socializing with him. A swimmer told me:

> I don't find the university athletic facilities to be hostile straight environments at all. I find people are much more vulnerable when they have all their clothes off. Some of the straight athletes may think homophobic things but they probably find that it's not cool to act on those sentiments anymore. If you're homophobic in an active way, you are not going to be accepted by too many people. It's more cool to think, "Well, that's fine as long as they don't do it to me."

Gay culture need not be restricted to predominantly gay environments. Mainstream culture can be infused with gay culture, making it a comfortable place for gay people. Gay pride is not limited to the festivities of Gay Pride Day, the Gay Games, or gay running, baseball, or volleyball groups.

The awkwardness that gay athletes have usually felt in mainstream athletic settings was the product of thinking in orthodox terms, that is, believing in the homosexual monster myth and the ethical superiority of orthodoxy. With the acceptance of paradox, the power that orthodoxy had over gay men begins to crumble. This is what it means to come out: the orthodox interpretation of gender myth and its standard of behavior are specious to those who know the paradox. There is good reason to be proud of being gay. Considering the deep ethical meaning of the gender and homoerotic paradoxes, it is clear that one should be proud of those dispositions. Gender is a myth that subjugates females for the social and economic benefit of males. The sexual relations that embody this mythic division of power are hetero-erotic; this is the orthodox attitude to the myth. Paradoxical gender is a deep intuition that is the rejection of that application of mythic power to oneself. One should, therefore, be proud of the paradox because it is a rejection of despotic power. It is a rejection that is deeper and more personal than politics or other conscious criticisms of the world in which we find ourselves. It is a profound psychic rejection of gender power, which, for most of us, dates back to our youngest years when that power was first being thrust upon us, when we were first learning that we are supposed to be boys, which is to say, eventually to become heterosexual men. The homoerotic paradox is the erotic expression of this paradoxical view of the gender myth. Being proud of being gay is like being proud of being a fine artist, a superb athlete, or an insightful thinker. It is the pride of accomplishment. And the accomplishment is to reject an orthodoxy that is unfair, exploitive, and ultimately cruel.

With the confidence of gay pride, gay athletes can live their lives openly. But orthodoxy, the traditional stance of men in our culture, resists that honest self-expression. Homophobia, being the fear of exposure, which is the fear that the fragile, mythical, and, in fact, chimerical nature of masculinity will be shown for what it is, tries to keep the paradox under wraps. It does this by expecting men to behave like "men," that is, straight. Most men seem to agree with this convention, and by adhering to standards of "normal" behavior exert considerable pressure on those who disagree to act straight also. This is especially the case in athletic settings. And so gay men will often feel compelled to "butch it up" when at the gym. But as gay pride grows with the maturing awareness of the integrity of the paradox, the need to conform to that inferior standard diminishes. In the light of the paradox, the masculinity of athletics loses its orthodox significance, thus making it easier for gay men to become athletes; they come to see paradoxical rather than orthodox significance in athletics and muscles. Gay pride has made it possible for multitudes of gay men who were "sissies" in school to go to their gyms, YMCAs, or university athletic facilities and not feel compromised, or at least too inhibited. A man told me that he is now becoming more comfortable being himself at the university athletic center.

> I'm still slightly concerned about totally camping it up in the weight room, but I'm less concerned than I used to be, partly because I'm confident enough there that I now view it as my territory and I'll bloody well behave as I want to behave, and because it's clear that even when I'm behaving more restrainedly, that I'm not one of those guys, so I'm not going to get to spot them or go off on whatever camping, jerk-off weekends those fucked-up little closet queens have. So, I thought, I don't have much to lose, and because I like it enough that I'm not going to be driven out. There are lots of gay men who don't like the place because of the jerks. But I like it there for a whole bunch of reasons.

There is great power in the use of camp in mainstream settings like athletics. Personally, it overwhelms the sway that orthodoxy has over one's perceptions and allows one to see things with the clarity of a gay ironic perspective. Orthodox masculinity is dismissed as insignificant and paradox is allowed to shine. So that while lifting heavy weights one needn't pretend to be what one is not. You can think: "Isn't it ironic that a queen like me is lifting these butch weights." It proves that you don't have to be butch to be strong; you don't have to be masculine to be an athlete. That insight has great power. It destroys the athletic arena of masculinity, exposing athletic masculinity as nothing more than a myth. Irony is power, the power to destroy superficiality, in this case, orthodox masculinity. It is a refusal to play by orthodox rules, declaring oneself to be above those rules. This is the triumph of paradox, the victory of irony: being a fine, strong athlete doesn't mean you are straight.

Living by orthodox standards is not only fruitless but also inauthentic. And so more and more, gay men are not hiding the fact that they are gay in athletics. But being known to be gay can sometimes be awkward. A body builder told me:

David and I used to belong to a weight-training specialty gym. So we went there, then we stopped going because other men were making remarks under their breath about "these fucking faggots," and that we were after them, and "Why the hell didn't they go somewhere else." It was quite clear, we didn't have the interests that the others had. We were by ourselves and were a little more expressive in the weight room. The owners knew we were gay, up front, but the people that went there learned over time, and when comments were made, and they would cut in and take the bars and go elsewhere, and sometimes you'd get into word battles. I didn't need that. I don't relate to [straight athletes] now. I don't have anything to do with them in a direct relationship.

A basketball player told me:

Most of the time I was in the closet, so very seldom would [athletes say anything to me]—they never directed anything at me while I was in competitive sports, but now that I'm more out and people sort of know that . . . We have a situation at the "Y," I'm playing in a competitive "straight" league, basketball, and we were playing this team with this really obnoxious straight person on it, whom nobody likes, even his own teammates. He's 6'5", 220 or so, and I'm a small person, 5'10" and 200, for basketball. So, anyway, my team was beating his team and we were both tied for first place and whoever won this would be first place for the playoffs, and the frustration of the game, etc. At one point during the game, he had a breakaway, and if he had got it he could have tied it up and possibly put his team ahead, so I dove for the ball, and in the process of knocking the ball out of bounds, I knocked him over. And he took the ball and called me a faggot and threw the ball at me. So I picked the ball up and threw it back at him about ten times harder than he'd thrown it at me, and just walked up to him, face to face, and said, "You'd better be prepared to back up those words." And then his teammates were pulling him back and mine were pulling me back, and it all happened so quickly and there was almost this big fight. His teammates were telling him, my teammates told me later, that he was in the wrong and to shut up and just play basketball. So we got the ball out of bounds anyway. And we won by two points! I don't think the people were necessarily being gay-positive, my straight teammates, I think they were just supporting me because I was on their team. And things like that should be completely extraneous to sports. And his other teammates apologized to me afterward: "He was out of line, he shouldn't have said that." They didn't come right out and say, "We know you're gay," but their attitude was, we respect you because you're a good basketball player.

Homophobia in athletic facilities is not unknown, although it is seldom given direct expression to gay men who make a point of being openly gay. Making it clear that I am gay, and having been in phys ed and having spent time in athletic settings and attended swim meets over the years, I have never been personally confronted with homophobia in those settings. However, Gerry Oxford, who is also a swimmer, said:

I'm not usually quick to notice homophobia. But there's a guy who works in the key office at the university athletic center—he's been working there for a year, I'm in there virtually every day, by now he has to know what my name is. Yet he insists that I tell him my name in order to get my card back. There is another fellow who works there; when he thinks I'm out of sight, he takes a fresh towel in order to pick up my towel, so that his hands won't touch my towel, he makes a face and one of the other neanderthals behind the counter laughs. There is another guy, who is about to become a medical doctor, he hangs around the weight room a lot. He once said to one of my teammates, "How can you swim with a fag team?" She replied, "Well, you know what, I even swim in the same lane with them!"

Knowing that there are other gay people at one's gym, pool, or track makes it easier to feel comfortable. A swimming instructor commented on the reassuring sense he has of knowing there are other gay men around.

It's sort of like an invisible community in a lot of ways. When I'm walking around the university, even though people know I'm gay, I would think that most people would automatically assume I'm heterosexual. So I don't feel as comfortable casually dropping comments about my boyfriend in front of these people because of their assumptions. So it's a real relief to run into my gay friends or straight friends who know, and to realize that I don't have to be on guard every minute of the day.

Another man said:

At the "Y"—there are many gay people there—not 90 percent . . . And I find there's a sense of community, running into people, talking to people, not always knowing people, but just saying "Hi." It says, "We're everywhere!" Not only that, but our lives are very diverse and complex, they aren't lives just pursuing sex and one-night stands, whatever. Our lives include relationships of all sorts. I enjoy seeing gay people working out, riding their bikes, being with male and female friends, walking their dogs. I think all that just gives a sense that there are a lot of choices in life, it doesn't have to be one-dimensional or two-dimensional, but it's multidimensional.

Who's Who: The Gay Gaze

Even the somewhat covert knowledge that there are other gay men around gives one strength in overwhelmingly heterosexual environments like athletics. Gay men are able to subtly communicate their shared worldview by a special gaze that seems to be unique to them. Although it is not always possible to tell who is gay—some men are very effective at hiding it and one therefore occasionally mistakes a gay man for a straight man—most gay men develop a canny ability to instantly discern from the returned look of another man whether or not he is gay. This gay gaze is not only a lingering, but also a visual probing, a sometimes satisfying search for recognition. Almost everyone I interviewed said they could tell who was gay by the presence or absence of this look.

> When I was coming out, it was one of the big questions. "How do you know somebody is gay, other than going to bed with them? How do you know?" And everybody would say, "You just know; you get a sixth sense." And they would say, it's little things, it's how long they hold your eyes, they'd catch your eyes, will they look away or look at you, how the body language is, how meticulously they dress, when they are walking along the street, how they look at things—do they look at the butch red cars and say "Oh wow," or do they look at the flowers. It comes back to a man being gay and what that means.

A wrestler and college teacher said:

> You can usually tell by the look in a man's eyes, the way he either does or does not make eye contact. You can just tell. I've had gay students whom I've known were gay from the moment they set foot in my office, and it turns out, two or three years later, they are coming out and you get the story. I knew before them. Something about the way gay men move or approach the world. . . .

Young homosexual boys can become aware of the gay gaze without quite comprehending its significance. A swimmer told me: "I remember that when I was a boy, I would meet some of the men friends of my parents and they would look at me in a knowing way, and I wondered what it was that they knew. And now, of course, I know." In Stanley Kubrick's movie *The Shining,* there is a similar recognition between an older man, a chef, and a little boy. Their recognition is not of gender paradox, but it is of a special gift of insight. The chef takes the boy aside and tells him

267

that although he doesn't understand his gift at this young age, eventually he will. These are cryptic shared worlds.

In addition to the look, there is also a deportment that is a sign of gayness. "I think gay men have *learned* to carry themselves a little bit differently, and I don't mean limp wrists and swinging hips and so on. I don't know . . . projecting a little . . . 'look at me.' " Another man said, "There is an intensity and sometimes a certain kind of expressed sensitivity. Perhaps because it's not entirely comfortable, there is a certain kind of manner, a certain kind of awareness that makes for a vibration. It is purposeful behavior. I think they are more aware of the need to adjust than the need to have other people adjust to them."

The gay look and deportment are the products of the knowledge of paradox and estrangement, and of adjusting oneself to a world in which one doesn't fit. Having had this experience, gay men can recognize it in each other: "It takes one to know one." One man said that he can almost always tell if a man is gay "by observing in them things that I recognize in myself." Confirming this sense of recognition, another said: "There's something that twigs when you are in the presence of a gay man." He explains:

Straight men don't make, or at least maintain, eye contact. Gays will hold a glance for longer than is polite, and they are glancing in the first place. Straight men will talk to you but they don't give the deep, lingering look.

Gay people are also more self-conscious of doing certain things and therefore won't do it. For instance, straight boys will scratch their ass crack or rearrange their genitals—a gay person would see that as a sexual gesture and therefore wouldn't do it—a straight guy will do it because he is itchy. It's strange, but straight boys are much less self-conscious of those things.

Sometimes the look imparts sexual desire.

Gay men who are out, if they are interested in you, you can usually tell because the eye contact is slightly longer than otherwise. That's a dead giveaway. If a guy looks in your eye and holds it for more than three or four seconds, it's a dead

268

giveaway. With the guys who I'm not sure of, who are not open, I can usually tell too. Especially in sports and athletic situations where you're changing together and you're nude together and realizing how sneaky my eyes can be in a shower. I'm very good at picking it up when somebody else is taking a boo.

The gay gaze is an ironic clue to paradoxical masculinity. A man may be regaled in all the trappings of orthodox masculinity: muscles, deep voice, football jacket, high fives, stiff wrists, cocky swagger. . . .[25] But with just one look, that masculine facade is peeled away, revealing the truth of paradox. By this ironic gaze, gay athletes usually know of their sometimes silent, paradoxical fraternity.

Integration

No more is it necessary to pretend to be straight if you want to be athletic. Inspired by gay pride, knowing that you are not alone, you can be a gay athlete among straight athletes. This often means carving out a space for oneself. The most effective way to do this is to make oneself known as a gay man. When nongay people get to know gay people, the monster myth disintegrates. The playwright Alan Stratton said, "The witness of a human life in action is more powerful than all the fact sheets in the world. When we come out, we change hearts and minds."[26] Normand Boucher said: "This is my personal militancy: Gay Pride Day is fine, but the best way for me to touch people is to be openly out and openly gay in society, at the school where I teach, and be a model of what a gay man is, and this is how people will learn."

The integration of gay men in mainstream sports, and in any other social setting, is only possible if it's known that there are gay people there. In the masters swim club at my university, homosexuality is a non-issue among the members; there are straight men on the team who don't seem to have any reaction to it at all. One straight fellow slipped up only once when he referred to a bar as a "fag bar"; realizing his blunder, he made a point of apologizing. Most of these men simply ignore the homosexuality of their teammates. Said one of my gay teammates, "I suppose that if there were any hostile reactions, those people just would not keep swimming with our team, since homosexuality is a normal reality there."

In New York City there is a gay soccer team, the Ramblers, that plays as one of the nine teams in the United Nations Soccer League. It is the only non-UN team and the only openly gay team. Fighting for their gay honor on the soccer field adds to the team's spirit of competition. Said one of the coordinators: "I wouldn't mind losing as much to another gay team, but when we lose to a UN team we get down on ourselves. During a game you can feel that members of other UN teams are sweating just as much as we are. Probably a bit more so, because they don't want to lose to a gay team."[27] Pitting themselves against their traditional foes, gay teams in a number of major cities compete against police all-star teams. In New York, the gay Big Apple League's best team plays annually against the New York City Police Department's all-star team. After one of those games, the two teams, with lovers and wives, gathered at the Spike, a leather bar in Manhattan. After a few drinks they socialized quite amiably.[28]

Commenting on playing with straight volleyball teams, Normand Boucher said:

In Montreal, the gay team used to play straights, and it was extremely political—the straights didn't want to lose to us. Not because we were better, but because we were a team of fags. And that year we won the championship—we really wanted to beat them too. We knew the fags on some of the straight teams and that was kind of interesting because they were closeted and we weren't.

The happy social, even sexual, integration of gay and straight athletes can occur. There was a party after a meet between the masters swim teams of the Central "Y," the University of Toronto, and the Downtown Swim Club (a gay swim club). The party was at the home of one of the straight University of Toronto swimmers (Paul).[29] One of the gay swimmers (Kevin) brought along his beautiful blond female (straight) roommate (Jacqueline) and another gay male friend (Brent). Gay Brent tried to pick up straight

FIG. 32. *Gay sports clubs and competitions offer lesbians and gay men the opportunity to express themselves not only athletically but also culturally. The above shows the start of the triathlon at Celebration 90, The Third Gay Games and Cultural Festival, held in Vancouver in August 1990. It was an almost magic time, during which intensely happy, healthy lesbians and gay men came together and delighted in their lives and being together. The mood was often euphoric. In mainstream competitive sports the athletes seldom look this cheerful just before beginning a gruelling event such as the triathlon, but the joyful spirit of the games overwhelmed much of the anxiety of competition. PHOTO BY DANIEL COLLINS*

FIG. 33. Over 7,200 athletes from 26 countries participated in 29 different sports at Gay Games III in Vancouver. This man from Toronto was just about to make his first pole vault attempt in the decathlon.

PHOTO BY DANIEL COLLINS

MEN

FIG. 35. *Enthusiastic Australian athletes flew to Vancouver in chartered jumbo jets. This group from Sydney attests to the play of paradox in gay sports. Their rugged masculine appearance is subtly undermined by the presence of a simple string of pearls on a black T-shirt. While the games looked in some ways to be just like mainstream sports, there were numbers of men who made a point of emphasising the gay ironic sensibility by wearing pearls over their more traditional athletic outfits.*

PHOTO BY JAKE PETERS

FIG. 36. The opening and closing ceremonies of Gay Games III brought together in the domed stadium, BC Place—home of the BC Lions football team—athletes, cultural festival participants, and fans in excess of 25,000. At the opening ceremonies athletes were marshaled for their entrance according to their home cities. The above is from backstage at the closing ceremonies, where athletes congregated by sport.

PHOTO BY JAKE PETERS

FIG. 37. Before the Games, Christian fundamentalists lobbied to have them prohibited, arguing that the earthquake in San Francisco was God's revenge on that city for hosting Gay Games I and II and that the "sodomite invasion" brought on by the Games in Vancouver would so anger God that He might cause Vancouver to fall into the ocean. The weather, as it turned out, was perfectly sunny the entire week. People at the Games ignored fundamentalists' limp protests.

PHOTO BY JAKE PETERS

FIG. 38. The condemnations of anti-gay activists had no effect on the pervasive joy of being gay and celebrating that fact at the Games.
PHOTO BY DANIEL COLLINS

FIG. 39. Many participants in gay sports take their gay athletic endeavours very seriously. The atmosphere around the pool at the Games' water polo event was one of the sober team sportspersonship.
PHOTO BY JAKE PETERS

FIG. 40. To do one's personal best was the competitive tenor of the Games. At the swim meet, athletes with a wide range of abilities challenged themselves and each other.

PHOTO BY DANIEL COLLINS

FIG. 41. The earnestness of gay swim meets is usually given its antidote in the camp of the pink flamingo relay, now a standard event at these competitions. The point is for two swimmers from each team to don plastic pink flamingo hats; while one swims the arm pull of the breast stroke, the other does the kick while grasping the legs of the first; at the other end of the pool, they exchange hats and another two complete the race. Over the years this relay has grown into a camp extravaganza, with teams in radical drag making grand entrances. The above picture of the West Hollywood Swim Club was taken by Jake Peters at the 1989 International Gay and Lesbian Aquatics meet in Vancouver.

FIG. 42. *There is a move in the gay sports world to copy the orthodox athletic sensibilities of mainstream sport. But there is considerable resistance to that among many gay athletes. Camp is a major element of the Judy Garland Memorial Bowling League experience.*
COURTESY OF JIM PULLEN

FIG. 43. Dan Gawthrop was one of the organizers of the hockey
tournament at Gay Games III. Hockey is traditionally seen as a
powerful expression of orthodox masculinity. As a gay hockey player
who eschews that orthodoxy, Dan has here taken the traditional
symbols of athletic masculinity and undermined them with camp
sensibilities that give full expression to the paradox. The question
remains open as to whether the hockey stick he is riding should be
read in its phallic significance or in reference to the broomstick of the
Wicked Witch of the West in The Wizard of Oz.

PHOTO BY DANIEL COLLINS

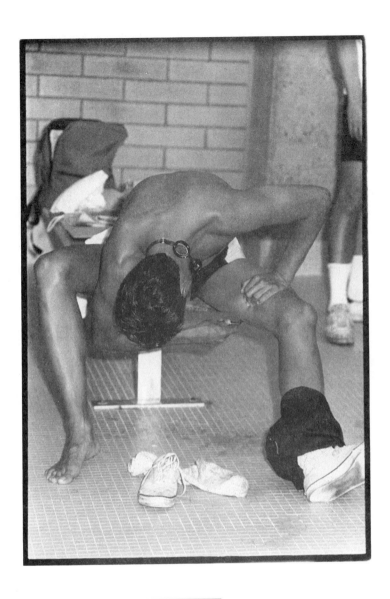

FIG. 44. *It is traditional for swimmers to shave down before major competitions. And many at the Gay Games did so, thus presenting an interesting amalgam of homoerotic and camp ironies. This picture speaks of the homoerotic desirability of athletic masculinity, a masculinity that is somewhat undermined by the camp sensibility of a man shaving his legs, a masculinity that in other circumstances could be salvaged by the fact that it is customary for male swimmers to do so. But the shaving was taking place at a gay meet where the preservation of orthodox masculinity should have little credibility—especially if one considers the significance of the pink flamingo relay (see* FIG. *41).*
PHOTO BY DANIEL COLLINS

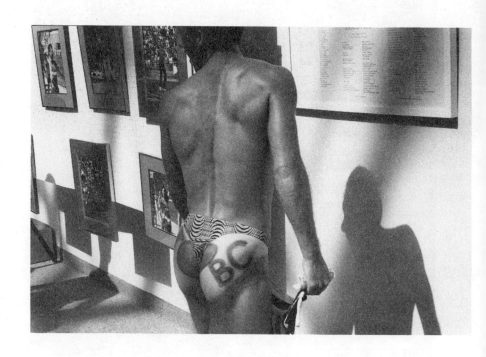

FIG. 45. Every day during the Vancouver Gay Games an arts fair was held in a large glass edifice, called the "Palace of Nations." Bathed in natural sunlight, various gay groups and artisans sold their wares. The Sisters of Perpetual Indulgence, an irreverent order of gay male nuns, were selling T-shirts. The man in this photo is one of the Sisters, showing "her" affection for the Canadian province (British Columbia) that played host to the Gay Games.

PHOTO BY JAKE PETERS

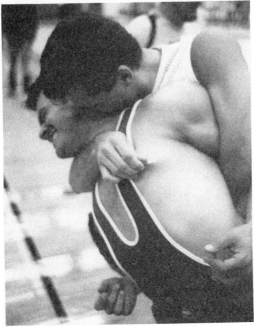

FIG. 46. More explicitly than most sports, wrestling plays on the homoeroticism of masculine struggle. At the Gay Games this event attracted large crowds and many photographers. While the official wrestling was serious Greco-Roman style, the erotic play of the wrestlers when not competing officially affirmed the homoerotic desirability of the sport.

PHOTO BY JAKE PETERS

FIG. 47. *The physique finals for men and women was one of the most lavishly produced athletic events of the Gay Games, held in the most elegant theater in Vancouver. This was the first time there has been a competition for same-sex pairs. The crowd went wild. The above duo are Raymond Vanden Heavel and Neil Trubukovich from New Zealand.*

PHOTO BY DANIEL COLLINS

These pictures of gay athletes show a subtle but important difference between the erotic sensibilities of the pornography industry and of gay athletic culture as it is actually lived. In porn, the gay athlete is an object for consumption. In gay athletic culture, the athlete is someone with whom one shares an erotic world and a way of being in it. At the Gay Games, immersed in that shared world for a week, most of us couldn't stop smiling. The erotic desirability of that truly gay pleasure is an integral part of the gay sports experience.

Paul; Jacqueline came over and started coming on to Paul also. Paul was clearly interested in Jacqueline. Brent saw what was going on and finally confronted Paul and said, "Are you straight or something?" Paul reported that he didn't really know what to say; he thought it would be rude to say yes, so he didn't say anything. Jacqueline ended up spending the night with Paul. Kevin picked up some other man. That, according to one of the gay swimmers, was not particularly significant: "Gay men pick each other up all the time. But getting a man and a woman together, now that's a real achievement. They don't do that sort of thing easily, you know."

This whole story was described by Paul in the showers after a workout. Here there was the delightful irony of straight men and gay men giggling about perceptions of who's gay and who's straight. About that, one of the gay swimmers said, "I liked it a lot. This is integration. Paul had a lot of fun with a woman and all because of a gay swim team."

The integration of gay and straight athletes is not only a possibility but also a reality in some places. But, of course, integration is not possible if gay athletes keep their paradox a secret. Being out in sports is obviously good for the integrity of those athletes who *are* out. Perhaps even more importantly, being out offers strength to young gay athletes who are estranged, feel alone, and have no positive image to give them hope. All the high-performance athletes I interviewed told me they wished they had known of other gay athletes. "It would be one thing off your mind. You could concentrate fully on swimming." John Goodwin discovered years later that one of his coaches was gay. Had he known when he was a young competitor, he said:

> It would have been great, a wonderful revelation. Would probably have saved me a lot of anxiety. I probably would have driven him crazy asking questions, wanting to know more about everything. Ideally speaking, I think it would be important regardless to have a gay coach somewhere, a gay anything. You think of all the sports and all the competitors and there wasn't one person I knew who was gay. It could

have been a hockey player, it could have been anybody, not just a rowing person. The anxiety that I experienced would have been diminished a lot.

GAY MUSCLES

"I don't know what it is but there is something about men's tits that just does a number on my brain! A man's chest is just irresistible," said a gay gymnast.

Although not everyone sees it as being equally important, muscular development has blossomed as a concern of many gay men. Over the last two decades there has been a growing popular awareness that body shape is plastic, malleable, and that, through exercise, anyone can affect the lines of his body. George Smith, who is now in his fifties, remembers that as not always having been the case.

> This business that one could make over one's body into the images that one desired, it was never true before the seventies. People who looked good in gay bars looked good because they were young and they had that kind of body "naturally." And nobody thought anything about changing themselves into that kind of an image. I never ever thought of changing myself into an image in the way one could change oneself into a clone or exercise one's way into this new "gay man." Gay culture was not there in any way. No one ever thought that you could *become* hunky. No one ever thought that you should go to a gym and work out and make yourself into a sex symbol. No one ever thought of dressing up to do that. I'd go out to a bar the same as I would go out to school, which was coat and tie. It was just ordinary. Men used to wear baggy suits and cover up their bodies—they weren't sex symbols.

The fashion and fitness industries have given men the means to transform themselves physically into the images that they desire. But the molding of bodies is not restricted to the fitness in-dustry. The more established athletic disciplines also have their plastic effects. A former pro tennis player told me, "I've talked to divers who have got into diving because they like the way divers look, their bodies." Many athletes know that they can derive both athletic and aesthetic, or perhaps more accurately sexual, benefits from their activities. A swimmer told me: "I work out because I like the athletic experience, although one can't possi-bly downplay the importance of what this is doing to my body. I don't like rowing very much but I do it religiously because I know it's having a good effect on my body. It's not the bottom line but it's always there."

Another man said:

> Being gay encourages me to take care of my body. Being in shape is important for gay men because it makes them more marketable. I think that gay men know more about their bodies, they know what the various parts look like, because it's part of gay male sexual activity—sexual activ-ity is not just genital. Because you are interested in bodies similar to your own, you are interested in your own body. You realize that there are differences between bodies and that you can mold them.

The "new gay man," mentioned above, is the man who has developed his body to reflect his desires and therefore his under-standing of himself. Although this may seem to some to be merely a fashion, and certainly in some respects it *is* fashion, it is also much more. This presentation of oneself, which is, after all, the product of a great deal of work, intentionally signifies the para-dox. The paradox used to be indicated by more obviously effemi-nate signs. A fellow told me that he was once walking with an older friend; they passed a young man with big pectoral muscles, and the older man said, "When I was a budding queen like that, we wore angora sweaters and a swish." Muscles, especially the pectorals, have replaced the sweater and swish as predominant gay signs. The paradox is now being played with greater, perhaps double, irony, emphasizing a masculine appearance. Rather than undermining masculinity by *effeminate* gestures and appearance, (single irony) gay men, not being masculine in the orthodox sense, undermine their seeming masculinity by the use of *masculine* signs like muscles (double irony). The muscular body of the "new gay man" is an embodiment of gender paradox that finds its erotic expression in the homoerotic paradox. The "new gay man" is synonymous with the "hot jock" (which I described in Chapter Five), which is the homoerotic paradox *lived* in its Apollonian phallic and anal versatility.

Gay muscles are the embodiment of gender paradox. Because of that significance, they are enticements to the sexual experience of the homoerotic paradox. This is the "number" that they perform on the brain of the gymnast whose quote introduced this section. The paradoxical meaning of gay muscles emerges for gay men ironically. Now, this irony, emerging from the lived experiences of the paradox and estrangement, is also the product of a pervasive contemporary sensibility, postmodernism. And so to understand the full significance of gay muscles, and to add the last refinement to our understanding of the gay ironic view, we should briefly turn our attention to the postmodern sensibility.

Over the last two hundred years or so, in Western culture there has gradually developed a deep and important shift in thinking. This is a heightened awareness of the way that forms influence our perceptions and understandings. Philosophers know this as the loss of the "transcendental object," an insight that can be traced to the eighteenth-century philosopher Immanuel Kant, who said that human understanding is like a candle in a dark room; that which we see is that which is illuminated by the candle. We cannot know things as they are in themselves; we know them only as the candle illuminates them. And so our perceptions are bathed in the candlelight of our human understanding. This has led to a growing skepticism about the veracity of our thinking. What we know is only what our candle of understanding shows us.

Inspired by Kant, subsequent thinkers have concerned themselves with the way the candle works, and great suspicion has developed around the authenticity of our candlelike understanding. This has led to an awareness of the structure of understanding. Cross-cultural anthropology has given empirical evidence that shows that understanding is culturally based. And so, the certainty that fueled Western thinking, especially in the shadow of the Christian claim to absolute truth as it is supposedly revealed in the Bible and sacraments, is now viewed skeptically as just one among many claims to truth. This awareness of *claims* to truth and the consequent disappearance of certainty is postmodernism. These claims are just cultural forms, balloons easily deflated by the pinprick of skepticism. Postmodernism is skepticism born of the awareness of the insubstantiality of forms.

That awareness of forms is a sensitivity to the seemingness of things; it is an ironic awareness. And so postmodernism is an ironic mode. In postmodern expression, an image or form is presented not because it is meant to be believed, and not because it is meant not to be believed, but because it is meant to be both true and false. It is the ironic *analysis,* as opposed to *synthesis,* of thesis and antithesis. Facade is of the essence. The irony of postmodernism is expressed, among other places, in architecture. The pseudo-classical columns that are so popular in postmodernist architecture are not supposed to be taken at face value. Their irony is a cynical allusion to the high-minded ideals of classical form. It manifests the failure of such exalted ideals at the close of the twentieth century. Most of all, postmodernism in its preoccupation with artifice reminds us of the impossibility of being natural. As Oscar Wilde pointed out, "naturalness" is a pose, a style that one affects.

Chief among the "natural" forms to undergo the scrutiny of postmodern skepticism is gender. Generally speaking, feminism has seen through the "naturalness" of gender and revealed a misogynist culture that subjugates and exploits women. At a less conscious, but perhaps more personally profound, level, the "naturalness" of gender has also been scrutinized by the gender and homoerotic paradoxes. What emerges from these paradoxes is gender ironically transformed: masculinity and femininity exposed as facade. The masculinity expressed in gay muscles only *seems* to be masculine, just as the ornamental columns of postmodern architecture only seem to be classical. Paradoxical masculinity looks masculine when, in fact, if read correctly through an ironic lens, it is the disintegration of masculinity. Gay muscles seen in their paradoxical context are postmodern muscles, a facade that must be understood *as* a facade. In this way, gay muscles, like postmodern architecture, are camp; they are "the lie that tells the truth."

Certainly, there are homosexual men who "take their muscles seriously," which is to say that they see their muscles as proof of their masculine status in the myth of gender. But this is an inauthentic, superficial understanding of themselves in the myth of gender. It is the product of the sensibility of de-emphasis, which is a willful ignorance of the meaning of the paradox. Having a profound paradoxical insight into the way that power as gender works in our culture, these men turn away from their intuitions in an attempt to identify with masculine hegemony, a power that their deepest erotic desires desire to undermine.

Gay muscle-men who pay attention to the paradox see their muscles in a different light. Gay muscles are butch drag, that's why they are popularly known as "tits." "Tits" invite the ironic interpretation of their paradoxical masculinity. Erotically, gay muscles are enticements to the homoerotic paradox; they set up a world of masculinity that begs to be undermined. The orthodox muscular body is the embodiment of the myth of patriarchal heterosexual masculinity; it is a sign that is meant to overwhelm women in the erotic celebration of the myth and to thwart other men, preventing the mythic violation of masculinity. The paradoxical muscular body, on the other hand, has no interest in the erotic celebration of its mythic power over women; it is, instead, an invitation to the mythic violation of masculinity, welcoming the irony and the ecstasy of the homoerotic paradox.

SELECT BIBLIOGRAPHY

BOOKS AND PERIODICALS

Ackroyd, Peter. 1979. *Dressing Up: Transvestism and Drag: The History of an Obsession.* London: Thames and Hudson.

Adam, Barry. 1987. *The Rise of a Gay Liberation Movement.* Boston: Twayne.

Alderman, Harold. 1978. "Heidegger's Critique of Science and Technology." *Heidegger and Modern Philosophy.* Ed. by Michael Murray, 35–50. New Haven: Yale University Press.

Altman, Dennis. 1982. *The Homosexualization of America, the Americanization of the Homosexual.* New York: St. Martin's Press.

————. 1972. *Homosexual: Oppression and Liberation.* Sydney: Angus and Robertson.

Atkinson, Paul. 1978. "Fitness, Feminism and Schooling." *The Nineteenth Century Woman: Her Physical and Cultural World.* Ed. by Sarah Delamont and Lorna Duffin. London: Croom Helm.

Babuscio, Jack. 1977. "Camp and the Gay Sensibility." *Gays and Film.* Ed. by Richard Dyer. London: British Film Institute.

Barnes, LaVerne. 1971. *The Plastic Orgasm.* Toronto: McClelland and Stewart.

Barthes, Roland. 1953. *Writing Degree Zero.* (Preface by Susan Sontag, 1968.) Trans. by Annette Lavers and Colin Smith. New York: Hill & Wang.

————. 1957. *Mythologies.* (2d ed.) Trans. by Annette Lavers. London: Paladin, 1973.

Bauman, Zygmunt. 1978. *Hermeneutics and Social Science: Approaches to Understanding.* London: Hutchinson.

Bell, Alan, P., Martin S. Weinberg, and S. K. Hammersmith. 1981. *Sexual Preference: Its Development in Men and Women.* Bloomington: University of Indiana Press.

———— and Martin S. Weinberg. 1978. *Homosexualities.* New York: Simon & Schuster.

Benjamin, Walter. 1968. *Illuminations.* (Introduction by Hannah Arendt.) New York: Harcourt, Brace and World.

Berger, Peter, L., and Thomas Luckmann. 1966. *The Social Construction of Reality.* Garden City: Doubleday Anchor.

Bergson, Henri. 1900. "Laughter." *Comedy.* Ed. by Wylie Sypher, 61–192. Garden City: Doubleday, 1956.

Bernstein, Mashey. 1987 "Gays in the Gym." *Christopher Street* 10, no. 6: 52–57.

Bersani, Leo. 1987 "Is the Rectum a Grave?" *October* 43 (Winter): 197–222.

Betjeman, John. 1963. *Collected Poems.* London: John Murray.

Blachford, G. 1981. "Male Dominance in the Gay World." *The Making of the Modern Homosexual.* Ed. by Kenneth Plummer, 184–210. London: Hutchinson.

Blackwood, Evelyn. 1985. "Breaking the Mirror: The Construction of Lesbianism and the Anthropological Discourse on Homosexuality." *Journal of Homosexuality* 11, nos. 3 and 4 (Summer): 1–17.
————. 1984. "Sexuality and Gender in Certain Native American Tribes: The Case of Cross-gender Females." *Signs* 10, no. 4 (Autumn 1984): 27–42.
Bogdan, Robert, and Steven Taylor. 1975. *Introduction to Qualitative Research: A Phenomenological Approach to the Socical Sciences.* Toronto: John Wiley and Sons.
Booth, Wayne. 1974. *A Rhetoric of Irony.* Chicago: University of Chicago Press.
Britton, A. 1978. "For Interpretation—Notes Against Camp." *Gay Left,* no. 7: 11–14.
Bronski, Michael. 1984. *Culture Clash: The Making of Gay Sensibility.* Boston: South End Press.
Brownmiller, Susan. 1975. *Against Our Will: Men, Women and Rape.* New York: Simon & Schuster.
Butt, Dorcas Susan. 1976. *Psychology of Sport: The Behavior, Motivation, Personality and Performance of Athletes.* New York: Van Nostrand Reinhold.
Callender, Charles, and Lee M. Kochems. 1983. "The North American Berdache." *Current Anthropology* 24, no. 4 (Aug.–Oct.): 443–70.
Carpenter, Edward. 1916. *My Days and Dreams.* London: George Allen and Unwin.
Carr, David. 1974. *Phenomenology and the Problem of History: A Study of Husserl's Transcendental Philosophy.* Evanston: Northwestern University Press.
Carrington, T., B. Connell, and J. Lee. 1985. "Toward a New Sociology of Masculinity." *Theory and Society* 14, no. 5: 551–603.
Carter, Paul. 1987. *The Road to Botany Bay.* London: Faber.
Cass, Vivienne, C. 1983/1984. "Homosexual Identity: A Concept in Need of Definition." *The Journal of Homosexuality* 9, nos. 2 and 3 (Winter/Spring). 105–26
Chaikin, Tommy, and Rick Telander. 1988. "The Nightmare of Steroids." *Sports Illustrated* 69, no. 18: 82–102.
Chevalier, Haakon Maurice. 1932. *The Ironic Temper: Anatole France and His Time.* New York: Oxford University Press.
Coe, Roy. 1986. *A Sense of Pride: The Story of Gay Games II.* San Francisco: Pride Publications.
Cohen, D., and R. Dyer. 1980. "The Politics of Gay Culture." *Homosexuality: Power and Politics.* Ed. by Gay Left Collective, 172–86. London: Allison & Busby.
Cole, Susan G. 1985. "Child Battery." *No Safe Place: Violence Against Women and Children.* Ed. by Connie Guberman and Margie Wolfe, 21–40. Toronto: Women's Press.
Congregation for the Doctrine of the Faith. 1986. "The Pastoral Care of Homosexual Persons." *Origins* 16, no. 22: 377–82.
Connell, Robert W. 1983. *Which Way Is Up?: Essays On Sex, Class and Culture.* Sydney: Allen & Unwin.
————. 1987. *Gender and Power: Society, the Person and Sexual Politics.* Cambridge, England: Polity Press.
Core, Philip. 1984. *Camp: The Lie That Tells the Truth.* New York: Delilah Books.
Crimp, Douglas. 1987. "How to Have Promiscuity in an Epidemic." *October* 43 (Winter): 237–71.

Crisp, Quentin. 1968. *The Naked Civil Servant*. Galsco: Fontana.

Crompton, Louis. 1985. *Byron and Greek Love: Homophobia in Nineteenth-Century England*. Berkeley: University of California Press.

Cucchiari, Salvatore. 1981. "The Gender Revolution and the Transition from Bisexual Horde to Patrilocal Band." *Sexual Meanings: The Cultural Construction of Gender and Sexuality*. Ed. by Sherry B. Ortner and Harriet Whitehead, 31–79. Cambridge, England: Cambridge University Press.

Dover, K. J. 1978. *Greek Homosexuality*. London: Duckworth.

DuBay, William H. 1987. *Gay Identity: The Self Under Ban*. Jefferson, N. C.: McFarland.

Dunning, Eric. 1986. "Social Bonding and Violence in Sport." *Quest for Excitement: Sport and Leisure in the Civilizing Process*. Ed. by Norbert Elias and Eric Dunning, 224–44. Oxford: Basil Blackwell.

————. 1986. "Sport as a Male Preserve: Notes on the Social Sources of Masculine Identity and Its Transformations." *Quest for Excitement*. Ed. by Norbert Elias and Eric Dunning, 267–83. Oxford: Basil Blackwell.

———— and Kenneth Sheard. 1979. *Barbarians, Gentlemen and Players: A Sociological Study of the Development of Rugby Football*. Oxford: Martin Robertson.

————. 1973. "The Rugby Football Club as a Male Preserve." *International Review of Sports Sociology*, 5–21.

Dyer, Kenneth. 1982. *Challenging the Men*. St. Lucia: University of Queensland Press.

Dyer, Richard. 1977. "Its Being So Camp as Keeps Us Going." *The Body Politic*, no. 36 (Sept.): 11–13.

Eitzen, D. 1984. *Sport in Contemporary Society: An Anthology*. New York: St. Martin's Press.

Elias, Norbert. 1986. "An Essay on Sport and Violence." *Quest for Excitement*. By Norbert Elias and Eric Dunning, 150–75. Oxford: Basil Blackwell.

————. 1978. *The Civilizing Process*. New York: Urizen Books.

Eliot, T. S. 1949. *Notes Toward the Definition of a Culture*. New York: Harcourt Brace Jovanovich.

Ellmann, Richard. 1987. *Oscar Wilde*. London: Penguin.

Empson, William. 1977. *The Structure of Complex Words*. London: Chatto and Windus.

Enright, D. J. 1986. *The Alluring Problem: An Essay on Irony*. Oxford: Oxford University Press.

Epstein, Steven. 1987. "Gay Politics, Ethnic Identity: The Limits of Social Constructionism." *Socialist Review* 17, nos. 3 and 4: 9–54.

Fledermaus, ed. 1988. "Fetish Feature: Wrestling and Boxing." *Drummer* 115 (Apr.): 26–41.

Fone, Byrne R. S. (n.d.) *Hidden Heritage: History and the Gay Imagination: An Anthology*. New York: Avocation.

Foucault, Michel. 1984. *The Uses of Pleasure: The History of Sexuality, Vol. 2*. Trans. by Robert Hurley. New York: Vintage, 1986.

————. 1977. *Discipline and Punish: The Birth of the Prison*. New York: Pantheon.

————. 1976. *The History of Sexuality, Volume 1: An Introduction*. Trans. by Robert Hurley. New York: Vintage, 1978.

Fox, John. 1984. *The Boys on the Rock.* New York: St. Martin's Press.

Freud, Sigmund. *On Sexuality: Three Essays on the Theory of Sexuality and Other Works.* Trans. by James Strachey. Harmondsworth: Penguin, 1977.

————. 1917. *Introductory Lectures.* Trans. by James Strachey. Harmondsworth: Penguin, 1973.

————. 1918. *Totem and Taboo.* New York: Moffat.

Fricke, Aaron. 1980. *Reflections of a Rock Lobster.* Boston: Alyson.

Gadamer, Hans Georg. 1960. *Truth and Method.* Trans. by Garret Barden and John Cumming. New York: Crossroad, 1986.

Gagnon, J., and W. Simon. 1973. *Sexual Conduct: The Social Sources of Human Sexuality.* Chicago: Aldine.

Gauld, Alan, and John Shotter. 1977. *Human Action and Its Psychological Investigation.* London: Routledge and Kegan Paul.

Geertz, C. 1973. *The Interpretation of Cultures.* New York: Basic Books.

Genet, Jean. 1949. *The Thief's Journal.* Trans. by Anthony Blond. Harmondsworth: Penguin, 1965.

————. 1953. *Querelle of Brest.* Trans. by G. Streatham. Fogmore: Panther, 1966.

————. 1953. *Funeral Rites.* Trans. by Bernard Frechtman. London: Anthony Blunt, 1969.

Geringer, Dan. 1988. "A Better Deal This Time?" *Sports Illustrated* 69, no. 12 (March): 23–29.

Gleason, Philip. 1983. "Identifying Identity: A Semantic History." *Journal of American History* 69, no. 4: 910–31.

Goldstein, J. 1984. "Sports Violence." *Sport in Contemporary Society: An Anthology.* (2d ed.) Ed. by D. Eitzen, 91–97. New York: St. Martin's Press.

Gould, S. J. 1981. *The Mismeasure of Man.* New York: Norton.

Gouldner, Alvin. 1965. *Enter Plato.* New York: Basic.

Greenberg, David. 1988. *The Construction of Homosexuality.* Chicago: University of Chicago Press.

Greer, Germaine. 1970. *The Female Eunuch.* London: Paladin

Guberman, Connie, and Margie Wolfe, eds. 1985. *No Safe Place: Violence Against Women and Children.* Toronto: The Women's Press.

Harding, Sandra. 1986. *The Science Question in Feminism.* Ithaca: Cornell University Press.

Hargreaves, J. 1982. "Theorising Sport: An Introduction." *Sport, Culture and Ideology.* Ed. by J. Hargreaves. London: Routledge and Kegan Paul.

Harris, Janet C. 1981. "Hermeneutics and Sport Research: Understanding Cultural Interpretations." *Sociology of Sport: Diverse Perspectives.* Ed. by Susan L. Greendorfer. West Point: Leisure Press.

Harry, J. 1982. *Gay Children Grown Up: Gender Culture and Gender Deviance.* New York: Praeger.

Hawkes, Terrence. 1977. *Structuralism and Semiotics.* Berkeley: University of California Press.

Heidegger, Martin. 1962. "Modern Science, Metaphysics and Mathematics." *Basic Writings.* Ed. by David Farrell Krell, 247–82. New York: Harper & Row, 1977.

————. 1961. "On the Essence of Truth." *Basic Writings.* Ed. by David Farrell Krell, pp. 117–42. New York: Harper & Row, 1977.

————. 1957. *Identity and Difference.* Trans. by Joan Stambaugh. New York: Harper & Row, 1969.

————. 1954. "The Question Concerning Technology." *Basic Writings*. Ed. by David Farrell Krell, 287–318. New York: Harper & Row, 1977.

————. 1926. *Being and Time*. Trans. by J. Macquarrie and E. Robinson. New York: Harper & Row, 1962.

Helmes, R. 1978. "Ideology and Social Control in Canadian Sport: A Theoretical Review." *Working Papers in the Sociological Study of Sport and Leisure*, 1, no. 4.

Hellyer, C. R. 1914. *A Vocabulary of Criminal Slang with Some Examples of Common Usage*. Portland, Oregon: Modern Printing.

Herd, Gilbert, 1981. *Guardians of the Flutes*. New York: McGraw-Hill.

Hix, Charles. 1983. *Working Out*. (Photography by Ken Haak.) New York: Simon & Schuster.

Hobbes, Thomas. 1651. *Leviathan*. Ed. by C. MacPherson. Harmondsworth: Penguin, 1968.

Hoberman, J. 1984. *Sport and Political Ideology*. Austin: University of Texas Press.

Hocquenghem, G. 1972. *Homosexual Desire*. Trans. by D. Dangoor. London: Allison & Busby, 1978.

Hodges, Andrew, and D. Hutter. 1977. *With Downcast Gays*. Toronto: Pink Triangle Press.

Horowitz, Gad. 1977. *Repression: Basic Surplus Repression in Psychoanalytic Theory*. Toronto: University of Toronto Press.

Horowitz, Gad, and Michael Kaufman. 1987. "Male Sexuality: Toward a Theory of Liberation." *Beyond Patriarchy: Essays by Men on Pleasure, Power, and Change*. Ed. by Michael Kaufman. Toronto: Oxford University Press.

Huizinga, J. 1955. *Homo Ludens: A Study of the Play-Element in Culture*. Boston: Beacon Press.

Hume, David. *The Philosophical Works*. Ed. by Thomas Green and Thomas Grose. Darmstadt: Scientia Verlag Aalen, 1964.

Humphreys, Laud. 1972. *Out of the Closets: The Sociology of Homosexual Liberation*. Englewood Cliffs, N.J.: Prentice Hall.

————. 1979. "Exodus and Identity: The Emerging Gay Culture." *Gay Men: The Sociology of Male Homosexuality*. Ed. by Martin Levine, 134–47. New York: Harper & Row.

Hyde, Montgomery. 1964. *A History of Pornography*. London: Heinemann.

Johansson, Warren. 1981. "The Etymology of the Word 'Faggot.' " *Gay Books Bulletin* 6 (Fall): 16–18.

Jullian, Phillipe. 1969. *Oscar Wilde*. London: Constable.

Kant, Immanuel. 1781. *The Critique of Pure Reason*. Trans. by Norman Kemp Smith. New York: St. Martin's Press, 1929.

Katz, Jonathan. 1976. *Gay American History: Lesbians and Gay Men in the U.S.A.* New York: Crowell.

————. 1983. *Gay/Lesbian Almanac: A New Documentary*. New York: Harper & Row.

Kaufman, Michael, ed. 1987. *Beyond Patriarchy: Essays by Men on Power, Pleasure and Change*. Toronto: Oxford University Press.

Kendrick, Walter. 1987. *The Secret Museum: Pornography in Modern Culture*. New York: Viking.

Kessler, Suzanne, and Wendy McKenna. 1978. *Gender: An Ethnomethodological Approach*. Chicago: University of Chicago Press, 1985.

Kett, Joseph. 1977. *Rites of Passage: Adolescence in America, 1790 to the Present.* New York: Basic.

Kidd, Bruce. 1984. "The Myth of the Ancient Olympic Games." *Five Ring Circus.* Ed. by Alan Tomlinson and Gary Whannell. London: Pluto.

————. 1986. "Play, Performance and Power." From the radio program "Ideas." The Canadian Broadcasting Company. Oct. 2, 9, 16, 1986.

————. 1987. "Sports and Masculinity." *Beyond Patriarchy: Essays by Men on Pleasure, Power, and Change.* Ed. by Michael Kaufman. Toronto: Oxford University Press.

Kierkegaard, Sören. 1841. *The Concept of Irony with Constant Reference to Socrates.* Trans. by Lee M. Capel. Bloomington: Indiana University Press, 1964.

Kinsey, Alfred, W. Pomeroy, and C. Martin. 1948. *Sexual Behavior in the Human Male.* Philadelphia: W. B. Saunders.

Kinsman, Gary. 1987. "Men Loving Men: The Challenge of Gay Liberation." *Beyond Patriarchy: Essays by Men on Pleasure, Power, and Change.* Ed. by Michael Kaufman. Toronto: Oxford University Press.

Kirkup, James. 1957. *The Descent Into the Cave and Other Poems.* London: Oxford.

————. 1959 *The Prodigal Son: Poems 1956–59.* London: Oxford University Press.

Kleinberg, Seymour. 1987. "The New Masculinity of Gay Men and Beyond." *Beyond Patriarchy: Essays by Men on Pleasure, Power, and Change.* Ed. by Michael Kaufman. Toronto: Oxford University Press.

————. 1980. *Alienated Affections: Being Gay in America.* New York: St. Martin's Press.

Knight, Richard Payne. 1786. *A Discourse on the Worship of Priapus and Its Connection with the Mystic Theology of the Ancients.* London, private printing.

Knox, Norman. 1961. *The Word "Irony" and Its Context, 1500–1755.* Durham, N. C.: Duke University Press.

Kopay, David, with P. Young. 1977. *The David Kopay Story: An Extraordinary Self-Revelation.* (2d. ed., 1988) New York: Donald I. Fine.

Krippendorf, K. 1980. *Content Analysis: An Introduction to Its Methodology.* Beverly Hills, Calif.: Sage.

Lapchick, Richard E. 1986. *Fractured Focus: Sport as a Reflection of Society.* Lexington, Mass.: Lexington Books.

Lawrence, D. H. 1920. *Women in Love.* New York: Viking.

Lee, John Allen. 1979. "The Gay Connection." *Urban Life* 8, no. 2: 175–98.

————. 1978. *Getting Sex: A New Approach: More Fun, Less Guilt.* Don Mills, Ontario: Musson.

Levin, David Michael. 1988. *The Opening of Vision: Nihilism and the Post-Modern Situation.* London: Routledge & Chapman & Hall.

————. 1985. *The Body's Recollection of Being: Phenomenological Psychology and the Deconstruction of Nihilism.* London: Routledge & Kegan Paul.

Levine, Martin. 1979. "Gay Ghetto." *Gay Men: the Sociology of Male Homosexuality.* Ed. by Martin Levine, 183–203. New York: Harper & Row.

Lewontin, R. C., S. Rose, and L. Kamin. 1984. *Not in Our Genes.* New York: Pantheon.

Leyland, Winston. 1983. *Physique: A Pictorial History of the Athletic Model Guild.* San Francisco: Gay Sunshine Press.

Lofland, J. 1984. *Analyzing Social Settings: A Guide to Qualitative Observation and Analysis.* Belmont, Calif.: Wadsworth.

MacDonald, Boyd, ed. 1982. *Flesh: True Homosexual Experiences from S.T.H.* Vol. 2. San Francisco: Gay Sunshine Press.

McIntosh, M. 1968. "The Homosexual Role." *The Making of the Modern Homosexual.* Ed. by Kenneth Plummer, 30–43. London: Hutchinson.

McKee, Leila Mitchel. 1982. " 'Nature's Medicine': The Physical Education and Outdoor Recreation Programs in Toronto Volunteer Youth Groups." *Proceedings of the 5th Canadian Symposium on the History of Sport and Physical Education.* Ed. by Bruce Kidd, 128–39. Toronto: School of Physical and Health Education.

MacLeod, David. 1983. *Building Character in the American Boy: The Boy Scouts, The YMCA, and Their Forerunners.* Madison: University of Wisconsin.

Madsen, Scott. 1985. *Peak Condition.* New York: Simon & Schuster.

Mailer, Norman. 1988. "A Piece of Harlot's Ghost." *Esquire* 110, no. 1 (Jul.): 80–90.

————. 1983. *Ancient Evenings.* Boston: Little, Brown

Mann, T. 1960. "The Art of the Novel." *The Creative Vision: Modern European Writers on Their Art.* Ed. by Haskell Block and Herman Salinger. New York: Grove Press.

Marks, Neil. 1978. "On the Underground Railroad to Cabbagetown." *Gaysweek* (21 Aug.): 11, 19.

Marshall, J. 1981. "Pansies, Perverts and Macho Men: Changing Conceptions of Male Homosexuality." *The Making of the Modern Homosexual.* Ed. by Kenneth Plummer, 133–54. London: Hutchinson.

Mead, Margaret. 1949. *Male and Female: A Study of the Sexes in a Changing World.* New York: William Morrow.

Meggyesy, Dave. 1971. *Out of Their League.* New York: Paperback Library.

Merchant, Carolyn. 1980. *The Death of Nature: Women, Ecology and the Scientific Revolution.* San Francisco: Harper & Row.

Meredith, George. 1877. "An Essay on Comedy." *Comedy.* Ed. by Wylie Sypher, pp. 193–254. Garden City: Doubleday, 1956.

Merleau-Ponty, Maurice. 1945. *The Phenomenology of Perception.* Trans. by Colin Smith. London: Routledge and Kegan Paul, 1962.

Millet, Kate. 1969. *Sexual Politics.* New York: Ballantine, 1978.

Mishima, Yukio. 1970. *Sun and Steel.* New York: Grove Press.

Mitchell, Juliet. 1974. *Psychoanalysis and Feminism.* London: Alan Lane.

Mitzel, J. 1976. "An Approach to the Gay Sensibility in Literature." *The Gay Alternative* 11 (Spring).

Money, John. 1975. *Sexual Signatures: On Being a Man or a Woman.* Boston: Little, Brown.

————. John Hampson, and Joan Hampson. 1955. "Hermaphroditism." *Johns Hopkins Bulletin* 97: 284–300.

Monick, Eugene. 1987. *Phallos: Sacred Image of the Masculine.* Toronto: Inner City Books.

Muecke, D. C. 1970. *Irony and the Ironic.* London: Methuen.

Napolitano, George. 1986. "Rick Rude: Come Home with the Ravishing One!" *Superstar Wrestler* (1986): 18–23.

New Yorker. 1987. "The Talk of the Town: Notes and Comment." (Aug. 24) vol. 63, no. 27: 19–20.

283

Newbolt, Henry. "Vitaï Lampada." *The Ontario Readers Fourth Book.* The Ministry of Education for Ontario, 325. Toronto: T. Eaton, 1925.

Nichols, J. 1977. "Butcher Than Thou: Beyond Machismo." *Gay Men: The Sociology of Male Homosexuality.* Ed. by Martin Levine, 329–42. New York: Harper & Row.

Ortner, Sherry B., and Harriet Whitehead, eds. 1981. *Sexual Meanings: The Cultural Construction of Gender and Sexuality.* Cambridge, England: Cambridge University Press.

Palmer, Richard E. 1969. *Hermeneutics: Interpretation Theory in Schleirmacher, Dilthey, Heidegger and Gadamer.* Evanston, Ill.: Northwestern University Press.

Peckham, Morse. 1969. *Art and Pornography: An Experiment in Explanation.* New York: Basic.

Pleck, Joseph. 1980. "Men's Power with Women, Other Men, and Society: A Men's Movement Analysis." *The American Man.* Ed. by Joseph and Elizabeth Pleck. Englewood Cliffs, N.J.: Prentice Hall.

Pleket, H. W. 1970. "Games, Prizes, Athletes and Ideology: Some Aspects of the History of Sport in the Greco-Roman World." *Arena* I, no. 1: 49–89.

Plummer, Kenneth. 1981. "Building a Sociology of Homosexuality." *The Making of the Modern Homosexual.* Ed. by Kenneth Plummer, 17–29 London: Hutchinson.

————. 1981. "Homosexual Categories: Some Research Problems in the Labelling Perspective of Homosexuality." *The Making of the Modern Homosexual.* Ed. by Kenneth Plummer, 53–75. London: Hutchinson.

Potvin, Dennis. 1977. *Power on Ice.* New York: Harper & Row.

Pronger, Brian. 1990. "Gay Jocks: A Phenomenology of Gay Men in Athletics." *Sport, Men and the Gender Order: Critical Feminist Perspectives.* Ed. by Michael Messner and Don Sabo. Los Angeles: Human Kinetics Publishing.

————. 1989. "Athletics." *The Encyclopedia of Homosexuality.* Ed. by Wayne Dynes. New York: Garland.

Reimer, J. 1977. "Varieties of Opportunistic Research." *Urban Life* 5, no. 4: 467–77.

Robinson, John Mansley. 1968. *An Introduction to Early Greek Philosophy: The Chief Fragments and Ancient Testimony, with Connecting Commentary.* New York: Houghton Mifflin.

Rodgers, Bruce. 1972. *Gay Talk: A (Sometimes Outrageous) Dictionary of Gay Slang.* New York: Paragon.

Rodway, Alan. 1962. "Terms for Comedy." *Renaissance and Modern Studies,* vol. 6: 102–24.

Rose, F., and G. Bennett. 1980. *Real Men: Sex and Style in an Uncertain Age.* Garden City: Dolphin.

Roselini, Lynn. 1976. "Gay Pro Athletes." *Blueboy* (Apr.) 7–9.

Ross, E. R. 1987. "Sportsex" in *Jock* (Jul.) 38–40.

Roszak, Theodore. 1972. *Where the Wasteland Ends: Politics and Transcendence in Post-Industrial Society.* Garden City: Anchor.

Rotundo, E. Anthony. 1987. "Patriarchs and Participants: A Historical Perspective on Fatherhood in the United States." *Beyond Patriarchy.* Ed. by Michael Kaufman, 64–80. Toronto: Oxford University Press.

Rougemont, Denis de. 1940. *Passion and Society.* London: Faber and Faber.

Rowberry, John W. 1986. *Gay Video: A Guide to Erotica.* San Francisco: Gay Sunshine Press.

Rowland, C. 1986. "Games People Play: The Burgeoning World of Gay Athletics." *The Advocate* 462 (Dec. 23): 42–47, 108–09.

Russo, Vito. 1976. "Camp." *Gay Men: The Sociology of Male Homosexuality.* Ed. by Martin Levine, 205–10. New York: Harper & Row.

Sabo, D., and R. Runfola. 1980. *Jock: Sports and Male Identity.* Englewood Cliffs: Prentice Hall.

Sade, The Marquis de. 1785. *The 120 Days of Sodom and Other Writings.* Ed. and trans. by Austryn Wainhouse and Richard Seaver. New York: Grove Press, 1966.

Sartre, Jean-Paul. *Being and Nothingness.* Trans. by Hazel E. Barnes. New York: Washington Square Press, 1956.

Schaap, Dick. 1987. "Death of an Athlete." *Sports Illustrated* 67, no. 4, July 27: 26–32.

Schifellite, Carmen. 1987. "Beyond Tarzan and Jane Genes." *Beyond Patriarchy: Essays by Men on Pleasure, Power, and Change.* Ed. by Michael Kaufman, 45–63. Toronto: Oxford University Press.

Schneider, John, and D. Stanley Eitzen. 1986. "The Structure of Sport and Participant Violence." *Fractured Focus: Sport as a Reflection of Society.* Ed. by Richard Lapchick, 229–44. Lexington, Mass.: Lexington Books.

Schutz, Alfred, and Thomas Luckmann. Trans. by Richard M. Zaner and H. Tristram Enggelhardt Jr., *Structures of the Life-World [by] Alfred Schutz and Thomas Luckman.* London: Heinman, 1974. [Evanston, Ill.: Northwestern University Press, 1973.]

Shaw, Gary. 1972. *Meat on the Hoof: The Hidden World of Texas Football.* New York: St. Martin's Press.

Sheard, Kevin, and Eric Dunning. 1973. "The Rugby Football Club as a Male Preserve." *International Review of Sports Sociology,* 3–4.

Slaate, Howard, A. 1968. *The Pertinence of Paradox: The Dialectics of Reason-in-Existence.* New York: Humanities Press.

Smith, Michael D. 1986. "Sports Violence: A Definition." *Fractured Focus: Sport as a Reflection of Society.* Ed. by Richard Lapchick, 22–28. Lexington, Mass.: Lexington Books.

—————. 1983. *Violence and Sport.* Toronto: Butterworths.

Smyth, John Vignaux. 1986. *A Question of Eros: Irony in Sterne, Kierkegaard and Barthes.* Tallahassee: Florida State University Press.

Sontag, Susan. 1988. *AIDS and Its Metaphors.* New York: Farrar Straus & Giroux.

—————. 1966. "Notes on 'Camp.'" *Against Interpretation and other Essays,* 275–92. New York: Farrar Straus & Giroux.

Steakley, James D. 1975. *The Homosexual Emancipation Movement in Germany.* New York: Arno.

Stevens, Wallace. "Adagia." *Opus Posthumous,* p. 63. New York: Knopf, 1957.

Stratton, Allan. 1988. "Moving Mountains," *Xtra!* no. 108 (Sept. 16): 9.

Styles, J. 1979. "Outsider/Insider: Researching Gay Baths." *Urban Life* 8: 135–52.

Thompson, Mark. 1987. *Gay Spirit: Myth and Meaning.* New York: St. Martin's Press.

Tripp, C. 1975. *The Homosexual Matrix.* Scarborough: New American Library.

Troiden, Richard. 1979. "Becoming Homosexual: A Model of Gay Identity Acquisition." *Psychiatry* 42 (Nov.): 362–73.

Trout, Hank. 1980. "The Great Wrestling Match (or the Spoils of Victory)." *Drummer* 4, no. 36: 8–17.

Tutko, Thomas, and William Burns. 1976. *Winning is Everything and Other American Myths.* New York: Macmillan.

Underwood, John. 1984. "Brutality in Football." *Sport in Contemporary Society: An Anthology* Ed. by D. Stanley Eitzen, 89–90. New York: St. Martin's Press.

Vadasz, Danny. 1986. "Aussie Rules: The Hottest Game in Town!" *Outrage* 41 (Oct.): 29–31.

Valverde, Mariana. 1985. *Sex, Power and Pleasure.* Toronto: The Women's Press.

Van Druten, John. 1950. *Bell, Book and Candle. Best American Plays Third Series.* Ed. by John Gassner. New York: Crown, 1952.

Vanggaard, Thorkil. 1969. *Phallos: A Symbol and Its History in the Male World.* London: J. Cape, 1972.

Vaz, Edmund. 1972. "The Culture of Young Hockey Players: Some Initial Observations." *Training: Scientific Basis and Application: A Symposium.* Ed. by Albert W. Taylor, 222–34. Springfield, Ill.: Thomas.

Vidal, Gore. 1949. *The City and the Pillar.* London: John Lehman.

Warren, C. 1977. "Fieldwork in the Gay World: Research Issues in Phenomenological Research." *Journal of Social Issues* 33: 93–107.

————— and B. Ponse. 1977. "The Existential Self in the Gay World." *Existential Sociology.* Ed. by J. Douglas and J. Johnson, 273–91. Cambridge: Cambridge University Press.

Warren, Patricia Nell. 1974. *The Front Runner.* New York: Bantam.

Watney, Simon. 1987. *Policing Desire: Pornography, AIDS and the Media.* Minneapolis: University of Minnesota Press.

Waugh, Tom. 1987. "Hard to Imagine: Gay Erotic Cinema in the Post-War Era." *Cineaction!* no. 10 (Fall): 65–72.

Weber, Max. 1930. "On Protestantism and Capitalism." *Theories of Society,* vol. 2, Ed. by Parsons, Shils, Naegele, and Pitts, 1253–65. New York: The Free Press of Glencoe.

Weeks, Jeffrey. 1986. *Sexuality.* Chichester: Ellis Horwood.

—————. 1985. *Sexuality and Its Discontents: Meanings, Myths and Modern Sexualities.* London: Routledge and Kegan Paul.

—————. 1981. *Sex, Politics and Society: The Regulation of Sexuality Since 1800.* London: Longman.

—————. 1981. "Discourse, Desire and Sexual Deviance: Some Problems in a History of Homosexuality." *The Making of the Modern Homosexual.* Ed. by Kenneth Plummer, 76–111. London: Hutchinson.

—————. 1980. "Capitalism and the Organization of Sex." *Homosexuality: Power and Politics.* Ed. by Gay Left Collective, 11–20. London: Allison & Busby.

White, Edmund. 1980. "The Political Vocabulary of Homosexuality." *The State of the Language.* Ed. by Christopher Ricks and Leonard Michaels, 235–46. Los Angeles: University of California Press.

Wilde, Oscar. 1895. *An Ideal Husband. Two Society Comedies.* London: E. Benn, 1983.

Wilden, Anthony. 1987. *Man and Woman, War and Peace: The Strategist's Companion.* London: Routledge and Kegan Paul.

Williams, Raymond. 1976. "Sensibility." *Keywords: A Vocabulary of Culture and Society.* London: Croom Helm.

Wooden, Wayne S. 1982. *Men Behind Bars: Sexual Exploitation in Prison.* New York: Plenum.

286

Woods, Gregory. 1987. *Articulate Flesh: Male Homoeroticism and Modern Poetry*. New Haven, Conn.: Yale University Press.

FILMS/VIDEOS

The following list of films and videos is incomplete because pornographic films quite often do not give full information in their credits.

All the Right Moves, dir. Michael Chapman, 1983.
Basket Practice.
The Bigger the Better, dir. Matt Sterling, 1984.
Classe de Niege, dir. Jean-Daniel Cadinot.
The Cyclist, dir. Richard Fontaine, 1949.
Deliverance, dir. John Boorman, 1972.
Down for the Count.
Games, dir. Steve Scott, 1983.
Gregg Donovan as the Jock, prod. by Nova.
GymNasty.
HARDball.
Hot Shot, dir. Rick King, 1987.
The Idol, dir. Tom de Simone, 1979.
Jock Dreams, dir. Tony Price, 1983.
Jock Empire, dir. Kenneth Holloway, 1984.
Jock Itch.
Jockstrap Romances.
The Jogger.
Like a Horse, dir. Matt Sterling, 1984.
Knockout, dir. Kenneth Holloway, 1984.
The Last Surfer, dir. Toby Ross, 1984.
Lifeguard, prod. by HIS Video.
Lockerroom Fever, dir. Robert Walters, 1985.
A Matter of Size, dir. Matt Sterling, 1984.
North Shore, dir. William Phelps, 1987.
The Other Side of Aspen II, prod. by Falcon.
Pumping.
Sizing Up Before Your Very Eyes, dir. Matt Sterling, 1985.
Skin Games.
Some Like It Hot, dir. Billy Wilder, 1959.
Spring Training, prod. by Falcon Studios.
Take It Like a Man.
Tough Competition, dir. Richard Morgan, 1985.
These Bases are Loaded, dir. William Higgins, 1982.
Track Meet.
Triple Workout.
Winner's Circle, prod. by Brentwood, 1982.
Wrestling Meat, dir. Tony Prince, 1983.
The Young Olympians, dir. William Higgins, 1983.
Youngblood, dir. Peter Markle, 1985.

PORNOGRAPHIC MAGAZINES AND EPHEMERA

Cocksucking Jocks
Drummer.
Jock Fuckers
Ass Eating Jocks
Jock Loads
Inches
Like a Horse
Tall Timber
The Big Fantasy
Huge
In Touch
Jock
Never Big Enough
They Grow 'Em Big
The Jock Book
Stars

NOTES

PREFACE

1. Blackwood, "Breaking the Mirror," p. 6.

CHAPTER 1

1. The word "psychic" may be confusing to some readers. By psychic, I am not referring to the mystical world of crystal balls, palm reading, out-of-body experiences, and the like. By "psychic," I mean that which pertains to the psyche. It has become common to use "psychological" when "psychic" is meant. People will say that so-and-so has a "psychological" problem. But psychological refers to the *study* (logo) of the psyche, not the psyche itself. Only those interested in the study of the psyche have "psychological" problems. This inappropriate use of "psychological" creates a false identity between the discipline that studies the psyche, "psychology," and the psyche itself, as though the discipline of psychology had special claims to the content of the psyche. Although it is becoming commonplace to ignore the distinction between "psychic" and "psychological," I think it is an important distinction and will not join in its obfuscation by ignoring it here.

CHAPTER 2

1. Shaw, *Meat on the Hoof.* p. 234.
2. Kidd, "Sports and Masculinity," pp. 252–53.
3. See Rotundo, "Patriarchs and Participants," pp. 64–80.
4. Kidd, *op. cit.,* p. 255. See also, Kett, *Rites of Passage;* McKee, "Nature's Medicine"; MacLeod, *Building Character in the American Boy.*
5. See Dunning and Sheard, "The Rugby Football Club as a Male Preserve."
6. See Dyer, *Challenging the Men.*
7. Kidd, *op. cit.,* p. 258.
8. Smith, *Violence and Sport,* p. 45.
9. Norbert Elias has written extensively on the historical development of the "civilizing" process in Western culture. See Elias, *The Civilizing Process.*
10. Henry Newbolt, "Vitaï Lampada."
11. *Globe and Mail,* July 31, 1970, p. 24.
12. Chaikin and Telander, "The Nightmare of Steroids," pp. 82–102.
13. Lapchick, *Fractured Focus,* p. 220.

14. Underwood, "Brutality in Football," p. 83.
15. Rose, *Real Men*, p. 80.
16. *Ibid.*, p. 79.
17. Goldstein, "Sports Violence," p. 92.
18. Shaw, *Meat on the Hoof.* See also sports psychologist Thomas Tutko, *Winning is Everything and Other American Myths.*
19. Shaw, *op. cit.*, p. 207.
20. Kopay and Young, *The David Kopay Story*, p. 152.
21. *Ibid.*, p. 53.
22. See Vaz, "The Culture of Young Hockey Players: Some Initial Observations," pp. 222–34.
23. Fox, *The Boys on the Rock*, pp. 19–20.

CHAPTER 3

1. For an excellent introduction and concise bibliographic review of this subject, see Hawkes, *Structuralism and Semiotics.*
2. See Levin's *The Body's Recollection of Being: Phenomenological Psychology and the Deconstruction of Nihilism,* in which he argues that the foundation of our understanding of life lies in the experience of embodiment and motility.
3. *Ibid.*, p. 121.
4. Merleau-Ponty, *The Phenomenology of Perception,* p. 238.
5. *The 120 Days of Sodom,* by the Marquis de Sade, is a compendium of epicurean sexual techniques.
6. There are "chromosomal abnormalities" in which there are variations in the numbers of X and Y chromosomes. Although such variations raise some interesting questions about the attribution of gender, their incidence is too rare to warrant discussion here.
7. See Money, *Sexual Signatures.*
8. That gender is a cultural category without biological basis is now well established. Cross-cultural studies indicate that gender is constituted differently in different cultures. Some societies have more than two genders and others have as many as six. See DuBay, *Gay Identity*, p. 44.
   Margaret Mead's famous iconclastic study of seven remote societies of the South Seas indicated that our conceptions of masculinity and femininity for men and women respectively are not reproduced in all cultures, thereby illustrating the cultural foundations of gender. See Mead, *Male and Female.*
9. Connell, *Gender and Power*, p. 76. He is referring to Kessler and McKenna, *Gender.*
10. There is also evidence that females in North American Indian culture crossed gender. See Blackwood, "Sexuality and Gender in Certain Native American Tribes." For a review of the literature on *berdache,* see Callender and Kochems, "The North American Berdache."
11. Connell, *op. cit.*, p. 77.
12. See Barthes, "Myth Today," pp. 109 ff.
13. See Mead, *Male and Female.*
14. Carter, *The Road to Botany Bay.*
15. See Hannah Arendt's introduction to Benjamin's *Illuminations.*

16. The myths of gender are not the same as the actual subjugation of women by men. The *exercise* of men's power over women is the actual forcing of women in sexual acts, the using of them as cheap domestic labor, the marginalization of them in the work force. While the myths are instrumental in the power men have over women in that they justify and create a context for that power, they are one step removed from the actual seizing of power. Whereas it's true that men do sometimes actualize their power and behave aggressively and violently, some more frequently than others, allusion to the gender myth is more or less constant.

17. Carrington, Connell, and Lee, "Toward a New Sociology of Masculinity," pp. 590. Emphasis mine.

18. Barthes, *Mythologies,* p. 151.

19. In *Mythologies,* Barthes says that the principle of myth is that it transforms history into nature, p. 129.

20. Foucault, *The History of Sexuality, Vol. 1,* pp. 92–93. Emphasis mine.

21. It is essential to note that masculinity is not the only expression or instrument of power. Capital, class, and the control of information are just three examples of other instruments of power.

22. See Money, *Sexual Signatures.*

23. Here I am drawing a parallel with Heidegger's argument about the insidiousness of Hellenic thought.

24. The anthropologist Clifford Geertz, paraphrasing Max Weber, said that "man [sic] is an animal suspended in webs of significance he himself has spun." (*The Interpretation of Cultures,* p. 5.)

25. See Cucchiari, "The Gender Revolution and the Transition from Bisexual Horde to Patrilocal Band," pp. 31–79. See also, Mead, *Male and Female.*

26. Blachford, "Male Dominance in the Gay World," p. 187.

27. It would be inappropriate in this study to pursue deeply the ontology of ecstasy—that task will be left to a more fundamental study of sex and human beings. The interested reader, however, may wish to consider Heidegger's discussion of the "ecstases" in *Being and Time* (pp. 329 ff).

28. Heidegger points out that the "world" is inauthentic, a concealment of the truth of human beings—although he does not himself speak of gender as an element of the "world." Because I have shown that gender is the creation of culture and culture is very much part of the "world" of which Heidegger speaks in *Being and Time,* it is appropriate to consider gender in this "worldly" way. See Heidegger, *Being and Time,* Division One: Chapters 3, 4, and 5, pp. 91–224.

29. Regarding the question of being, Heidegger says: "This question has today been forgotten. . . . It is one which provided the stimulus for the researches of Plato and Aristotle, only to subside from then on as a theme for actual investigation. What these two men achieved was to persist through many alterations and 'retouchings' down to the 'logic' of Hegel. And what they wrested with the utmost intellectual effort from the phenomena, fragmentary and incipient though it was, has long since become trivialized." With these words in the introduction of *Being and Time* (p. 2), Heidegger begins the retrieval of the (ancient) appreciation of being to which *Being and Time* is meant to lead us.

30. Plato, *Symposium,* as quoted in Kierkegaard, *The Concept of Irony with Constant Reference to Socrates,* p. 216.

31. From Anthony Wilden, *Man and Woman, War and Peace: The Strategist's Companion,* as quoted in *TLS* (4, 457) Sept. 2–8, 1988, p. 971.

32. It may be true that in regard to physical strength some men have a slight genetically based physical advantage over women. But this genetic difference is really only borne out at the most elite level of athletics, and even there the significance is highly debatable. At the 1988 Seoul Olympics, thirteen-year-old girls were swimming faster than Mark Spitz, multiple gold medal winner at the 1972 Olympics. See Kenneth Dyer, *Challenging the Men.*

33. There are men who are critical of patriarchal culture who nevertheless are erotically attracted to women. The "men's movement" has many such men. One of the primary concerns of the "men's movement" is to make masculinity respectable in the light of the feminist critique of male hegemony. But maintaining any sense of masculinity amounts to little more than coating a fundamentally patriarchal myth with a patina of egalitarianism. See Carrington, Connell, and Lee, "Toward a New Sociology of Masculinity."

34. Connell, *op. cit.,* 215.

35. That women are more concerned about love than men is born out by the fact that popular women's magazines often dwell on love themes. Men's magazines are more concerned with technique and erotic body signs. Harlequin Romances are geared almost entirely to women; there is no equivalent for heterosexual men.

36. It's interesting to point out that "paradox" can have the connotation of being the "correction of a vulgar error." It often has the implication that that which is paradoxical is "marvelous or incredible." (OED)

37. My understanding of primordial existential human being in its relation to culture I take primarily from Heidegger's explication in *Being and Time* of authentic Dasein struggling with the inauthenticity of the world; the essentiality of Dasein's embodiment I draw from Levin's *The Body's Recollection of Being* and Merleau-Ponty's *Phenomenology of Perception.*

38. Sartre, *Being and Nothingness,* p. 572.

39. *Ibid.,* p. 568.

40. I mention transsexualism or antidoxy here only to indicate the range of the spectrum of intuition available to people within the gender myth. An examination of the meaning of transsexualism within this context would be interesting but is not appropriate here.

41. The "homoerotic paradox," emerging as it does from the cultural construction of gender, is unlike the early theories of homosexuality that tried to explain it in terms of gender, being biological in its origin. Gender paradox sees homosexuality as a form of knowledge, an interpretation of the myths of gender, whereas early theories of homosexuality conceptualized it as a biological essence. From the early nineteenth to the mid-twentieth centuries, homosexuality was viewed by medicine as a disorder that arises out of problems of the biological origins of gender. Early medical theorists of homosexuality, such as Karl Heinrich Ulrichs and Richard von Krafft-Ebing, who wrote extensively on the subject from the 1860s to the 1890s, identified the "problem" as being a congenital malformation. They both believed that in the embryonic stage during which male or female genitals developed in the respective embryos, the complementary masculine or feminine mental characteristics did not develop in that part of the brain that was responsible for sex drives. This resulted in a "feminine soul" in a male body or a "masculine soul" in a female body (Marshall, "Pansies, Perverts and Macho Men," pp. 142–43.). A nat-

ural consequence of a man having a feminine mind, it was reasoned, would be a psychic predisposition to having sex with men rather than women.

In 1895, Edward Carpenter published an essay on the subject of "the intermediate sex" that argued that homosexuality is the product of the combination of masculine and feminine gender. Like his predecessors, he believed that gender has a biological basis. Magnus Hirschfeld conceptualized homosexuals as "the "third sex"—a species that combined not only the mental qualities but also the physiological features of men and women" (Marshall, "Pansies, Perverts and Macho Men," p. 144). In the world of nineteenth-century sex theory, there clearly was a sense that homosexuality had its origins in the biological formation of gender. The obvious fallacy here is that gender is not a biological phenomenon, but a cultural one. Gender and its eroticization is the subject of mythic interpretation rather than the object of biological determination.

42. Betjeman, "Narcissus," *Collected Poems*, pp. 345–7.

43. *Ibid.*

CHAPTER 4

1. See Wooden, *Men Behind Bars.*

2. Weeks, "Discourse, Desire and Sexual Deviance," pp. 78–81.

3. Herd, *Guardians of the Flutes*, pp. 2, 3.

4. Foucault, *The History of Sexuality, Vol. 1*, p. 141.

5. *Ibid.*, p. 146.

6. Gagnon and Simon, *Sexual Conduct.*

7. Ibid., p. 17.

8. Weber, "On Protestantism and Capitalism," pp. 1253–65.

9. Jeffrey Weeks points out that Foucault and others have argued that the growing importance of the norm since the eighteenth century has been instrumental in setting the stage for the categorization of homosexuality. Guy Hocquenghem, in *Homosexual Desire,* also refers to Foucault and to what he calls the "growing imperialism" of society that attempts to give a social status to everything. The result of this has been the increasingly tight definition of homosexuality and its marginal status.

10. Weeks, *op. cit.,* p. 107.

11. Carter, *The Road to Botany Bay,* p. 18.

12. See Merchant, *The Death of Nature.*

13. Katz, *Gay/Lesbian Almanac,* p. 16.

14. Foucault, *op. cit.,* p. 43.

15. Congregation for the Doctrine of the Faith, "The Pastoral Care of Homosexual Persons," pp. 377–82.

16. DuBay, (*Gay Identity,* p. 50) has pointed out that "although the ancient Romans and Greeks were familiar with our modern concepts of 'family' and 'child,' these meanings were lost in Europe after the sixth century until the late seventeenth century. For a long time 'family' referred to property and meant the household of servants, wives and children." The family as we know it has become the "traditional" family. As Heidegger (*Being and Time,*

p. 43) said, "Tradition takes what has come down to us and delivers it over to self-evidence." The family is understood as a natural, ahistorical, self-evident structure when, in fact, it is the creation of history.

17. See Plummer, *The Making of the Modern Homosexual.* See also, DuBay, *Gay Identity.*

18. McIntosh, "The Homosexual Role," p. 32.

19. See Carrington, Connell, and Lee, "Toward a New Sociology of Masculinity," on the pervasiveness of role theory in the literature on masculinity. Gleason, in "Identifying Identity," suggests that in the 1950s the social sciences acquired a reputation for being able to "unlock the secrets of the human condition." (This is not surprising since the positive sciences in general, on which the human sciences have been most inadequately modeled, have been credited with the ability to reveal enduring truth.) Many of the theories of the human sciences acquired a prestige, both popularly and among academic intellectuals, that precluded critical examination of their fundamental assumptions. The jargon of the social sciences has worked its way into the popular vocabulary, invoking an understanding of life that is not only largely unquestioned but also at odds with the truth.

20. DuBay, *op. cit.,* p. 5.

21. See Carrington, Connell, and Lee, *op. cit.* This perspicacious article, in its review of the literature on masculinity, offers a devastating critique of role theory.

22. Plummer, "Building a Sociology of Homosexuality," p. 23.

23. See Bell and Weinberg, *Homosexualities.*

24. See my brief discussion of primordial human being in its relation to culture on pp. 43ff and p. 61. See also, Heidegger, *Identity and Difference.*

25. Foucault, *op. cit.,* p. 43.

26. See Hodges and Hutter, *With Downcast Gays.*

27. Schaap, 1987, p. 27.

28. Schlegel, as quoted in Muecke, *Irony and the Ironic,* p. 24.

29. Kierkegaard, *The Concept of Irony,* pp. 271–72.

30. Rodway, "Terms for Comedy," p. 113.

31. Booth, as quoted in Enright, *The Alluring Problem,* p. 2.

32. Van Druten, in Gassner, *Best American Plays, Third Series,* p. 597.

33. As quoted by Patrick Parrinder in a letter to the *TLS* (4, 437), June 24–30, 1988, p. 705.

34. Warren, *The Front Runner,* p. 141.

35. These signs, of course, are also shaped by the cultural contexts of class, ethnicity, and so on.

36. See Adam, *The Rise of a Gay Liberation Movement.*

37. *Ibid.,* p. 73.

38. *Ibid.,* p. 78.

CHAPTER 5

1. Because pornography is an issue dominated by the interests of a variety of moralists, its definition is highly contentious. "Pornography" is often considered a pejorative term. Conservative moralists categorize any representation

of sexuality as "pornographic." Liberal moralists call "pornographic" those representations of types of sexuality that they find distasteful. Portrayals of sexuality that they deem acceptable, they call "erotica." Walter Kendrik has written an interesting book, *The Secret Museum,* on the historical development of definitions of pornography. Readers who are interested in the art versus pornography argument may want to look at Morse Peckham's *Art and Pornography.* The definition I use, and that I believe is the common-sense understanding of pornography among gay men, at least those who enjoy using it, is not pejorative, is almost empty of moralism, and is a more or less simple statement of fact. Pornography is any representation used for erotic stimulation.

2. According to the cover of *Jock,* Feb. 1988.
3. Tom Waugh, "Hard to Imagine," p. 66.
4. Foucault, *The History of Sexuality,* Vol. 1, pp. 92–93.
5. Pierre de Coubertin, the founder of the Modern Olympics, said: "At the Olympic Games the primary role [of women] should be like the ancient tournaments—the crowning of the victors with laurels."
6. Crisp, *The Naked Civil Servant,* p. 155.
7. Genet, *Funeral Rites,* pp. 250, 251, and 254.
8. The *Dictionary of Slang and Unconventional Usage* says that originally "fuck" as a transitive verb can be applied only to males, which is to say that only men can "fuck" women. More recently, the growing emancipation of women has mitigated against this sharply hierarchical usage. Nevertheless, the original sense still carries considerable cultural weight.
9. Susan Brownmiller, in *Against Our Will: Men, Women and Rape,* points out that rape has become an institutionalized aspect of war. Victorious soldiers see it as their prerogative, even duty, to rape the women of the defeated side.
10. Woods, *Articulate Flesh,* p. 53.
11. Mailer, *Ancient Evenings,* pp. 288–89.
12. Fox, *The Boys on the Rock,* pp. 135–36.
13. Crisp, *op. cit.,* p. 62.
14. Levine, *Gay Ghetto,* p. 137.
15. The first ad is from *New York Native* (271), June 27, 1988, p. 61. The second ad is from *Now* (vol. 7, no. 47), Aug. 4–10, 1988, p. 59.
16. From a story entitled "Sportsex," by E. R. Ross, in *Jock,* July 1987.
17. Mishima, *Sun and Steel,* p. 45.
18. *Jock,* Sept. 1986, p. 72.
19. Kirkup, "The Body-Builder," *The Prodigal Son,* p. 26.
20. Hume, "Of Tragedy," *The Philosophical Works.*
21. Woods, *op. cit.,* p. 9.
22. Vanggaard, *Phallos.* The first quote is from p. 56 and the second, p. 62.
23. Woods, *op. cit.,* p. 52.
24. Peckham, *Art and Pornography,* p. 171.
25. MacDonald, (ed.), *Flesh,* p. 130.
26. *In Touch* (no. 129), p. 67.
27. *Physique Pictorial,* Spring 1959. As Quoted in Waugh, "Hard to Imagine," p. 70.
28. Readers interested in gay pornography from this should see Winston Leyland's *Physique: A Pictorial History of the Athletic Model Guild.* Those inter-

ested in a more critical discussion may want to look at Thomas Waugh's "Hard to Imagine: Gay Erotic Cinema in the Post-War Era," *Cineaction!*

CHAPTER 6

1. Sandra Harding, in her book *The Science Question in Feminism,* discusses the way in which gender bias constructs scientific research, thereby predetermining the sexist facts it produces.
2. Lawrence, *Women in Love,* pp. 262–63.
3. Woods, *Articulate Flesh,* p. 94.
4. *Ibid.,* p. 72.
5. Vidal, *The City and the Pillar,* p. 34.
6. Marks, "On the Underground Railroad to Cabbagetown," p. 11.
7. Kirkup, "Football Action Shots," *The Descent into the Cave and Other Poems,* p. 33.
8. Shaw, *Meat on the Hoof,* p. 22.
9. Denis de Rougement, *Passion and Society,* p. 254.
10. Meggyesy, *Out of Their League.*
11. Vadasz, "Aussie Rules," p. 31.
12. Rose, *Real Men,* p. 79.

CHAPTER 7

1. See Carrington, Connell, and Lee, *Toward a New Sociology of Masculinity,* re: modernizing hegemonic masculinity.
2. Crisp, *The Naked Civil Servant,* p. 33.
3. *Ibid.,* p. 114.
4. *Ibid.,* p. 61.
5. Kate Millet, *Sexual Politics,* as quoted in Edmund White, "The Political Vocabulary of Homosexuality," p. 240.
6. Ken Popert is the first person I have heard use this term and I would like to thank him for bringing it to my attention.
7. McIntosh, "The Homosexual Role," p. 37.
8. Hellyer, *A Vocabulary of Criminal Slang with Some Examples of Common Usage,* as quoted in Johansson, "The Etymology of the Word 'Faggot,'" pp. 16–18.
9. See Wayne Booth's discussion of the steps of stable irony in *A Rhetoric of Irony.*
10. White, "The Political Vocabulary of Homosexuality," pp. 235–46.
11. Sontag, "Notes on 'Camp,'" p. 290.
12. Core, *Camp: The Lie That Tells the Truth,* p. 9.
13. Oscar Wilde, *An Ideal Husband.*
14. Sontag, *op. cit.,* p. 280.
15. *Ibid.,* p. 288.
16. *Ibid.,* p. 291.
17. Quoted in Byrne Fone, *Hidden Heritage: History and the Gay Imagination: An Anthology,* p. xviii.

18. See Lee, *Getting Sex.*
19. See Nichols, "Butcher Than Thou: Beyond Machismo." See also, Marshall, "Pansies, Perverts and Macho Men"; Kleinberg, "Where Have All the Sissies Gone?" *Alienated Affections,* pp. 143–56.
20. See Hoberman, *Sport and Political Ideology.*
21. Tom Waddell, as quoted in Coe, *A Sense of Pride,* p. 13.
22. *Ibid.,* p. 29.
23. *Ibid.*
24. That competitive sport is not necessarily a healthy occupation is evidenced by scams around the use of drugs by athletes, like anabolic steroids, cocaine, and amphetamines (among professional athletes who must play games night after night while flying from city to city). Evidence of the physical and psychic damage done to athletes as a result of overtraining and bad coaching is extensive. For a discussion of the negative effects of competitive sports, see Dorcas Susan Butt, *Psychology of Sport: The Behavior, Motivation, Personality and Performance of Athletes.*
25. Tom Cruise, in *All the Right Moves,* delivers a compendium of these butch signs.
26. Alan Stratton, "Moving Mountains," p. 9.
27. Rowland, "Games People Play," p. 47.
28. *Ibid.*
29. Because I was unable to locate those involved in this anecdote to get permission to use their names, I am using pseudonyms here.

INDEX